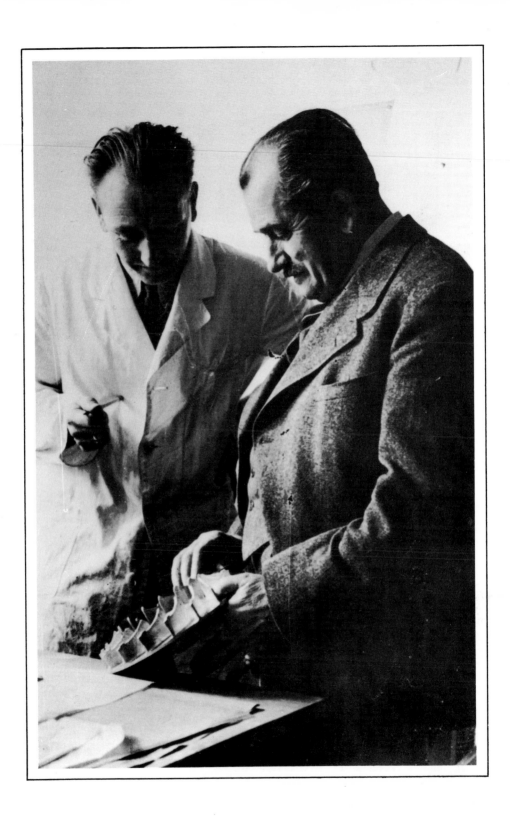

THE VW STORY

Jerry Sloniger

 Patrick Stephens, Cambridge

Frontispiece *A view of Ferdinand Porsche, the VW papa, with Reimspiess who did much of the Beetle design as well as drawing the VW emblem still used.*

For Edy
Who has been bemused by Volkswagens at least as long as I.

First published 1980

British Library Cataloguing in Publication Data

Sloniger, Jerry
  The VW story.
   1. Volkswagenwerk—History
  I. Title
  338.7'62'920943   HD9710.G44V6

ISBN 0 85059 441 3

Text photoset in 10 on 11 pt Plantin by Manuset Limited, Baldock, Herts. Printed and bound in Great Britain, on 120 gsm Huntsman Velvet coated cartridge by The Garden City Press, Letchworth, Herts, for the publishers, Patrick Stephens Limited, Bar Hill, Cambridge, CB3 8EL, England.

Contents

Acknowledgements

Among the countless people who gave so freely of their time, memories and photographs
to enliven this volume, I would especially like to thank the press departments of
Volkswagen and Audi as well as leading engineers of both firms. Particular thanks are due
to Dr Bernard Wiersch, head of VW archives, for both files and photos; as they are to
those early Beetle supporters Ghislaine and Herbert Kaes, Hans Klauser, Professor W.
Rixmann, Joachim Fischer and Major Ivan Hirst. I hope they, and so many others, will
find the result justifies their unselfish assistance.

Makers of a legend

'As long as the automobile remains transportation for a preferred circle only, it will be difficult to accept its class-dependent, even its sadly class-dividing, character. Therefore, the car must become transport for the entire volk.' *Adolf Hitler*

'Hitler's backing was simply necessary to put my ideas across.' *Ferdinand Porsche*

'When somebody can built a better or cheaper car than mine, it will be all right with me.' *Henry Ford*

'I realized full well that the greater part of the responsibility would lie on my shoulders—and carried this burden gladly.' *Ferdinand Porsche*

'It was very special for young people to work for Porsche. He had a special feel for them.' *Hans Klauser*

'The autobahns can only be successful in conjunction with the Volkswagen; with a car which at least every tenth German can afford.' *N.S. Kurier*

'This vehicle doesn't even fulfill the basic technical requirements which any automobile must meet.' *Rootes Commission*

'The Beetle is as full of faults as a dog is of fleas.' *Heinz Nordhoff*

'Nordhoff was something of an enigma to ordinary mortals like myself.' *Major Ivan Hirst*

'You know, Herr Nordhoff, this is the way I always imagined it. But I didn't know I was right until you proved it.' *Ferdinand Porsche*

'Even if all car sales should come to an end some day, the last automobile purchased will be a Volkswagen . . . Germany should follow where Volkswagen leads, not the other way around.' *Heinz Nordhoff*

'Volkswagen was such an exemplary model of the problems, goals and lessons in industrial politics that it would have to be established as the text book if it didn't already exist.' *Kurt Lotz*

'Building an automobile is a matter of taste. Our philosophy was to build a car for people who like to drive.' *Ludwig Kraus*

'First they all said we were too stolid—then they said we were moving too fast with new models. Never follow short-term trends.'   *Rudolf Leiding*

'Nobody could design a proper automobile in Wolfsburg.'   *Ludwig Kraus*

'It is comforting to know I drive the most thoroughly-engineered car in the world.'
                                                                            American customer

'Hard-won test results are the better results.'   *Ferdinand Piëch*

'You have to know what you want.'   *Ernst Fiala*

'The golden age of the automobile is behind us.'   *Toni Schmücker*

The plant today, from the air.

Chapter 1

That elusive thing called a 'Volks' car

The Volkswagen itself is an automobile born out of debate and nurtured by controversy, so it seems only appropriate to preface any examination of its convoluted life with a possibly-contentious statement:

While a great many interesting post-war cars have done their best to project some aura of universal recognition which would equate with fame, there remains only one which may be absolutely sure it would be identified instantly, no matter where in this world it might come to rest—from Park Lane penthouse to the last igloo in Antarctica. That one car is the VW Beetle.

In fact, this curious machine could still lay honest claim to the title of most popular four-wheel vehicle in the century even if it had not managed to underline that bare boast by topping even the Model T legend with sales of nearly 20 million (and still climbing). Such overwhelming success naturally makes one wonder just what might have been so special—perhaps even unique—about the background or birth of this Beetle.

It is a truism that any highly-visible automobile star has enjoyed exceptionally shrewd (or lucky) timing at some point in its career. But in the case of the Volkswagen, the luck on its side was plain extraordinary and sorely needed more than once. This may be the only car in motoring history which was launched, largely by chance, at precisely the right moment—twice over. Not only was the original presentation timely from the standpoint of support from a bottomless state purse, but the car then basked in ten further years of 'cost-no-object' military testing before facing its actual public presentation. It is certainly true that no comparable project could have found such friendly financing on the open money market. And probably at least as true that this VW could never have become the commercial proposition it was after 1948 without all that 1939 fanfare. Admitting both points, we still must concede that the most important launch factor of all remained a small clique of true believers.

We even find that the Beetle's ultimate success was not really based on an array of exotic design modes or futuristic materials after all—although many VW features did indeed break new ground—but far more on the fact that a handful of obstreperous, opinionated but dedicated men happened to want something they could logically promote as a 'volks' car, and that they all wanted this same thing at roughly the same point in time.

Men like Hitler, Ferdinand Porsche—even Ivan Hirst, Heinz Nordhoff or Toni Schmücker after the war—all played key roles in the VW story. The first of them threw the full powers of his muscle-flexing new state behind the much-debated engineering theories of the second, a bull-headed man who had proved decisively that he could never function properly within an established motor industry. But it was left to a post-war man to wrap up their project and tie a shining bow around it.

When we consider this array of divisive elements in the VW heritage it becomes easy to suppose that this KdF machine, as the Nazi hierarchy came to call it, was simply predestined to succeed, regardless of all odds. There is a theory that if the Beetle had not appeared from pre-war Germany, somebody would have been forced to invent it later. This does ignore all the efforts Porsche made to launch something similar before the Beetle. In actual fact this car was a very close-run thing. Even if hindsight suggests the Volkswagen was an idea whose time had come, the truth is that the single-minded men behind it only barely managed to complete their chosen task.

For one thing, the very name of 'Volkswagen' had already been applied to too many failed Germanic small cars. Next, the VW proper was originally presented to a waiting world under the name of *Kraft durch Freude Wagen,* or Strength through Joy Car, hardly the most catchy of titles. Furthermore, both its engineering father and governmental godfather may have shared a single vision but the nominal overseers and selected promoters, Germany's motor barons, had a strong vested interest in squashing it without a trace—and damn near did just that. Finally, its actual birth was left to the mercies of bureaucrats.

Whatever minor miracles may have occurred down through 40-odd VW years, the real wonder of this whole Volkswagen tale is the pure fact that it was born at all. In the end, two driven men who had long dreamed of a peoples' car got together, each for his own reasons, and built one; with no regard for logic. One of those men was Adolf Hitler, a long-time car buff who once used the very last of his own party's inflation funds, in 1923, to buy a 60 hp Mercedes. Ten years later he had reached power so recently that he opened the 1933 Berlin automobile show in a dinner jacket, not a uniform, but he was already declaring a pet project: motorise the masses.

Hitler stated flatly that all car industry efforts along those lines up to that date were clearly insufficient when it came to matching his own seven-point programme. This hinged on the *Reichs-Autobahn* network begun that June (and owned originally by the state railroad, incidentally). This grand design called for 14,000 autobahn km/8,700 miles, of which 3,800 km/2,400 miles would be completed by the summer of 1942 at a cost of 5,655 million *Reichsmarks,* not even counting rest stops where the man who pumped your petrol also served the coffee.

Such a super highway network, able to carry good Germans to all corners of their land, obviously called for special car shapes which might utilise it fully. 'Streamlining' then meant a teardrop and that was achieved most easily with the rear-mounted engine in this early-30s era when any autobahn trip would make you a hero of the local car club.

As the automobile completed its first half-century, the cheapest proper car in Germany was a 20 hp, 700 cc, two-stroke DKW, selling for 2,350 Rmk (when £1 = 12.50 Rmk) and there was no guarantee it would survive a long autobahn trip. Between that and the 3,000 mark level, buyers had a choice of 1.1 to 1.3 litre cars from NSU/Fiat, Opel, Ford, Adler or Hanomag but three of those were built by foreign-owned companies, another thorn in Hitler's eye, and none was really within reach of the worker. A metal worker who built such cars earned about 42 Rmk per week and a top construction hand no more than 70, while a pound of beef or litre (quart) of beer went for 75 *pfennigs.* Hitler had ample reason to insist that his peoples' car would have to be far cheaper than any contemporary, before the average man could afford one. Or afford to run it, for that matter.

His first move, on April 10 1933, was to abolish the registration tax for any buyer of a new automobile or motorcycle. Current owners could make one final tax payment by October 1. When Ferdinand Porsche heard that speech, including the statement, 'we will lift the German industry to a place of world leadership', he commented, 'that sounds good at least'. That same September Jakob Werlin, the Munich dealer who had sold that 1923

Mercedes to Hitler and was to become his chief automotive adviser, visited Porsche in Stuttgart. He listened closely to the designer's broad ideas for a popular car, then invited Porsche to Berlin—without saying exactly why.

In Berlin the engineer was shown into a hotel room and told, 'Hitler will be right in. He's very interested, personally, in a small car project'. When they met Porsche was first bemused that the busy leader recalled a very casual first meeting eight years earlier at the Solitude races, then amazed to hear Hitler replay Porsche's own volks-car ideas back as the new state goals. It was only left for Porsche to ask what price would be set on this dream car. Hitler responded, 'any price you like, Herr Porsche . . . so long as it is less than one thousand marks'. Porsche was privately convinced that was pure fantasy but the two Austrians had found common ground so he agreed to send Hitler a memorandum or *exposé* of his peoples' car proposals anyway. This document distilled Porsche's life-long small-car dream into five points:

1—A small car could not be properly realised by merely reducing dimensions, at the expense of performance or longevity. Rather, it must be a utilitarian car of normal size but low weight, this to be achieved through new production means and materials.

2—Power must not be cut at the sacrifice of top speed. This must be a utility car capable of normal speeds and mountain-climbing abilities.

3—Neither size nor number of seats could be reduced by lowering comfort levels. This car must offer normal, accepted levels of space and comfort.

4—Such a new design should not be limited to one application—Porsche foresaw various car, truck and military vehicles, all based on one engine/chassis combination.

5—The car should avoid all complicated components which might require involved maintenance. The goal was fool-proof servicing.

His last two points had obvious appeal for any government which might soon be using unskilled military drivers. Hitler agreed whole-heartedly that his wonder car could not be cheaply built, only priced for the low-income buyer.

Porsche was determined utility could not take precedence over safety and proposed to realise a full-value car by applying new solutions to old problems. Even then he felt 1,000 Rmk was not logical and almost retired from the discussions when this became a fixed factor. Then he rationalised that Hitler could probably be eased up to an end price of 1,500 Rmk once he saw the first prototypes.

The Fuehrer was certainly far more intrigued by automobile technology than Porsche by politics. There was a fashion in the first post-war years to lump the Czech-born designer with all Nazi industrial exploiters. His apologists over-reacted by claiming he was so naive he had not even noticed the mood of the German 30s.

Seen more objectively, there is simply no indication Porsche ever supported 'the' party, or any other, although he was made an honorary German on December 17 1934 when he obviously could do little more than comment wryly, 'there isn't much we can do about that'.

He was, and remained, an Austrian and a remarkably one-tracked solver of technical problems, not in the least naive when it came to finding the right lever which might set his pet machinery in motion. Once he produced a new design he saw no possible reason to withhold it from the people and if the Devil himself had offered land for a factory, with all the forces of the nether world to market its product, I'm sure Porsche would have named his car Diablo, added low-cost air conditioning and begun prototype tests.

Porsche was never a selfless god. He simply felt a peoples' car would be the culmination of his life work. He was a hard-headed, self-taught genius at spotting correct solutions hidden in the chaff, a restless man never satisfied with himself or others. This son of a

An early Porsche design from his electric period with Lohner of Vienna.

Bohemian tinsmith was first attracted to electricity, then to electric automobiles, starting with the Lohner-Porsche *Elektrochaise*, built in Vienna. It founded his four-wheel fame by winning acclaim at the 1900 Paris fair. In 'improved' form it also opened his life-long love affair with competition. Ferdinand won his first race in it at 14 kph/9 mph. This doubtless convinced him the idea was right and he would always be a hard man to shift from an idea, once conceived. Porsche clung to electrics, only grudgingly moving on to a mixed-drive car with petrol engine generating power for electric hub motors.

This won a 1905 Austrian prize for best construction of the year but even that could not persuade Lohner to underwrite Ferdinand's expensive ideas any longer. He became a very young technical director at Austro Daimler where he finally built his first pure petrol automobile, named Maja for the sister of Mercedes Jellinek. This Maja became not only the most successful seller in pre-war Austria but also the machine which brought the works team medals in the 1909 Prince Henry Trial.

When Porsche then studied the Prince Henry rules for 1910 he realised weight and wind resistance would have to be cut much further so he evolved the tulip shape which added 10 kph/6 mph to the top speed and, incidentally, introduced a forerunner of streamlining to the land. This car also featured an improved six-cylinder engine by race week and proved as successful as its predecessor.

During the first war Porsche revived his petrol/electric drive theory for a 100 hp howitzer tractor-train which worked so well the Vienna Technical University awarded him his first honorary doctorate, in 1917. He would never be one to drop a good idea entirely.

Now general director of Austro Daimler, Porsche used his power to launch the first visible result of his small car ideas, the one-litre Sascha which earned laurels in the Targa Florio precisely because it broke with the 'bigger is better' school of racing car design.

Since the first women began to drive at the turn of the century Porsche had sought easier car control. As early as 1909 the press had noted that his first small car idea would still be full-value transport. However, the Austro Daimler board felt its future lay with

One of the earliest 'small' Porsche cars, the Austro-Daimler Sascha named after Count Sascha Kolowrat (in the seat) and a successful Targa racer although it never reached production (one reason why Porsche left Austro-Daimler).

fewer, fancier cars. Austria, in fact, was not the land to preview mass transport as both the Sascha and his small Steyr proved. Porsche had proved too expensive for his firm once again so he moved on, to Daimler in Stuttgart during June 1923.

Within a year he had reworked their supercharged two-litre engine and set Daimler on the path of single-ohc, inline sixes they follow today. The 1926 merger of Daimler with Benz increased tensions for Porsche whose intuitive leaps and reliance on instinct rather than mathematical explanation often dismayed the staid board. He left.

After three stormy decades with five firms (including Steyr briefly) it was apparent, even to Porsche, that he was not meant to be an employee, not even at the top. With characteristic disregard for the 1930 Depression, he opened his own design offices in Stuttgart where he could contemplate the popular car in peace, if not in wealth at first. On August 10 1931 he filed the patent for one of the key features of his rich career, the torsion bar suspension which became a major victory in his unending battle against weight and complication, as well as the basis for everything from peoples' transport to the Auto Union racing car.

Late in September 1931 Porsche gathered his small, élite team together and announced they would now design a cheap, high-quality car for everyman. If neither Austro Daimler nor Daimler Benz could see such a clear light, he would simply do it on his own, well ahead of Hitler we note. Porsche might have added that virtually every top motoring designer up to that point had tried such a thing as well. The fact that none had solved the price/size puzzle would only have spurred Porsche on. His own list of similar projects included the 130 H Mercedes with central tube frame and rear engine, dropped once he left Daimler Benz but revived for the 1934 Berlin auto show.

There would even be an air-cooled, flat-four engine in the American White Horse, running as a prototype about the time Porsche made his first US visit, but he almost certainly never saw one. The call for a low-priced car was at least as old as the December

1904 issue of *der Motorwagen,* the thought of doing it more or less the Beetle way was not a lot younger.

Boxer engines go clear back to the 1898 Benz *contra motor.* More to our point, Bela Barenzi suggested the opposed piston or boxer powerplant in his 1926 student thesis and Ledwinka had put a twin in the tail of his 1924 Tatra, then fitted a fan-cooled four in 1928. Not to forget the Viennese Avis, a small car propelled by a boxer twin, which Josef Kales sketched well before he joined Porsche's team. These and several similar forerunners tend to reduce the impact of claims by Josef Ganz who insisted later that the Volkswagen had been stolen from his designs.

As editor of the magazine *Motor Kritik,* Ganz sponsored rear engines, independent suspension and the backbone frame for a decade so we can hardly ignore his contributions. He also designed cars, including suggestions for Zündapp in 1929, and one actually built by Ardie in 1930. That carried their 175 cc bike engine ahead of its rear swing axles. A more powerful, 1931 Adler by Ganz was even called *maikaefer* or May Beetle.

Standard was next to take up the Ganz theme, in 1932, when its 1,590 Rmk Superior was advertised as a 'German Volkswagen'. This carried a boxer twin ahead of the rear axle. Some 700 orders for this car were booked at the 1933 Berlin show where both Goering and Hühnlein admired the design and rushed to engage its creator—until they discovered he was a Hungarian Jew. So they jailed him for a month of questioning instead, then forbid the Ganz byline on any future articles.

Drawing the logical conclusions, Ganz moved to Switzerland in 1934 and to Paris in 1948 where he worked on another small car before emigrating to Australia. He found time there to back his claim as the true father of the Volkswagen. He insisted an unknown man had copied his Ardie, then passed these drawings to Zündapp when a *Motor Kritik* editor happened to be present. Porsche supposedly took over the eventual VW layout from Zündapp.

Left *Porsche's son, Ferry (seated) and one of his father's most loyal colleagues, Karl Rabe, still under the parental eye.*

Right *Direct VW forerunner, the almost-Beetle car Porsche designed for NSU (who decided to stick to motorcycles as they had promised Fiat, in any case). At least one of the prototypes survived the war.*

The Professor replied that he had had the combination in mind for years—and that it was hardly original in any case. The French Claveau and Guerin cars both featured rear engines (the first even a flat four) with independent suspension as early as 1926-27. Rumpler and the Italian San Giusto used such features five years earlier still and Dornier proposed an air-cooled, V-twin diesel for a cheap car in 1924. In short; the trick lies in getting an idea produced, not in merely having one.

Heinz Nordhoff probably put Ganz in proper perspective when he noted in a 1959 speech that many young engineers had been spurred on by Josef Ganz and his magazine which had the courage to attack established firms with biting irony. Ganz has his place in car history for vision and devotion to the affordable automobile. To be fair, he always esteemed Porsche personally and blamed the Nazis for all the 'thefts'.

Come to that, the KdF was far from Porsche's first try along Beetle lines. During 1932 he was delighted to find a backer for his volks idea, even if it meant mounting Zündapp's pet water-cooled, radial five in the tail of a semi-streamlined 900 kg/1,980 lb car on a 250 cm/98.5 in wheelbase. Son Ferry Porsche does claim that this engine was at least partly his father's choice as well.

It produced 26 hp from 1.2 litres and lost all its oil in the first 10 km/6 miles of its maiden outing but that was not the sole reason Zündapp paid the 85,000 Rmk fee and dropped the project. They were primarily motorcycle builders and two-wheelers had entered upon a new boom meanwhile. This setback very nearly prompted Porsche to take the Russian government up on an offer to control all things motorised in their land, however. In the end Russia proved too far from home and the people there spoke the wrong language.

Before he could regret that decision, another motorcycle builder nibbled at his popular car project; in 1933. These NSU prototypes were the real VW forerunners, featuring a lineal descendent of Porsche's own first air-cooled, boxer engine. That had been a 2 litre, ohv twin built for Austro Daimler way back in 1912. Expanded to four cylinders with

NSU prototype and pre-war KdF Beetle meet after the war.

dimensions of 80 × 72 mm/3.15 × 2.84 in, this NSU powerplant carried its fan on the crankshaft nose (about 25 years too soon) and produced 20 hp from 1.45 litres.

The wheelbase had been stretched to 260 cm/102 in but the car only weighed some 790 kg/1,660 lb while carrying a payload of 370 kg/775 lb and reaching 90 kph/55 mph. 320,000 km/200,000 miles and a war later, one of these NSU prototypes would still touch 72 kph/45 mph. It featured the patented Porsche torsion bars—which his mechanics called spring bars—and was excessively noisy, as NSU had noted in the early 30s.

Larger and roomier than the Zündapp, this car also fell foul of recovering bike sales, plus the fact that NSU had sold its car side to Fiat and promised not to go into direct competition. So Porsche designed another racing car, his standard consolation when a small car project foundered. He also showed the NSU prototype in France where Citroën took out a suspension licence and Mathis adopted torsion bars. Unlike the eventual VW, this NSU had only one arm of the front suspension on each side connected to the torsion member.

This pair of pre-Volkswagens did help settle Porsche's thinking. When his exposé then reached Hitler's desk in mid-January 1934 it was well formed and perfectly timed to give the Fuehrer material for his second public attack on the German car industry, again at a Berlin show opening: 'I would like to see a mass-produced German car which could be purchased by any person with sufficient funds to buy a middle-class motorcycle', the leader announced. 'It is bitter to think that millions of sturdy, hard-working citizens must be barred from a means of travel which would not only be useful to them but, above all, a source of happiness on Sundays and holidays.'

Each of his speeches, opening the annual Berlin motor shows, would echo this same mass-motoring theme with little specific reference to the VW. In 1936, for instance, the theme was bringing Germany on to par with Ford's America.

The coming car itself was left to government-inspired articles which began to appear regularly after 1934. It was obvious that the chancellor intended to push his car industry into a new future and equally clear that German manufacturers might be willing to do their own volks versions but they had no intention of producing a joint car. And even less interest in any work from the Porsche design office.

Still, Hitler held the reins, so the *Reichsverband der Deutsche Automobilindustrie* or RDA, which ruled over all car production, announced it would 'make all means available to Porsche'. That translated into a contract, signed on June 22 1934, giving him 20,000 Rmk a month for ten months. They were ordering up a near-miracle on a ridiculously tight budget, so remained confident little could ensue.

Porsche realised clearly that his preparations must be minutely thorough, and that 'all responsibility lay on his shoulders', but he was willing to carry that *if* the industry would do its part. The almost-insulting fee, incidentally, had to cover himself, his co-workers and all costs apart from business trips. Fortunately his young crew felt privileged to work for Porsche who had a special rapport with up and coming men. One recalled, 'he wasn't always what you might call a comfortable man to work for—impatient like all his type—but he was a good boss and always fair'.

Next Wilhelm von Opel told Porsche, with some condescension, 'it's a wonderful contract, Herr Porsche. Ten months on good pay and then you tell our leaders their project is impossible'. To be honest, that rather matched Porsche's own assessment but the jibe made him just stubborn enough to take on the fiercest battle of his hardly calm career.

He had always disliked the downsizing factor in all previous popular car attempts and even though he began with the NSU prototypes in his garage, his basic conviction was that all existing cars could be bettered by a wide margin. The VW was touted quite early as a car in a class all its own, the 'classless car', which it soon became in fact.

Porsche's original parameters, followed with amazing fidelity, included a 250 cm/98.5 in wheelbase and 120 cm/47.3 in track, a one-litre engine producing 26 hp at 3,500 rpm, and an empty weight of 650 kg/1,435 lb. He calculated these figures would meet his goal of a 100 kph/60 mph top (and also cruising) speed with consumption of 8 l-100 km or 35 mpg. He expected all this to cost about 1,500 Rmk, not a figure mentioned prominently around Berlin.

First they had to build the pre-prototypes, using hand tools in the four-car garage of his own Stuttgart villa where his wife's laundry room held the lathe and power drill. Subsequent propaganda photos would show Plant I, built a few years later, instead.

Chassis layout proved far less of a problem than hand-built bodies which, in turn, were a cinch compared to early engine woes. This last problem stemmed from a Porsche fixation on the two-cycle system as the only way he could even approach Hitler's price limit. Unfortunately two-stroke engines would not stand up to steady, full-speed autobahn runs despite ample use of rare alloys, variations between twins, triples and radials, even fuel injection and/or dual-piston layouts. They even brought in a specialist from Puch before eventually realising that few motorcyclists run flat out for very long, due to wind and weather.

Next Porsche experimented with a four-stroke using sleeve valves actuated at first by rods which promptly broke, then by cams and torsion bar return springs. But he did not finally abandon the two-stroke idea until 1938. Other byways investigated, despite time pressure, included turbocharging (gas flow proved too meagre) and a Roots supercharger which gave 40 hp.

For most of 1935, however, he 'improved' the two-cycle twin of 960 cc or worked around a four-stroke twin which could not push the car to more than 85 kph/53 mph, even using dual carburettors, and that was clearly too slow once the first autobahn segment was open. After all, his VW would become the first German car priced below 5,000 Rmk and capable of all-day cruising at 100 kph/60 mph. On the body side he persuaded the RDA to authorise a third test car to be built entirely of steel, alongside the wood-framed pair in his original contract. By now it was clear too he could never meet the first deadline and a 12-month extension was granted.

One of the first turning points in VW development came at an August 1935 meeting when the head of Ambi-Budd, a body producer, suggested there could be little or no price gain in reducing interior space. This was the first industry support for Porsche's concept of the full-value basic car.

There were several such skirmishes, leading up to a full session of the RDA committee in Berlin on February 24 1936, where industry leaders examined the original pair of prototypes and conferred at length. The Porsches, father and son, were faced on this occasion by top managers from Ambi-Budd, Adler, Auto Union, Bosch, Hanomag, Hansa-Lloyd, Mercedes, NSU, Opel and Stöwer, as well as several RDA engineers. Werlin and von Opel were notable absentees, as was Maybach, while BMW had declared that the bus was your only real means of 'volks transport'.

The RDA was quick to praise interior space and the cars' new features but doubted that the public would ever buy such an odd shape. There was obvious self-satisfaction in their comment that Porsche must admit his two-cycle engine was a clear failure in the one car while the four-stroke twin in the other lacked adequate power.

All present agreed 1,000 Rmk was an illusion for the cars presented, insisting it would not even cover materials. After emphasising strict secrecy the chairman added they could hardly give their Fuehrer a rosy report on that point, in good faith. The remainder of this pivotal meeting was largely devoted to wrangling over possible production pricing. Body estimates ranged from 550 Rmk by the RDA to 320 from Porsche who leaned heavily on his hopes of using advanced American know-how, although Auto Union countered that 75 per cent of the price differential lay in materials so a low US wage hardly mattered. Bosch added that Great Britain, with its depressed pound, was the better comparison and no true four-seater there sold for less than 1,500 Rmk.

The two sides were a little closer on chassis pricing—712 versus 755 Rmk—but even if they accepted Porsche's lower estimate and assumed a cheaper body might somehow be built, they were still discussing a 1,350-1,400 Rmk automobile, no longer a 'volks' car but a direct competitor for Opel and Auto Union. These firms felt it would share an annual market of 75-80,000 sales, yet the VW was projected for an eventual 100,000 by itself and propaganda releases dreamed of the million-car factory.

At this point in the meeting Opel's man read a prepared statement contending that the VW price was too close to their own, thus unfair competition. The government should let his industry get on with its own various small car projects. NSU chimed in that the cars shown were virtually what Porsche had done for them and those had been 'full of flaws'. The mistake, as NSU saw it, 'lay in hiring a chassis man who lacked body experience'.

Porsche was in a corner—trying to justify a price he did not believe himself. He turned to defending details, such as keeping the parallel-arm front suspension but dropping its ball joints. A one-arm model would only save 11 Rmk and not work nearly as well. He had already abandoned Silentbloc engine mounts on price grounds and skipped a limited slip differential although it was filed away for later military use.

After extensive bickering Daimler Benz suggested one or two RDA member firms might build pilot cars to obtain a clearer price picture. The project was not that advanced, in fact, but it was the first, oblique suggestion that a separate VW factory might be necessary, a most unappetising concept for the small car producers. Opel countered that somebody should try and sell such cars—to see if any German would buy one—before considering a plant.

The upshot of this first full meeting was a decision to have Daimler Benz project chassis costs while Ambi-Budd would calculate body prices more carefully and Adler (with Hanomag, who had not said a word) should price actual production on the basis of 100,000 units. Meanwhile, RDA engineers would drop all other work to monitor lists and drawings which Porsche agreed to provide by June 30 against the threat that otherwise the industry would have to take over his entire project. When the RDA continued to debate his pricing Porsche recalculated with the aid of US specialists and found they might even come close to his figures with new methods. He actually found leeway for a few improvements within the cost framework.

Shortly after this meeting Porsche published again. He argued that less than four—even five—seats would be unsocial, and that only latest methods to match the advanced designs would ensure that this car would not be technically outdated before it even appeared. He also admitted a four-stroke engine might be 'easier to export', without giving up the two-stroke. Porsche was always changing designs to conform with his latest idea. He was a man of grand concepts, often leaving design of a workable mechanism as such to the eternally loyal Karl Rabe.

The turning point on price came in considering production numbers previously unknown in Europe. That January Hitler had declared, in his show speech, they could be very happy such a brilliant engineer was making such fine progress. He expected first tests by mid-year, an illusion, but even Porsche could not delay the decision on an engine type much longer.

The Fuehrer's curious 'American complex' had also surfaced in that speech. It was another fixation shared with Porsche. Both men thoroughly admired Ford's output for the price, and the spread of popular motoring in the US. The only dislikes Porsche had of America were over-iced beer, a sacrilege to any man from Bohemia, and the inevitable butter at every meal since he had an abhorrence of that food. As for the VW, Hitler pointed out that if it could cost only 900 Rmk, one could be purchased by a German working the same number of hours as his American counterpart laboured to buy a car. This ignored the fact that one German hour only bought three quarts of fuel, about a tenth as much as an hour of American work.

Porsche's team realised full well that buyers would have to earn at least 400 Rmk a month to afford even a 1,000 mark car plus expenses. They hoped Hitler would see it too but he was blinded by the idea that existing cars split Germans into classes while even the poorest should be able to save for a VW.

First they had to provide a car for Hitler to admire. And that meant a boxer four as engine. It was short, a vital factor for rear mounting, easily air-cooled, cost-effective with only four cam lobes, inherently balanced for primary and secondary forces and—once rigidity problems could be solved—promised a long life. Franz Reimspiess got the job of putting it all on paper and while he was not overwhelmed with the original concept, he did an engine very like that still built today, and one which weighed little more than their own twin. This earned him a spontaneous 100 Rmk bonus from Porsche.

Iron cylinder barrels reduced cost but thermal expansion variations between magnesium crankcase, aluminium heads (they risked an unusual amount of alloy for that era) and steel drive train parts would prove a long-term problem. Even after the critical oil cooler was added it was always hard to pinpoint proper valve clearances and the engine never liked to be lugged in a high gear. Wear limits were generous—piston ring gaps could triple before becoming critical.

This engine for owners who would park outdoors proved more rigid on the road than it

One of the original VW3 cars built at the Porsche villa by hand to demonstrate that the system would work, then tested in late 1936 to end phase one of the project.

had looked on paper. Piston speeds were restricted, in part because the first version had only three main bearings and no oil cooler, plus an electric fuel pump. Dual inlet ports in the first drawings were later turned into one passage for price reasons, when a carburettor cost 3.50 Rmk. Horsepower/cubic centimetre was hardly exciting but it could be refined into a long-living wonder, with testing.

Part one of an unprecedented test programme began on October 12 1936, despite imminent winter. Porsche was so far behind his target date there was no option. However, they had already done some private chassis testing through the Alps over Easter, using the two- and four-stroke twins.

Now the RDA scheduled 30,000 km/18,000 miles on each of three cars, a plan soon expanded to 50,000/30,000 apiece. This would be driven in two shifts a day, every day but Sunday, to cover 750 km/465 miles daily. It meant nearly 15 hours for each driver, accompanied by six young engineers recruited from Stuttgart and Berlin technical schools as observers. Driver/observer pairs stayed together for the entire test and drove the same car throughout, although they shifted from day shift to night shift and back each week.

Facing such a stiff test of a small car Porsche decreed that responsible designers from his office must go along as often as possible. Thus each car carried at least two men with a third of the distance driven four-up plus 30 kg/65 lb of 'luggage'. At times even Porsche's private chauffeur had to help with the driving and he was always on call with the family sedan and trailer to collect broken cars.

The RDA test chief admitted later his industry wanted no part of a success so they logged every squeak and groan, yet he felt his final report had been 'positive' and expressed real hope that outstanding problems could be solved.

Test teams left the Porsche villa at six each morning for 350 km/215 miles of back roads, mostly pot-holed gravel, through the Black Forest and over the car-killing Herrenalb gradient used to wring out Mercedes. Each ran alone and the public seemed unaware they were seeing the much-discussed peoples' car although some villages did wonder at the same car passing through at the same time every day. Following a checkover at the villa, there were 400 km/250 miles of highway plus the one completed bit of autobahn each afternoon, turning around in Frankfurt where the crankshafts always broke if they were going to because it made the longest tow home.

Since the story of 20 million Beetles begins here we might take a closer look at the stars; V1 and V2 were the wood-framed, metal-panelled saloon and convertible, weighing 825 kg/1,735 lb and 845 kg/1,750 respectively, while V3 was the 720 kg/1,515 lb, all-metal series of three test cars numbered I, II and III. They all looked more like the NSU than later Beetles since details like headlights in the wings, sketched by Kommenda months before, could only be fitted when time allowed.

The cars can be confused from old photos since components were swapped or replaced throughout the test. The half-lid in front, a Kommenda favourite, skinned the knuckles of every driver who changed a wheel but the body designer was not known for changing a design lightly, once made. The crew finally arranged a wheel change at the villa and invited Kommenda to hoist that spare out of its well, through the tiny opening. When his fingers were bloodied too, full length lids followed quickly.

V3-I opened testing with 8,000 km/5,000 miles clocked up from alpine runs and a forged crankshaft in three main bearings. Its troubles included a torn front axle mount, brake fade after 21,000 km/13,000 miles and a broken torsion bar which scarcely reduced its 55 km/35 mph average. On one occasion a passing pedestrian did call their attention to a wiring fire, on another day it was a burned exhaust valve and when number four connecting rod snapped after 43,997 km/27,340 miles, they swapped engines.

That first engine suffered total oil loss on the dynamometer during one of the Kamm Institute checks run every 6,000 km/3,700 miles, but matters like a broken gear lever (common to all three cars), sliding gently into a truck one icy day or running down a hart, merely enlivened the long slog. The venison, enjoyed with dumplings by the entire crew, reportedly came direct from von Opel's private hunting ground.

The chassis of VW3.

Above *Short lid of VW3 which caused scraped knuckles when the spare wheel was lifted out. The fuel tank is behind, with not much space for luggage.*

Below *Early test runs with closed and open VW3 cars, two of the three built.*

Test logs for V3-II and V3-III were quite similar. Most failures traced to the fact that there had been no time for materials checks before installation. V2 was barely run-in when the test began. On day one it lost compression on number four cylinder, then broke a gear lever. A day later the cast crankshaft broke for the first of three times in the first 13,397 km/8,325 miles, giving them a chance to time a complete engine swap. Four men had it out in 14 minutes, three others disassembled in 40 more. The basic VW concept of service ease was thus ahead of its time.

Even without hitting a motorcycle, V3-II would have been the most repaired car. It also broke a con rod, burned the same exhaust valve twice, broke a rear brake drum and suffered persistent front wheel flutter. V3-III shared that last trait although the all-metal car had covered 5,000 km/3,000 miles before the group test began. It recorded constant electric fuel pump woes and a loud noise in top gear. Following a broken rod—and a 12-hour tow home—they discovered there were no more crankcase halves so part of its run was covered with that under-powered boxer twin in the tail. Two earlier pilot cars, those shown to the RDA early in 1936, were also used as hard as possible when time permitted. This should explain the stories that Porsche actually built five 'prototypes' prior to the W30 series.

Alongside the set tests, cars might be used for special projects such as brake and clutch lining studies run on the notorious Gross Glockner in Austria. There was a side report that the VW would climb this famous pass in little more than twice the time a Porsche-designed Auto Union Grand Prix car of 600 hp required. Many of its peers could not make the top at all without boiling.

Despite the many dramas—on one occasion a hub fractured and threw the wheel through a window—all tests were completed just before Christmas 1936, as all drivers had firmly intended from the start. The cars were then checked minutely in early January and an eagerly-awaited report filed with the RDA on the 26th of that month. This 100-page record was icily correct, knowing full well this car was a pet of the Third Reich.

In essence the RDA had to declare the design purposeful with no basic flaws and no changes proposed to original dimensions. However, many alterations were needed in body details and mechanical brakes were criticised in full knowledge that royalties for foreign-made hydraulics had already been forbidden. Handling and performance were rated good, consumption acceptable.

The RDA virtually had to conclude that this car had qualities which would make a larger test sample worthwhile. More could be expected of batch two since these would be built by a proper car plant, to showroom finish standards. In effect, this was the starting signal for the Volkswagen as Porsche had always wanted it but the RDA was far from silenced. For one thing, Opel and Ford declined to attend a pricing conference on VW components, claiming a lack of plant capacity prevented their contributing. For a while longer improvisation would still rule the scene.

The RDA pointed out yet again that the car could never be produced for the target price and suggested (also again) that their members take over all further development, matching the next series of test cars against their own best offerings. A week after that idea was turned in the government told the RDA to return all files instead. The Fuehrer felt a victim of overseas (Opel/GM and Ford) intrigue. Henceforth the VW would be a pure state project and Porsche suddenly found himself operating with sufficient, even lavish, funds for probably the first time in his entire engineering career.

Chapter 2

From prototype to 'production'

The year 1937 began with press and public half-expecting an early Volkswagen. Hitler had opened the annual Berlin motor show with another of his surprise statements: 'final production preparations were virtually complete'. He was premature again, by years rather than months.

And von Opel again managed to further a project he despised by antagonising its principal backer. When Hitler reached the stand featuring Opel's new P4, von Opel said, 'and this, my Fuehrer, is *our* Volkswagen'. The leader stalked off, red-faced and speechless. He found his voice later to forbid Opel to drop the P4 price below 1,280 Rmk. That would put it too close to the VW.

Porsche's team soon grew to 100, funded by the *Deutsche Arbeitsfront* or DAF to which every German worker belonged perforce. And Werlin ordered the 30 prototypes from Daimler Benz for 'full' testing. As Porsche noted in a 1939 article, Hitler's backing was a simple necessity. This car was one part of his mass motorisation scheme, more than a model on its own. Industry leaders had underestimated this obsession.

It extended well beyond mere cars. During 1937 Porsche's design office drew up a light, cheap, air-cooled volks-tractor with 12 hp diesel engine in the rear. This Type 110 was

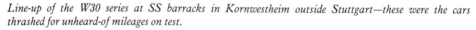

Line-up of the W30 series at SS barracks in Kornwestheim outside Stuttgart—these were the cars thrashed for unheard-of mileages on test.

Rear view of the W30 series showing front-opening doors and lack of rear window.

followed a year later by the 111 with air-cooled V-twin of a still-marginal 16 hp. Later they would try an inline twin using petrol as well. The design parameters were 3 kph/2 mph in rough going, twice as fast for easy work and 20 kph/12 mph on pavement.

As for those W30-series cars, testing began on a scale unknown anywhere. The project was based on an SS barracks outside Stuttgart where 200 army 'drivers' stood ready to thrash the cars in three shifts, around the clock, in temperatures ranging from −18 to +34 degrees C/0 to 93 degrees F. They even used the old section of Stuttgart for a 'city cycle' test.

Ferry Porsche often felt the SS was there more to record slips than merely drive. Every man had to sign a stern pledge of secrecy and promise not to smoke, drink or take pictures on duty. Drawn from every walk of life, these army men were mechanically inexperienced, an ideal test team which drove, abused and reported on the W30 range just as normal customers might have done.

Each car was to cover up to 80,000 km/50,000 miles, with the army told to show no mercy. A total effort of 1.35 million km/850,000 miles helped boost overall development costs to 30 million Rmk. It could be compared with the Ford practice of some 32,000 km/ 20,000 test miles for a new model then. Despite such obvious and massive exposure on open highways there were, in fact, very few photos taken by anybody since this test was officially a secret project, making it a crime for any civilian to notice.

The results were bound in a final report which noted that the 30 cars had averaged 7.42 l/100 km or 38.01 mpg overall and gone through an average of two sets of front tyres per car, but three sets of rears. 33,000 km/20,500 miles was the best tyre mileage for any car. Part of the distance was run on artifical, or buna, rubber which outlasted the natural kind. Two of the 30 topped 80,000 km/50,000 miles and one of those went on to log more than 100,000 km/62,000 miles.

Actual numbering began with 0, built by Porsche following V3 but included in the W30 series, making W29 the last number used. There were two cars bearing W2, following an accident to the first, and W6 got the body from W24 after both had been wrecked. Numbers 22 and 28 were actually show cars for high officials and seldom used on the SS route.

At times cars would be pulled out of the mass test for special work. In one case a car needed a wing exchanged in a small Austrian garage where the owner watched so closely that he could later confirm their basic design and thus win a patent suit brought by Tatra. Such alpine runs led them to consider a 1,131 cc engine option since this accelerated the car to 80 km/50 mph in 27.5 seconds, compared to 30 seconds for the standard 985 cc machine, which also had trouble reaching 100 kph/62 mph as planned. Porsche's office was also calculating production schedules, beginning with the high figure of 36.5 hours per car, reduced to 19 by December. That cut the wage share in half, to 56.91 Rmk per car, although 367.22 Rmk for chassis materials and 196.57 for the engine hardly dropped at all.

Meanwhile Karl Rabe, Porsche's long-time right hand, was listing design updates: 6:1 compression, rerouted fuel line, mechanical fuel pump, single intake passage, baffled oil filter and vented gearbox with stronger spring to protect reverse (later removed again), new front brakes, handbrake bracket and clutch cable, altered kingpin position, square three-piece torsion bar, improved boot lid attachment and (the most obvious need) a redesigned gear lever. The original ring-shaped oil cooler around the fan housing was soon replaced by an upright version used ever after.

Just as the test pace intensified it seemed that every Nazi crony wanted a private viewing, much to Porsche's disgust. Goebbels visited Stuttgart for a look, Goering was so

Checking early VW chassis—note the knobbly tyres. This makes the point that the car was easy to move around as needed.

Above *Compare W30 (left) and VW3, the forerunner.*

Below *The W30 model for the wind tunnel.*

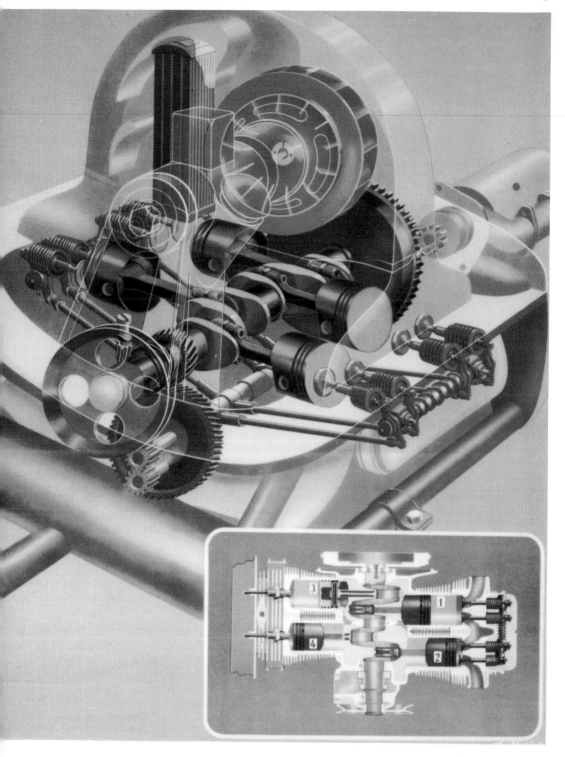

Left *Good schematic drawing of the basic Beetle engine which started it all.*

Left *Good schematic drawing of the basic Beetle engine which started it all.*

Right *Engine dismounted from car. A model with standing, rather than ring, oil cooler.*

heavy he tipped the car, which he did not like anyway since it cut into aeroplane quotas, and in November General von Blomberg, the SS boss, viewed a red saloon, dark blue cabriolet and a bare chassis. Then it was Party Treasurer Schwartz and, in December, Goebbels again with leaders of the four-year plan. This eventually led to an order for extra pre-series cars and an official public peek since these command performances were not only taking cars off the test run but were occupying the time of key Porsche men as well.

Germany even accommodated a few foreign journalists who pronounced the shape advanced, the interior spartan, acceleration loud but cruising speeds amazing and bad-road ride superior. Production planning continued to be euphoric: 17,500 workers on two shifts would build half a million cars a year. (In 1957 it would take 40,000 to build 450,000 VWs.) Porsche remained convinced, 'we can do it if the Americans can'. Since he actually had little idea what this factory he was supposed to head should look like he made two visits to the US, taking his secretary/nephew Ghislaine Kaes on the first and a full team a year later. Porsche himself spoke no English.

The late-1936 trip was devoted to prying about US assembly lines to his heart's content, timing procedures, and asking endless questions, all of which were answered freely—'except those about styling'. He also debated industry leaders like Ford who wanted no part of any joint venture with Germany. Henry I was convinced war was imminent, an idea Porsche discounted.

On the second trip stamping machines took second place to the idea of hiring back key, German-born production specialists. Werlin managed to convince several their future lay with VW; men like Kuntze who built the River Rouge power station; Mayer, a sheet metal technician who would body Beetles; Schneider for spot welding, a field little-known in Germany, and Werner, an expert on tooling. For some of these key men, VW salary offers were simply irresistible, many of the technicians were merely homesick, a few liked what they heard about the new Germany.

On the first trip Porsche bought a Packard to take home for study, on the second a Ford. It was during the 1937 trip that he also realised front-hinged doors were not only safer but the coming style as well so he wired home to have the W30 successor converted.

1937 was actually an uncertain year for the motor industry of Germany as von Schell produced his plan to throw out all overlapping models. Firms like BMW or Hanomag would be restricted to one capacity class while Auto Union could build in seven, Daimler Benz in six, Opel in five, including the key one where VW would be. It was also the year Porsche—as well as Heinkel and Messerschmitt—received national accolades for technical services to the Third Reich. Porsche was given an honorary German professorship since the Austrian honour was not recognised.

At the end of the year Reutter, the body works, received an order for another 30 cars, now labelled Porsche Type 60 or VW 38. These were very close to later production versions with a body designated 60 K 7, indicating the seventh *karosserie* or body style. The chief engine change was a test of aluminium main bearings (January 1938), leading to multi-layer mains.

In July Ferry led a team over their favourite alpine passes, matching the 303 (an improved W30) against direct rivals from Adler, DKW, Opel and Steyr. All except the DKW displaced roughly one litre and produced 20-25 hp but the VW outshone them all in top speed, consumption and autobahn durability, while 'costing' only half to a third as much. All this was part of its design brief.

Porsche people were at least as pleased when their baby also cornered better than front-drive contenders and proved vastly superior on the steep grades. They announced the design could progress to final pre-production polishing since the professor had always insisted it would only be a viable car when it was at least a step ahead of all existing small cars.

On October 12 the decision was made to follow VW38 (44 cars in the end) with VW39, 50 of which were to be completed by July 1939. That ignored war clouds and a military version which had really been a prime concern since the first and would be the only one after May 1938. After a showing to German generals all facilities were devoted to it as of June 1940.

Meanwhile, Hitler personally laid the cornerstone for a totally new factory in an all-new area on May 26 1938, attended by soft-top saloon, convertible and coupé prototypes. He took the Ascension Day occasion to stun even Porsche by naming the new car *Kraft durch Freude*, although signs surrounding the ceremony still said Volkswagen Werke. This KdF car would be built in a town of the same name on the new site, which most people did not like any better than they liked its title. In the end only the party's most faithful used KdF and Porsche commented it would be hard to sell many abroad under that name.

The cornerstone itself, with prominently carved swastika, very probably never even held the elaborate founding scroll which was not quite ready at the end of May. When it was broken open in 1945 the box was empty. Nordhoff could not stand the carving on a stone, apparently first set approximately where the high-rise office building is today, and had it buried in a ramp leading to the new canal bridge in 1959, probably under the pedestrian steps between the guard post gate and the car park. The exact location is not recorded.

The new plant came about after four RDA members made a belated offer to build the VW at 200 Rmk profit per car, too much for the dream of a million in Hitler's eyes. He would rather spend the 200 million on his own factory. The basic considerations were to build outside the existing industry, ignore plant construction costs, and be ready to turn

Above *The original cornerstone for the KdF plant, dated 1938. This apparently never contained the planned scroll and was later buried in the foundations of a bridge.*

Below *Hitler in the back of a machine he had just renamed KdF car, after the cornerstone ceremony, 1938.*

out cars by 1938. Hitler had used his pre-show Berlin dinner in February 1937 to add that Ley's DAF would embrace the VW task in all its ramifications; car, plant and town.

That same May Dr Bodo Lafferentz, husband of a Wagner granddaughter and Ley adjutant nominally responsible for arranging worker vacations, was saddled with the job of getting Volkswagens built at one remove from Ley. Lafferentz proved to be an organisational genius. 'Without him, the VW plant would never have been finished and perhaps not even begun, despite all Hitler's desires', as a post-war article put it.

The workers' front or DAF put up 20 million of an eventual 150 million capital outlay to found a new entity called the *Gesellschaft zur Vorbereitung des VW*, shortened to GEZUFOR or 'go ahead', a teutonic pun. Werlin and Porsche joined Lafferentz as directors and occasionally accompanied the doctor on his Junkers flights to scour north Germany for a factory site until he spotted the land just east of Fallersleben and north of Braunschweig (Brunswick) and said, 'the plant goes there'.

There is no indication Lafferentz was swayed by the fact that the 19th century poet Hoffmann who wrote the line, *'Deutschland über alles'* had come from Fallersleben. In any case, the lands of Count Schulenburg of historic Schloss Wolfsburg were soon invaded by unexplained testers of the ground who focused on the one-time village of Hesslingen, part of the estate since 1928. There was no crop or forestry reason for a survey, yet nobody could or would tell the Count where these surveyors came from. Schulenburg appealed to the land ministry and learned only that Ley had 'something in mind'. Decentralisation, as it turned out.

Lafferentz had picked the spot because it lay along the Mittelland Canal to be opened in 1939, had a highway and was close to a projected rail line and spur of the autobahn. Also it was 'central,' a rather north-German view. But chiefly, the entire site belonged to one man, eliminating time-consuming small-parcel deals.

The area between Hamburg and Berlin needed jobs and would be handy to the new Hermann Goering steel works at Salzgitter—actually the basis for Goering's objection. A car plant would syphon off his cheap labour. And his approval was not unimportant since he controlled the scarce dollars vital to buy US tooling. As for jobs, Popp of BMW pointed out that Bavaria had the same excess labour problem and since Nürnberg was a party mecca, buyers could attend a mass rally and drive their new car home in one trip. Since BMW built its cars in Eisenach, Bavaria had no car industry then but his plan found few backers. Berlin countered that Fallersleben had raw materials.

Even today, with modern Wolfsburg literally within sight of East Germany, they find both hard and brown coal, iron, lead, silver, copper and zinc within 100 miles of the town—but draw their steel from the distant Ruhr and most other components from the Rhine/Main area, truly more central to Germany. Materials were simply a convenient argument then.

Ley paid lip service to all complaints and named the site near Fallersleben anyway. Von Schulenburg countered with two nearby possibilities and was promptly told, 'the plant would be north of the canal, the city to the south, and would he care to sell for a "reasonable sum"?' He most emphatically would not, insisting he could not maintain the estate with its best parts sliced off. When even the minister of Lower Saxony suggested a better site, further east, Ley at least reduced the size of the land grab, probably pre-planned to soften the Count. In truth, it was sell or be dispossessed. Hitler had decided by January 1938.

Questions, such as vulnerability to air attack, were brushed aside with a bland, 'the war will be decided in the east and anyway, if you can't protect one plant, why do we have a Luftwaffe?' Schulenburg attended the last Berlin meeting but was not permitted a voice.

His last-ditch plea that the area was so mosquito-plagued it was uninhabitable was answered by sending in a bug expert who happily catalogued 70 varieties—before the swamp was drained.

The previous December Peter Koller, a happy-go-lucky 30-year-old Austrian architect and Speer protégé had already begun city studies precisely where Wolfsburg stands today. The full survey was made by a Braunschweig professor who apparently never got the Beetle promised for this task but Koller's city plan was chosen for the site. Braunschweig itself was given a sort of 'prototype plant' to produce both tooling and three-year apprentices schooled in all car trades.

In the rush to show drawings to Hitler, Koller set some buildings in the middle of the Aller River but soon had a master plan sorted out for a self-contained factory to turn out rubber, glass, both cold- and hot-rolled steel and all foundry parts. Only the foundry and assembly halls were built before the war. Declaring he could 'only build a new city where none exists, yet only put down roots where surroundings are prepared for them', Koller put the recreation area of pool, gymnasium, boat house, restaurant as well as the hospital within the factory walls. Speer's close involvement indicates this was to be the 'mother town' of National Socialism.

It was founded officially on July 1 1938 as 'Stadt des KdF' with grand plans for 30,000 inhabitants immediately and another 60,000 later. Actually they ran out of men and materials that same year with only 2,358 units built for an official 6,780 inhabitants by the end of 1941. That ignores 15,000 'imported' workers in barracks. By the end of the war KdF town would have 14,298 registered citizens and more than 18,000 impressed labourers, mostly Russian and Polish. It would not have a church, in deference to Hitler's mid-1940 ban on new religious buildings.

Nor did they ever build the crowning touch, an acropolis on the highest piece of ground, 165 feet above the living areas. This was to house party headquarters and a cultural palace, approached along an avenue 100 yards wide. More modest construction began in late February 1938 and almost immediately ran into a labour shortage, solved by importing the forerunners of those post-war 'guest workers' who would build the Beetles.

Apart from a few hundred Dutch showing solidarity, VW depended in 1938 on Mussolini who was happy to send his surplus Italians. They lived in red board barracks

Below left *Peter Koller, young architect (then) who first laid out KdF Stadt under Speer, having just returned from Russian prison camp to do Wolfsburg, as it became.*
Below right *The DAF variation on the emblem later used by VW with cog-wheel teeth et al.*

and ate in Cianetti Hall, often shown to guests. Chief beneficiaries of what was called the world's biggest ant heap, were apparently the local bars and midwives.

The rush had brought myriad problems, such as cement foundations to overcome the swamp—assembly lines had to move one floor up when cellars proved impossible. And no factory floors could be made of wood, in anticipation of incendiary attacks. Porsche soon asked if it was a car factory or a war plant. Hitler replied, 'a VW factory and nothing else'. But his aides stipulated no flat or angled windows which might reflect moonlight at hostile aeroplanes. Officially, German industry had gone on a 'wartime footing' four years before their army marched into Poland.

The cornerstone ceremony that May received saturation radio and newsreel coverage, including Ferry driving Hitler off in the new VW convertible, but the Fuehrer had proved less voluble than usual—perhaps considering his Czech annexation plans, set in motion two days later. New levels of censorship shortly thereafter meant that little more was said publicly about this plant. Much was said after the war, trying to prove the entire VW programme was a government swindle, but the fact that Germany pulled 3,000 workers away from KdF town in mid-1938 to build the West Wall indicates the state car project was still largely civilian, yet serious.

They did complete the portion of their factory which fronts the canal today and started nominal production in April 1939, using much specialised American machinery. The first 1,000 workers were soon expanded to 3,000 producing 10,000 vehicles in the final five months of the year against a projected 120,000 for 1940. That dream ended when the Air Ministry took over. As late as 1941 however, KdF town was still holding trainee workshops and graduating a class of 'customer service mechanics'.

Original plans for 17,500 on two shifts called for only 30 per cent of them to be skilled workers, well below industry norms. Trainees and apprentices from the Braunschweig facility would fill the ranks and hold down the labour cost. Skilled men received 1-1.20 Rmk per hour while 40 per cent of the salaried staff received only 200-350 Rmk a month, another 50 per cent from 350 to 650 Rmk. The token production they managed was sufficient, at least, to maintain the claim that a peoples' car was coming.

Sales and propaganda had always been as important as plant and product although it seems curious now, how little promotion was integrated with production. That famous savings fund was not used to build any part of the plant, for instance, although it was inseparable from the concept. In the end the entire fund plus interest was 'withdrawn' from post-war Berlin by the Russians.

The overall plan proceeded in four ponderous and totally detailed steps from the local or town branch of the workers' front, through county and *gau* or district levels to a central KdF office. Drivers' licences, insurance and purchase were centralised, amounting to state permission to possess this wondrous machine.

All that came five years after Hitler launched his vision in 1933, of course. Originally he declared the then-existing car industry vital to his nation's life and suggested that he would take the state clear out of the traffic scene. Apart from more roads and motor racing, that is. An industry showing several new small cars at the time liked that first speech better than most which followed.

Only a year later the theme was: such a favoured land should have 12 million cars not 500,000, so all should get to work on a volks auto along the lines of the brandless 'volks radio'. The German media naturally expanded on this theme, usually mimicking the official Volksbeobachter. 'An auto for every family', became the sub-heading to every car story. They were promoting the universal car.

Autobahns were not being built, 'so the rich can race'. (No mention of the supercharged 7-litre Grosser Mercedes favoured by officialdom.) This new super highway, 'belonged to the whole volk and could only be a success if used by a volkswagen'. At this point aerodynamics crept into every tale. Achieving the magic 100 kph (just over 60 mph) 'would obviously mean an engine in the back'. By 1935 the car 'tomorrow' had given way to phrases such as, 'a Volkswagen takes time'.

It was carefully orchestrated throughout. Once Hitler expressed the official line that this VW would tap new markets, not steal buyers from more expensive models, industry convictions that it would run them out of business had to be expressed very privately indeed.

By the time Hitler saw his first Beetle, at a private Obersalzburg showing, all dealer distribution ideas or traditional industry involvement had been dropped, saving the local mark-up against that 1,000 Rmk limit. Even the price prediction of 1,200 Rmk, which Hitler promptly spurned, made DAF control inevitable. In any case, the front banked some 50-80 Rmk per year per person with no accountability so they could easily finance a car too.

With sales under their wing the government had total control at last and Hitler's yearly speeches hardly mentioned details any more. There were sufficient leaks through the testing and few foreign journalist viewings. A Dutch paper noted in December 1937, for instance, 'that all reports indicate the car is close', even mentioning the savings plan which was not due to be officially launched before August 1 1938.

During the first half of 1938 Hitler restricted his car concerns to basking in praise of 'what Germany under the Fuehrer can achieve'. He even left it up to Lafferentz to present official data on size, price, performance and the imminent savings plan for the three VWs alongside the official stand at the cornerstone ceremony. By this point Werlin was declaring that 'Porsche had received his route map from Hitler clear back in 1934 and could only stand in awe of the Fuehrer's grasp of details'—which had come originally from Porsche himself, of course. The propaganda was slowly moving out in front of the actual car in government minds.

Hitler did remember to thank Professor Porsche for his labours, while giving Werlin and Lafferentz equal credit for the project, and for the car which 'could be in production by the end of 1939'. He finally had the date right. All this carefully-orchestrated build up, alongside the actual engineering work, meant that this VW—or rather, KdF—was finally a popular topic. Lacking mechanical facts, most people had only the plan for motorising small-wage earners to debate. This was the famous savings scheme, personally opened by Ley at a banquet celebrating the 75th anniversary of IG Farben's Leverkusen plant, a curious occasion.

'Sign up at any *Arbeitsfront* or KdF office', they trumpeted. 'Stick a 5 Rmk stamp in your savings book regularly and you will soon own the class-less car—our thanks to the Fuehrer.' In theory no one could buy a KdF for cash but there was no limit on the number of stamps purchased at one time.

Buying a KdF became the ultimate objective: 'driving is fun, driving strengthens the nerves and brings back the beauties of our land'. And public response exceeded their fondest hopes—until it came to putting down money. War seemed all too likely at the end of 1938 yet the DAF announced that any foreigner could buy into this dream too, 'provided he had a German residence'. Some 270,000 savers began immediately, a figure which doubled Opel's total annual production then and even exceeded a full year's production of German cars. Theoretical 1940 production was 'sold out' by the end of May 1939.

The core of this idea (Ford in the 20s and later Opel had flirted briefly with similar plans) went back to 1937 when Hitler decided even 900-1,000 Rmk would be too high for

Marken für Sonderausführungen und Transportkosten

	Sonderausführungen			
	Transportkosten			

Merkblatt beachten! Für verlorene oder sonst abhanden gekommene Sparkarten und -marken wird kein Ersatz geleistet.

Nur für den Dienstgebrauch:				
Wagenpreis e...schl.Versicherung	Entrichtet sind auf KdF-Wagen-Zusatzmarken		Erste Marke geklebt am	Letzte Marke geklebt am
Laut Karte 1 RM 250,-	RM		10. 1 39	14. 11.40
" 2 RM 250,-	RM	20,-	25 11 40	21 11.41
" 3 RM	RM			
" 4 RM	RM			
" 5 RM 500,-	RM			
Sa. 500,-	Sa.	20,-		

Type: Cabrio-Limousine Wagenpreis ab Werk: RM 990,-
Farbe: graublau Sonderausführungen: RM 60,-
Lieferungsort: Werk Versicherung: RM 200,-
Wochen-Mindest... Transportkosten: .... RM
Sa: RM 1250,-

(Unterschrift der KdF-Kreis-Dienststelle)

Die Deutsche Arbeitsfront

KdF-WAGEN-SPARKARTE
(Anschlußkarte)

NR.   Voraussichtliches Lieferjahr
Gemäß Gaubestellnummer

Vor- und Zuname (bei Frauen auch Geburtsname)

Wohnort: Position:
Straße: Schmittgasse Nr.

Geboren am: 16.6.11 in ...rne-Eickel
Genaue Berufsangabe: Graveur
Besitzt Führerschein: nein Klasse:

Diese Karte ist ausgestellt am: 18.12.1941
von der Kreis-Dienststelle: Siegburg
Gau: Köln-Aachen

(Unterschrift des Ausstellers)

Volkswagenwerk

Above *Famous saver's stamp book for a KdF car, from the Volkswagenwerk. This saver had no driving licence but had already filled the first two books and ordered an open-top car.*

Below *Front/back covers of the owners' handbook, the KdF car from A to Z.*

the new driving class he sought. At five marks, including the first year's insurance then, the state would not be able to charge off usual collection costs to the car price.

This is the point where DAF took over all control of owning or driving a VW, including an overview of servicing, although owners were expected to perform small jobs themselves. In November 1940 there was even a service bulletin which announced more to come. These would be issued in four colours of paper to expedite shop use. Despite such controls, an eventual 336,638 savers opened accounts, some as late as a year into the war. Two-thirds were buying their first automobile, but less than 2 per cent had been motorcycle riders, a class Hitler particularly sought. Just under 4 per cent were converts from some other car marque.

Average income among savers came out to 300 Rmk a month, leaving two-thirds of the nation below the KdF class. These savers provided the state with nearly 268 million Rmk plus another 35 million in interest. What is more, the rulers planned a motor sport magazine whose subscription would be mandatory for savers, but open to all. It was projected for four or five million copies at half a mark each.

Each applicant for a savings book was carefully checked to be sure he could afford the 5 Rmk each week, plus 4 Rmk stamps towards transport costs for those who did not intend to collect the car personally, and another 4 Rmk series towards the optional, 60 Rmk sun-roof.

The first of three stamp booklets cost one mark and indicated intent to buy but half the total had to be paid in before 'a firm order' was placed. A delivery number was not given until three-quarters of the price was saved. Less publicised was the option of changing your mind, losing 20 per cent for costs. An internal circular, not shown to buyers, also allowed withdrawal with full repayment for sufficient reason. Heirs could retrieve all money if a saver died before delivery.

KdF backers were sure insurance claims would be no problem due to 'good discipline'. Improper drivers could always be expelled. The master plan even allowed for post-delivery conversions on cars for the handicapped. A variation of the Type 60 had been foreseen with column gear change for invalids but none of this 67 were apparently built.

Once the programme became established, the government discovered nearly half its buyers already had a driving licence. About a third were self-employed, usually in one-man operations which badly needed transport. Here the KdF would have filled a clear need. Only 46 per cent chose the basic saloon with the rest willing to pay for the soft sun-roof. The actual convertible saloon was not offered initially. Just under half planned to collect their cars at the plant, saving that fee. In short, the savings scheme was also a statistical coup, telling planners which models would be wanted two or three years ahead, where they would be located and which groups were buying one. The stamp plan proved as valuable an economic barometer as it was for motorising the masses—who never got their promised cars anyway.

Unlike hopeful savers, a great many officials got rides and quickly dubbed this the 'universal car' for town, country, autobahn or alps. Goering had his painted in a special Czech-blended blue with ground fish scales, the colour used on all his cars.

A larger group of foreign journalists were sent from Berlin to Magdeburg, along the autobahn, in a 60-car convoy accompanied by SS men in full black regalia. 'So I suppose we might have been under some sort of pressure to like it', as one recalled. English writers got even by asking their immaculate driver to check the oil at the lunch stop. German papers quoted this group as declaring the car, 'a great success'. Later the men would recall that they 'didn't think a whole lot of it then because there wasn't any wood trim and very poor finish in the sense of very sparse'.

What did impress them was the idea of running along all day flat out. This was an era

1938 presentation of cars to foreign journalists in Berlin.

when even Rolls begged owners not to do that. Then there was that trickle of heat when you got the revs up. Few, if any, other cars even had a standard heater. The figures that the German papers quoted from this 'test' came out suspiciously like the official ones.

The state had now spent some 30 million Rmk on propaganda but gained far more in image polishing and distraction from the looming war. No chance was missed, from a special stamp from the post office down to first 'real road tests' by German motoring magazines who chose not to use the pre-written texts copied by almost every daily paper.

A first true test came from *Motor Kritik*, no longer edited by Ganz of course, and printed in September 1940. It was based on a drive in the pre-production car ten months earlier but there had also been several even-earlier peeks behind the curtain, which were clearly condoned. *Motor Kritik* had published a power curve as early as September 1938, plotting 24 hp against the 100 kph/62 mph top speed to prove that the streamlining was 'quite advanced'. No contemporary car could match a KdF without streamlining and a fifth gear.

Motor Kritik did add that price would matter as much as performance since rival cars offered more comfort. Three months later the magazine offered interior photos and a glimpse under the front lid. They had even heard the engine run, and paced test cars met by chance along the road, but lifting the rear lid remained *verboten*. As a Christmas present for its readers *Motor Kritik* then produced the first technical data and photos for chassis and engine. They now confirmed the all-independent suspension and backbone frame, noting the provision for a tow bar, then focused on two dashboard compartments and space for the promised KdF radio, fuel reserve lever on the floor board and central indicator switch—they might have been showing a post-war car.

A proper test of the pre-production, one-litre car came next. Features singled out were a complete winter run without chains, good weight distribution, low centre of gravity and soft ride. The easily-accessible engine with fine cold-start habits was praised for being so quiet you could hardly hear it at top speed. Not to forget the 'intense heat' and fine defrosting. The nose-mounted spare was lauded as a safety feature but storage in the nose was incidental compared to that 'big boot' behind the rear seat. Bumpers were standard for the price and the tester was overjoyed by adjustable seats (by wing nuts), readable dial and the simple, but well thought-out, interior generally.

This magazine weighed the car at 685 kg/1,510 lb, clocked a top speed of 102 kph/ 65 mph, exceeding all claims, but managed only 17 seconds for the 0-60 kph/35 mph run which was laggard. Steady consumption ranged from 48.6 mpg at 50 kph/30 mph to 41.5 mpg at 70 kph/43 mph. When they finally tested a production Type 60 a full year later—September 1941—*Motor Kritik* found fewer deviations from these figures than expected, despite 0.5 more hp which gave 24.5 at 3,300 rpm. Production weight was up by 45 kg/100 lb and top speed down a fraction but consumption was noticeably better; 52.2 mpg at a steady 50 kph/30 mph.

This brought further praise of the streamlining but they also raved about weight distribution which put half the weight on the rear wheels, a credit to Porsche's racing car experience, as was the 'fine handling'. Inside luggage space only seemed 'a good median' now but testers continued to find the engine extremely silent—which says a good deal about the car's peers.

If we drove a 1939 VW today it would be noise which would assault us first, then the oily exhaust smoke rather than heat through those heater vents, followed by amazement at the tail-happy handling. Seat/pedal positions have hardly changed for the current Beetle but the much-praised vast glass areas of a 1939 car would seem claustrophobic now. One feature still worth noting would be the flat undertray which did so much for performance. While it is true that testers then had to be somewhat circumspect, although there was no direct pressure for a 'good press', the cars available for direct comparison were hardly overwhelming. A 1.1 litre Opel had even less power yet cost twice as much.

As late as mid-March 1942 there were press reports praising the civilian model for its wealth of advanced ideas and careful detailing for ease of maintenance, as if anybody could buy one. Having said that, it was still just as well for their legend that the factory never had to actually try and build the promised car for the projected price. Considering the eventual export effort as well, it seems equally lucky that nobody seriously tried to build a VW with either the two- or four-stroke twins, nor even the original four until it had accumulated those years of war-time experience.

After laying the foundations for a legend ten years later VW converted to war-time production, which meant referring back to Porsche's own basic plan for a wide range of variations to one engine/chassis unit. This range soon proved to be far more varied than the best-remembered *kuebel* (bucket) and amphibian.

It was war-time need as well which prompted the change at last from that original 985 cc engine to the 1,131 cc version which was then available for post-war civilian models, when the Beetle could be taken off its shelf again. Meanwhile, KdF town tooled up for war.

Chapter 3

VW variety in the war years

When Volkswagen turned most, if not quite all, its attention to military needs the result was a one-model policy turned inside-out. They not only had many more models to deal with on short notice, but also a vastly greater number of people to satisfy—most of them generals with firm pre-conceptions of the ideal troop carrier.

These war years did provide the stiffest possible in-use test of components, in addition to the extended pre-war programme, but the first half of the 40s also showed clearly that the KdF plant outside Fallersleben was far from ready to build cars on its own, one of Porsche's tasks after all. What's more, Ley and the DAF did not even want it to, preferring to keep tight control until the promised early victory when they could again monopolise the giant project. A *kuebelwagen* or bucket car design was on test even before they had a plant but it became bogged down in bureaucratic manoeuvres more tenacious than all the sands and swamps of Hitler's combined invasions. On one hand, the VW simplicity attracted more open-minded generals who would admit their soldier-drivers seldom pampered any machine. On the other, there were at least as many advocates for designs from men as inventive as Ferdinand Porsche but less practical.

During the early 40s the Trippel amphibian, built in a Molsheim plant requisitioned from Bugatti, was considered more seaworthy than the VW and more intriguing to technically-bemused generals who overlooked the fact it could never be repaired easily in the field. In the end, a few middle staff, a good many inverted snobs and several top leaders setting the standard put their massive Horchs or Mercedes away and rode around in chauffeured Beetles—so many, Porsche had to set up a service garage in Berlin to maintain this fleet. At the same time, a great many officers, joined by their troops, were happy to ride in the topless bucket car which seldom gave up. This was the first VW-based, slab-sided carry-all, Type 62 which became Type 82 with many other numbers to follow.

VW/KdF terminology is a maze. There were Porsche design office numbers, government designations which sometimes overlapped, multi-digit tags for esoteric variations and even paper projects, all used before the British changed most numbers in 1945 and quite apart from Wolfsburg's own eventual system which they themselves began to ignore or obscure even before it was well-established.

Eventually, water-cooled models would come along to use the same numbers, in some cases, as air-cooled models still in parallel production. No table will ever please all purists but we can consider some basic numbers and their direct variants here. It began with V1-3 (except that there were two cars without numbers before that), followed by the W30 series and the VW38 range, very close to Type 60, that pre-war KdF Beetle. 60 was Porsche's number, qualified by K-numbers for different body designs. However K9, the convertible model, was not built until after the war—when it had a new number anyway.

K10 was also model 64, the 1939 streamlined special of which three were built for a

Berlin-Rome race which was never held. One of them, most probably the one Porsche used himself through the war, survives as the VW sports car Porsche always meant to build—or the forerunner of the first car called a Porsche, as you prefer. Other K-curiosities include K11, a plastic body solution to looming steel shortages which was apparently never built. Nor was Type 61, a down-sized Beetle drawn up during Porsche's battles with the RDA.

That brings us to Type 62, the off-road predecessor with altered chassis but original 985 cc engine and spare wheel countersunk in the nose lid. It dates from 1937 and was also called K12. Porsche was obviously concerned with a bucket car even before his Type 65-66-67 range of civilian Beetle variations with right-hand drive etc.

The first military-type VW to be produced, however, was Type 82, the *kuebel* whose name was as indirect as its design history. First *kuebels* had bucket seats and were called *kuebelsitzwagens,* soon shortened to *kuebel* since the whole thing looked like a square tub anyway. The first model actually delivered to the troops as a four-seat bucket car at 2,782 Rmk was Type 820, soon complimented by 821 with three seats, two seats and a siren numbered 822, 823 with machine gun turret and fake tank panels to serve as an armoured trainer, even a two-seat pick-up (825) and tropical van (826), not to overlook a wood-bodied bucket numbered 828.

Confusion began when the pick-up body was also fitted to a Type 92 chassis. Then 82E was not a bucket at all but a KdF body on the *kuebel* chassis, renumbered 51 in 1945. This same 82 chassis was also used for the *kommandeur* or command car, 827, which looked very much like a four-wheel drive *kommandeur* which was really Type 87.

In all there were some 50,000 of the Type 82 built between 1940 and April 1945. The biggest month of all came at the end when 2,030 buckets with various body variations were built in January 1945. Raw materials shortages restricted production in all those years. Total figures, including the 82E, are not certain, due in part to the unknown number of Type 62 forerunners built, but 51,352 would be close. Plus 630 KdF sedans in 1941-44 and the 14,276 amphibians with type numbers all their own. In the end something over 66,000 Volkswagens was not really a lot for five war-time years.

Kuebel or bucket car, the Porsche design on a VW chassis, with VW engine in the back, enlarged to 1.1 litres to carry all the soldiers. The first 'four-door' VW with only rear-wheel drive but lightness and panel simplicity (bodies made by Ambi-Budd in Berlin) and duck-board interior bearing one dial.

Opposite page top *A variation on the* kuebel *which was German army maid of all work: tracked version for snow or particularly deep mud, although it proved more complicated than need be.* **Centre** *Typical of the odd-ball Beetle offshoots, a short-chassis works pick-up.* **Bottom** *An amphibian on the VW base with shortened chassis to use as a scout car (or officer's duck blind). A water screw pivoted down and this 166 had four-wheel drive as well, plus a low-range gear driving front wheels only.*

Above *An amphibian chassis (the four-wheel drive chassis in longer, normal VW, wheelbase length with Beetle body) was then used for a very few special cars sometimes called Kommandeurs. This one was built after the war out of left-over parts.*

Below *Variety envisioned even by Porsche: postal vans on either* kuebel *or Beetle basis.*

Of course the builders had endless problems, not the least of which was a military weapons board dedicated to second-guessing. The first 'army' version came when SS test drivers on the W30 project put together a backyard platform car to see what a bodyless KdF might do. Official Beetle plans had called for three to four passengers or four soldiers, so requirements hardly varied.

In January 1938 word reached *Hauptsturmfuehrer* Liese, the head of the SS team, that a W30 should be prepared for off-road tests with projected weight limit of 950 kg/2,095 lb, including 400 kg/880 lb for three men and a machine gun. With only 150 kg/330 lb for bodywork, that would have to be light alloy. Otherwise VW dimensions fell right in the middle of proposed army limits, apart from the 24 cm/9.5 in ground clearance rule.

Porsche was ready to test by January 20 and ordered VW-size off-road tyres for the saloon, with wing flares under consideration. A first prototype was shown in Berlin on February 1, in saloon form however. The first actual bucket car, developed in six weeks for a mere 1,500-2,000 Rmk, reached procurement officials that November, two years before the first US Jeep was built. Its chief glory was the fact four men could right one which tipped over. The German army then used Horch, BMW 3-wheel and Tatra all-terrain vehicles but Rommel told Porsche later it was the bucket which had saved his life. The 82 was so light it crossed a mine field without setting any off while the Horch baggage carrier behind them was blown up.

Porsche needed no convincing that the last thing any army needed was complication. He pointed out there was no radiator for a bullet to hole. Early field tests of the KdF (to military types) or VW (to all others) were held in Polish mud where rival machines had to be towed out of places the *kuebel* managed easily. Rommel was sure it would be equally ideal for shifting sands. Eventually VW built 500 special cars for the Desert Fox with sand-shielded ignition, extra cooling capacity, front axle shield and larger, low-pressure tyres—then sent them all to the Russian front.

Meanwhile the 62 prototype was completed in 1939 and even shown publicly at the Vienna Fair. Debate centred on its engine, which soon proved it would start in extremes of heat or cold which disabled all others, on the rear engine location, which provided off-road traction in the absence of special gearing, and on the lack of four-wheel drive. Also, the ground clearance was still an inch or so below military minimums but the 82 solved that with rear hub drop gears which lifted clearance to 29 cm/11.4 in and simultaneously lowered overall gearing without a gearbox redesign. A limited-slip differential planned at

VW variety in the war years

Below left *Close to a 'production' car at last. Wooden body mock-up for the actual KdF at the Reutter shops in Stuttgart.*

Right *The 1,000th car, just after the war began. Now a* kuebel *of course.*

the same time was still giving trouble on test two years later.

A prime advantage of the bucket was its flat bottom, extended by skid plates front and rear. Historically this was the first 'production' car which featured a different body and various engine changes, breaking with the public's perception of a strict one-model policy.

So-called production then began in 1940, at about the point when first bombs fell near KdF town, an obvious target alongside the canal. They did no damage. The Allies hesitated to bomb at that time, knowing that much of the labour force was not volunteer nor German. This crew completed its 1,000th *kuebel* five days before Christmas, along with the first VW stationary engines, given Porsche numbers 121-122-123. Early KdF saloons had been built there relatively easily, 'to prove the tooling' but complete bucket cars were another matter.

They only had machinery in place to produce engines and transmissions, whereas the Air Ministry wanted to take over the plant for airframe repairs. As a compromise the workers' front contracted Goering's repair jobs while the few press tools made fuel cans or Ju 88 aeroplane parts. In the end probably no more than a third of the plant was ever used to assemble *kuebels,* and the body panels for those had to come from Berlin.

Ambi-Budd, originally American-owned, only released its US patents for all-steel bodies in exchange for an option to build the first alternate body to the Beetle in Berlin. The bucket car was that model and KdF town lacked presses for such a job in any case. That left a German government negotiating with a US firm on peace-time terms.

To begin with, few dared state in 1940 it would be anything but a quick victory, largely in the east. Also, there was still no firm decision to build the *kuebel* in 1940. General Staff Prussians took a dim view of any Hitler project on principle and maintained a very slow approval pace. Rommel was begging for the car when other commanders were returning buckets to Germany from their war zones. Finally, the army had its own four-wheel drive prototype design to favour—until it lost a direct face-off with the *kuebel*. General von Schell finally won his battle for standardisation when Hitler simply said, 'it will be the kuebel'. Of course the one he had received as a birthday present was rather

A harder-won milestone than surpassing the Model T in later years—at a time when many doubted VW would build ten cars or a hundred, the first thousand was phenomenal.

special, including four-wheel drive. But the leader's decision ended complaints from men like Borgward, head of military vehicle procurement for Lower Saxony, who naturally favoured his own firm's products.

Salvation for the *kuebel* came when Porsche fitted the larger engine to at least partially answer a well-founded complaint that the VW was under-powered. Fortunately 1,131 cc was possible from the same castings and while it added only one more horsepower, it spread the power around a little better. This 15 per cent capacity increase came from bore enlarged to 75 mm from 70, keeping a 64 mm stroke. 1,131 cc worked so well VW still used it in 1954 for cars and found it a sound basis for their stationary engines as well. These portable powerplants powered everything from an alpine cable tow with hydraulic drive to a tropical AC generator, an air compressor, balloon winch drives and even an assault boat.

Never prone to drop an idea, Porsche also revived the flat twin, now made of VW components, to produce a 12 hp tank generator and starter motor for heavy tractors. Going the other way his office also produced Type 274, a 33 hp aviation four used in the pusher-propellor Horten III flying wing in 1943. Attempts to revive sleeve valves as well—making the engine lighter and cheaper—faltered over high oil consumption and thermic overloads.

His 1,131 cc engine became the standard for all VW-based machines in March 1943, when the staff had finally cancelled all competitors and made the VW their sole light army carrier. Its 25 hp rating was actually the prescribed minimum for any German army vehicle, a fact conveniently overlooked until the added bore made it possible for a VW. When petrol became scarcer they forgot the rule again and built a Type 82 offshoot powered by a wood-gas generator mounted under a bulging nose. This model boasted all of 12 hp.

Further ahead in war-time developments, the lack of light alloys in 1942 led Porsche to design a fan cut from sheet steel to replace the original cast model. They discovered these new blades produced 50 per cent more air; more quietly as well. The following year lead-bronze bearings gave way to alloy, so successfully that main bearings were still done that way in 1959.

A different sort of model—a perfect KdF copy made for Hitler's birthday.

Meanwhile Porsche's design team had turned to other three-digit types as offshoots of the original VW. During 1940 they designed Type 128, an amphibian with four-wheel drive but based on standard VW dimensions, including the 240 cm/94.6 in wheelbase in particular. A year later this had passed through Type 138 to become the 'production' German amphibian, Porsche Type 166. Between 128 and 166, however, we have a vehicle whose proper designation causes endless argument, the Type 87. This mated a KdF-like body shape, with some details from the 82, to the longer 128 wheelbase.

The whole was developed from a Type 86 prototype and could be titled a 287 chassis with 877 bodywork. It is popularly called simply *kommandeur* and numbered 87, even by VW itself today, although that pains the purists. For one thing, there was the 870 as a four-seater with unitary body, the 871 with three seats and the 92 SS which also had four-wheel drive but a Beetle body. Visually the confusion is compounded by the 82 E and the plain 92 which both stood tall on tractor-tread tyres but had only two-wheel drive like the bucket. The command car title was often applied to two-wheel drive or four-wheel drive but here 87 means a 287/877 with 1,131 cc engine, 94.6 in wheelbase and drive to all four wheels.

Only 667 of these most specialised Beetles were built between 1942 and 1944, plus a pair built from leftover parts by the British forces in 1946. 1943 was peak *kommandeur* year when 382 were built with wider wings and bumpers. These weighed 790 kg/1,740 lb empty with a 450 kg/990 lb payload and really needed more than 25 hp.

Ground clearance was increased by drop-gear rear hubs plus tall tyres but the gearing generally was curious since front and rear differentials had unlike ratios of 5.31 and 7.31 while low range was 5.86, unsynchronised like the normal VW four-speed manual gearbox. These four speeds drove the rear wheels in normal manner, or turned all four if a second lever alongside the shift was moved forward one notch. Pushing it another notch forward gave low range but only for the front wheels. The crunch came on grades of soft sand when a driver had to decide on either four-wheel drive but normal first gear or lower gearing in front only. The sum of all those gears made this the only VW whose engine, when underway, was inaudible. Steering was very heavy with little self-centering to counter front drive shafts so a command car tended to weave about on pavement, even in two-wheel drive.

Even allowing for special desert and arctic manuals, the car's general complication and need for extra driving skill could explain why so few were built and why VW did not pursue that four-wheel drive bucket tested in the Baltic. Refinement was left for their amphibians.

When it came to testing, Porsche obviously favoured countries outside Germany where the going would be tougher. Apart from a Libyan run in mid-1941 there was an extended 'raid' through the Balkans that same August/September. A KdF sedan, two command cars (87) and a pair of buckets plus non-VW army transport and small tracked vehicles were shipped or driven to Greece and run for some 13,000 km/8,100 miles through Hungary, Yugoslavia, Bulgaria, Greece and Rumania. The KdF was taken along to evaluate for later Balkan sales.

They concluded a 1,131 cc engine would be needed abroad where good German service was lacking and that the 'spring bar' suspension and front axle carriers would have to be strengthened for colonial driving. Also, the fuel tank should be raised 5 cm/2 in. Furthermore, dust sealing around the lids was poor, windows jumped their tracks, and locks on both lids would be a must in the Balkans. A suggestion that carburettor air be drawn from inside the car to keep out dust had to be dropped on noise grounds.

Herbert Kaes, nephew to Porsche and brother of his private secretary, made this trek, living in tents and eating from a field kitchen. His notes on the 87 reported that sand got into the bores despite 'tropic preparation' and cooling became marginal when sand stuffed the cylinder ribs. Oil cooler seals failed regularly but vapour locks were rarer than expected. The sand problem was cured by a felt filter mounted provisionally in the left rear wing, and later tucked inside, while an oil temperature gauge would be vital in the desert. Both ZF and Rheinstahl limited slip differentials wore badly in two months while front-drive teeth proved weak as well. Low range proved ideal for the wilder Balkans, provided drivers remembered to disengage the normal box first.

Both 87s broke steering arms around the 3,500 km/2,200 mile mark, indicating loads with four-wheel drive needed further thought. Despite more front torsion bar leaves and a larger bar in the back they still hit the bump stops under load. Correlating these results with army reports Porsche decided that cold starting was fine but overheating and poor dust filtration must be cured, yet there were no basic problems to prevent their building the amphibian, under Ferry's direction.

Porsche did its best to apply family precepts of simplicity to this amphibian and Major Hirst, later to run VW for the British, felt they did very well indeed. 'We all admired the "schwimwagen" greatly. It was the right approach to the amphibian problem, a real boat hull with Volkswagen front axle outside. The US model was a horror, just a leaky hull around a Jeep chassis.'

In fact, Porsche was ahead of the Americans with Type 128 underway several months before even a road-going Jeep, and two full years before the US car went aquatic. The contract for an amphibian based on the four-wheel drive 87 was dated June 18 1940. This used the standard Beetle wheelbase with wider track matching off-road KdF cars then. With a curb weight of 1,350 kg/2,970 lb it was credited with speeds of 80 kph/50 mph by land, 10 kph/6 mph afloat. Once they switched the shaft seals from leather to butyl rubber it was non-leaking but too bulky. A three-blade screw which could be pivoted down in the back had a friction clutch in the drive system—a lay shaft at screw depth driven by roller chains from a crankshaft extension—to prevent debris breaking a prop.

Some 30 of this pre-production series were built with body welded to the floorpan. Next, numerically, came 129 called a 'special off-road amphibian' but never built. Type 138, or model B, had similar dimensions but a central frame, one step closer to the production machine, Type 166. Some sources claim up to 100 pre-166 amphibians were completed.

Along the test route Porsche added baffles and a water-proof distributor to solve the problem of water in the hull which flowed to the rear under acceleration on land, only to be thrown up by the fan pulley to drown the electrics. Drive shafts and winterising were improved as well.

Although VW built less than 15,000 of these specialised vehicles (some sources say over 16,000) between 1942 and 1944, with over half of them produced in 1943 and all built in KdF town, production still exceeded the US 'seep' whereas Jeep totals were vastly greater than eventual *kuebel* production.

Type 166 was favoured by the SS, although armaments officials did not want them, even after Porsche's design outshone all rivals. The SS saw it as a go-anywhere scout car, a four-wheeled motorcycle replacement. The first amphibian was shown to Hitler in August 1941, the same year VW capitalisation was doubled to 100 million Rmk, then raised to 150 million.

Smaller and lighter than the 128, with a shorter wheelbase, this C-model carried less equipment (no anchor but they kept the paddle brackets), yet it would seat four under a neat, folding canvas top and was famous for scaling steep grades, one reason so many of the survivors are found in alpine Austria. The drive line was virtually identical to that of the command car. This 166 was a dimensional maverick with its 200 cm/78.8 in wheelbase and narrow track which allowed it to slip through tighter places. Quoted speeds were the same but the 166 boasted a fifth more fuel capacity and larger off-road tyres. It cost the forces 7,667 Rmk and used many VW parts, such as the gearbox.

The prime purpose on paper was officer reconnaissance but a good many were also used as mobile duck blinds between battles. Much of the testing was carried out in the Tyrol where an amphibian, steered by its front wheels in the water, became a common sight on the Wörthersee where other boats were banned in war-time. When the amphibian proved a hit on the Russian front, Ferry found himself made an honorary (and unwilling) SS man by Himmler.

Having tackled movements on water successfully, Porsche's team found time for almost endless variations on the bucket, many parallel to equally wild US Jeep efforts. Searching for more power Porsche tried both a mechanical supercharger (Type 107) and a turbocharger (115), paths which pleased his son, Ferry. When his KdF with higher compression and dual carburettors proved too tame he shifted to a supercharged Beetle 'for test purposes'. The office also tried fuel injection and a diesel variant of the basic flat four.

Automatic transmission was explored as well as a fully-synchronised manual box and even one with five speeds. Such a richness of invention was the reason Hitler insisted at the end of 1941, when Porsche had to make a trip to the eastern front, that it could only be done in the Fuehrer's own aeroplane with his personal pilot. As Hitler said; 'he could always afford to lose a general or two in a plane crash. But he only had one Porsche'.

His favourite designer's ideas continued to flow. Design number 164 was another SS contract for a light off-road carry-all with six wheels and two VW engines, another idea which almost certainly never passed the prototype stage. An even earlier combination of the four-wheel drive 128 chassis with one of their convertible bodies almost certainly did not even survive the drawing-board stage. It was more important to test new winter travel systems, so vital in fact that they went to the 3,780 m/12,400 ft Gross Glockner in June 1942 rather than wait for winter snows. Model 166/3 was favoured originally since its flat hull planed over the snow but it persisted in bogging down when slowed so they turned to tracked options.

This led to Type 155, based on the *kuebel*, with either wheels or skis in front and various track systems on either normal road wheels or special bogey sets at the back. By the time they reached variation four it was clear the car must be rev-limited to 3,000 rpm to hold top speed below 30 kph/18 mph. Even then most tracks churned down into snow which supported the amphibian, while the 155 was better on deep new snow, indicating no single solution. Rear shaft bearings were not up to track drive either and they needed a steel-plate clutch as well. Porsche achieved excellent manoeuvreability with individual brakes for each track.

Appreciating the benefits of a road vehicle which could be converted quickly to run along railway tracks, it took Porsche just three weeks to design flanged steel discs which could be mounted on the road wheels without altering tyre pressures, in 8-12 minutes. The sole change was to reverse the wheels for more track width, using longer wheel studs. They avoided locked steering so wheels would centre themselves and not rub. These reached the front by the spring of 1944.

That same September Hitler viewed the first Type 276, a strengthened 82 for towing an anti-tank or munitions trailer. This unit, presented at the Wolfschanze, that massive bunker complex on the eastern front, only managed 65 kph/40 mph on the road, suffered brake and acceleration problems and used three times the normal amount of fuel. Its limited slip differential was prone to fail every 4,000 km/2,500 miles too.

By this time the KdF plant, which had employed 12,700 at the end of 1943 and built over 60,000 vehicles of various types, had been heavily bombed on several occasions. On May 1 1944 Hitler visited the plant and declared it a 'model works', entitled to fly the DAF banner with golden wheel emblem and golden fringe.

By the end of that year two-thirds of the factory buildings were destroyed and 73 employees had been killed. Dispersal to prepared sites nearby was ordered. Basic assembly machinery remained in the plant, however, and production was never halted completely despite damage eventually estimated at some 156 million Rmk. In addition to bomb damage there was considerable wanton destruction later by the workers— particularly the forced labourers—once they realised their hated guards had vanished, literally overnight, at the war's end.

German civilian managers desperately wanted advancing American units to take over security and protect the 17,000 left in town, half of them Germans, but US tanks had halted some 10 km/6 miles to the west by Fallersleben because none of their maps showed any more towns to the east. The non-city once called KdF town quickly made up a delegation including a French pastor from the labour force, plus a man who spoke impeccable American slang. They made the risky journey through wandering Russian patrols and left-over SS groups in search of Americans.

A young US officer in command of forward tanks was somewhat astonished to be begged in best American to push just a little further, but the news that fellow-American citizens were in danger in KdF town (the speaker was one of the ex-Detroit men of course) prompted him to rush on. Rough order was quickly established by the GIs who kept eastern forced labourers and German civilians apart until zones could be drawn up and the factory, as well as the town, turned over to its British overseers. KdF people were more than willing to seek some sort of peaceful existence again, even to dream of civilian car production some day; but nobody quite dared hope that this really would, or even could, come about from this non-town in the ravaged middle of 1945 Germany.

That it did, and beyond the wildest dreams of even Hitler's pre-war planners, was due largely to a young British Major of the Engineers who now formed the indispensable bridge between KdF and VW.

Chapter 4

The town God forgot

As the war ran down in mid-1945 the would-be town with the unregistered name of KdF-Stadt was really little more than a refugee way-station and nobody—least of all Major Ivan Hirst, REME—had the slightest inkling that the woebegone souls left there might be on the verge of launching a legend.

They could equally well have been on the verge of complete dispersal, of course. During the first month the British Element of the Control Commission for Germany, or CCG, had more than enough on its hands merely trying to contain foreign labour to its barracks or ringing the plant with troops to prevent further plundering.

The town itself had officially been called Wolfsburg since the first meeting of the new town council under British control, on May 25. Although some recall the name as American, VW today believes it was British and taken from the nearby 16th century castle, built on the site of a 13th century keep. This castle had passed to the town during the war but few of its new 'owners' cared much about that in May of 1945.

Germany's near-total national collapse was all too clear in 'the town God forgot', as a German magazine would dub it only 15 years later, but long after those once-forbidden churches had been built. At the end of the war Wolfsburg was a plant two-thirds destroyed, a handful of houses, a permanent home for unmarried mothers and a large cluster of barracks spared by bombs since they lay south of the Mittleland Canal.

While the town had not been hit it was still less than the focus of industrial might or workers' showplace as envisioned a decade earlier. The division of Germany left it well off the main routes and in the first months—even years—of the Occupation, its shifting citizenry was uncertain whether there would ever be an employer there. The symbolism was unintentional but the town which would see near-complete turnover of inhabitants yearly until the end of 1947, had a refugee from Danzig as first mayor. Siegfried Zaayenza was installed on October 1 1945, when the British had a grip on things.

To be clear: the British Army did not run Wolfsburg. The Military Government, or MilGov, handled civilian affairs even though most of its men were army officers at first, with a sprinkling of RAF and RN. Eventually a good many of them switched to civilian status but kept their same jobs. On the other hand, army vehicle repair was a military job and that came under the command of one Colonel McEvoy who, by further chance, had actually driven a KdF prototype and appreciated it during the 1938 Berlin motor show. When he discovered Fallersleben was in the British Zone, McEvoy quickly put in a 'holding party' of Royal Engineers to oversee local labour on the repair job.

The workers were 80 per cent eastern refugees from Russian rule at first and the spectre of radical politics was only one of the daily crises. When Hirst ran into an acute labour shortage in 1946 he proposed transporting in Yugoslav DPs on the condition they be used for special jobs such as rubble clearance, well apart from his German workers.

Many Germans would contend later the British were only interested in the status quo

Left *Major Ivan Hirst, TD, REME, Military Government's senior resident officer at Volkswagenwerk, 1945-9.*

Below *What the British found when they took over soon-to-be Wolfsburg after the war—the plant in rubble—here Hall 3.*

Below right *Almost as soon as they built cars, they needed dealers. Thanks to the GB operation, these were gathering even before VW became a German firm again.*

with no conceivable interest in reviving the firm but the British recall their role more benignly and documentation supports them. It was only natural for Germans to be nervous—and more—about reparations. Rumours were endemic that the whole plant would be dismantled and shipped—east or west—at any moment. Without the plant, however marginal, there would be no Wolfsburg. The hardest task was implanting hope at a time when one cigarette would buy three times what man could purchase with an hour's hard work. In any case, car production was far from the first priority in the 'alternating euphoria and disorganisation of the months following May 1945', as Hirst termed the era.

Since the Russians had thrown patrols well to the west of Fallersleben before withdrawing reluctantly, Wolfsburgers found the British most welcome instead. The plant itself was even named Wolfsburg Motor Works briefly, since some felt 'Volkswagen' had Nazi connotations. Since no higher authority then or later wanted to rule on it, Hirst simply kept the VW emblem without the surrounding DAF cog wheel teeth. He would also propose the car badge of wolf and castle somewhat later.

The British badly needed light transport to match the Jeep and since there were few cars left to requisition the Army soon asked MilGov whether those repairmen could not start up small-scale assembly as well. Several young officers of the repair team had already assembled a *kuebel* or two from stray parts, discovering that German technicians who happened to be left were willing to help. If production began it would be a MilGov responsibility so they sent in an officer during August 1945. This was Ivan Hirst who had been second in command of a tank overhaul shop in Belgium using largely local labour. He imagines that is the reason a Major inherited both plant and town at the age of 39.

Hirst was destined to play the key transitional role, tying the Porsche era to that of Nordhoff who would reign over German rebirth. He came from a background of watch

First actual public VW, built right after the war and still using the drop-gear back axle (note ride height).

importers and clock manufacturers and studied optical instrument engineering himself before infantry duty during the 1940 battle for France. Hirst transferred to the REME in 1941. He arrived in Wolfsburg to find vast damage but believes much was done by Nazi demolitions men out of spite, rather than by bombing. There was little actual damage to the sketchy machinery still in place. Outside components were virtually unobtainable at first, of course, and he had to arrange finance as a bank loan through the county Military Finance Officer. But Hirst was a man who liked the Beetle. He even said, 'we might manage to build a few', and Germans of that time still relate his glee in matching their amphibian against a Jeep, with the VW winning every time. When the Army of the Rhine put in an order for new Volkswagen cars he was happy to go into business.

Wolfsburg actually built 1,785 new Volkswagens—this name was universally used again—by the end of 1945, largely for the British army and control commission, although the allies were interested too. The French happened to see a post-war *kommandeur* built by the experimental shop for fun and requested another for evaluation by their Black Forest officials. The forestry men wanted a series but there were no more ex-amphibian front axle units and the dies had been lost, probably in Silesia.

That same experimental shop later turned out a dual-carburettor Beetle credited with 160 kph/100 mph while the French not only made do with a fleet of Beetles for staff cars, once their officers learned to tolerate, then appreciate, them, but even set up a service shop for VWs in Baden Baden.

The Major used one command car, the one which never left Wolfsburg and now graces the works museum, as a winter staff car to seek out brown coal, carburettor jets or whatever. He improved the design with a roller across the nose so it would not dig the nose in while crossing ditches and tried a second limited-slip differential in front—which proved near-fatal on ice. And it was unusually icy in the 1945-46 and 1946-47 winters when Wolfsburg was shortest of power station coal. This generating giant survived the war undamaged to become an albatross for the British who could never get enough coal to fire it economically. The only alternative power line ran in to the Russian zone so Hirst negotiated a deal with Braunschweig which plugged VW's plant into the city grid and assured VW adequate coal rations.

Both British and Germans wanted to document a new start so they assigned new numbers to many models, only some of which were actually built, to confuse nomenclature further. The basic machine of that first hour became Type 51, meaning a Beetle body and 1,131 cc engine on the two-wheel drive Type 82 chassis with drop-gear hubs at the back. In rough sequence 53 became the same with sliding roof, 55 would have been the convertible saloon.

The Type 82 *kuebel* was renumbered 21, although its body dies were lost in Berlin anyway, and the rest of the 20-series went to a fire tender and van variants. That left 81 and 83 for Beetle offshoots such as a canopied delivery van, and another with a closed box in the back (both for the post office). Porsche had suggested similar vans under different numbers.

To support their 'new leaf' theory the basic Beetle without off-road hubs but using the 25 hp/1,131 cc engine, was eventually called Type 1 to start a numerical run still used. Variations were then 13 for the sun-roof and 14 and 15 for cabriolets. The British seldom used the term 'Beetle', simply calling the car Type 11 or Volkswagen.

Since this basic Type 1 became the all-time best seller in motoring history we might fix its 1945 form. Engine dimensions remained Porsche's, compression was 5.8:1 and power output 25 hp/3,300 rpm. Gearbox ratios were 3.6, 2.07, 1.25 and 0.80 with a final drive ratio of 4.43:1. Wheelbase was its eternal 240 cm/94.6 in and the car measured 405 cm/

Modest beginnings for one of the production phenomena of our time—the GB era was most definitely 'make-do' and the key light alloy castings prove it.

Above *Variation for the post-war post office. Just what had been planned earlier, here using the* kuebel *chassis.*

Below *The engine now in the form it would keep for years.*

Below right *Proper chassis, model one from 1945-8, under British control.*

160 in by 154/60.8 by 150/59.1. Empty weight then was 725 kg/1,590 lb with a payload of 400 kg/880 lb. This was more than the VW target of 650 kg/1,435 lb but still well ahead of the class. The top speed remained the 62 mph that Porsche planned, which looked far better as a metric 100 kph. An early German magazine test exceeded that speed and recorded a 0-100 km/62 mph time of just under 23 seconds with average consumption of 7.9 l/100 km or 35.5 mpg.

The British were satisfied to turn out transport without adding frills to either the plain exterior or grey interior with a cream dashboard panel and two lidless compartments flanking a semaphore switch and starter button. The 'crash' gearbox required clever footwork, cable-operated brakes liked a strong foot, while the steering responded best to a delicate hand. At least they had a runner with flair when the few other factories were concentrating on pre-war designs which pre-dated the Beetle.

It is a fair measure of how advanced Porsche had been in 1936 when we note what a fresh design it seemed in 1945, or even three decades later, come to that. For all these reasons Hirst did his level best to build Beetles. He explained: 'originally I was resident military government officer, then senior resident officer, but both jobs came down to finding work'. He had arrived to find three other officers and 20 to 30 men of all ranks to run a whole factory. They were executors for an ownerless undertaking in effect, since DAF, the owner on record, no longer existed.

The actual army, not under Hirst's command, kept order and 'bought' Beetles—which pleased him even more. The 'company' invoiced repairs or cars to local German authorities who paid such bills as a charge against occupation costs. Almost from the first

VW was a commercial firm in fact, however curious its ownership. British officers lived in the one-time VW guest house, the ranks in a former 'bachelor's home', and their German counterparts wherever they found space. Apart from a few middle-management ex-Americans, most German managers had worked before at Ford or Opel. All developed a close relationship with the British to get Germany back on its feet somehow.

'The key man then', as Hirst recalls, 'was Rudolf Brörmann, a Porsche protégé with Opel training, yet another unconscious boost from von Opel. Brörmann had been chief inspector for KdF and, once cleared by a British de-Nazification board, became top German at the plant. Then clearances were handed over to the Germans who promptly declared him unsuitable. Hirst believed it was a settling of old grudges but Brörmann died a broken man and VW was left with no plant manager at first.

Another chief aid, briefly, was American-trained former works manager Meyer, later jailed on child neglect charges (those of Polish girls at the plant). After acquittal he did not return to VW. Such changes indicate the VW climate at first. At another point a directive arrived forbidding any ex-Nazi to have supervision over fellow Germans and they 'lost most of the foremen overnight', since party membership had been almost universal during the war.

Housing was little better than morale at first since the best huts had gone to UNRRA as a transit camp for Poles and Balts, leaving only the most derelict barracks. Hirst had to establish sanitation before he could build cars and organise transport from surrounding villages for a good part of the work force. Yet he still found time to obtain permission for a works council. As Hirst put it, 'relations were never bad but once the men somehow perceived that MilGov meant to be benevolent they even became good, based on mutual trust and respect'.

The biggest problem remained turnover for the first 18 months in a shifting land, so Hirst was happy that the British and German police trained a works protection force for what he later described as 'probably lawless days in some respects'.

Dick Berryman who joined the British team in early 1946 recalled Hirst as a perfectionist whose devotion to good workmanship led to every man on the assembly line becoming his own inspector, although the very first cars were predictably not of very high finish standards. The only whole car Wolfsburg had ever produced was the bucket car, after all, and the dies for that were lost to the Russians so Hirst and his Germans began to think Beetle immediately. First they sprayed a couple of left-over cars army green and sent them to headquarters for evaluation, receiving a handsome order in return.

Hirst is careful to claim no credit for launching the post-war Beetle, believing it was never the result of any clear overall plan. A need was evident, the *kuebel* was ruled out, and they had some Beetle tooling handy. Senior officer McEvoy already liked the design so the choice was obvious. His team eventually built some 20,000 before the plant returned to German control on January 1 1948, for Americans and French as well as the British. Even the Russian forces took a few. They maintained a small unit in the town, possibly to assess chances for reparations, a cloud which hung over German dreams for most of the earliest post-war years.

'War plants' as a class would be automatically dismantled while tooling from other operations, which might be declared 'surplus to post-war German industry', would be available to the various Allies as needed. Volkswagen was placed on this second-level list but the British soon slapped a four-year reserve on it as 'essential to occupation requirements', meaning that Wolfsburg was never actually inventoried or truly evaluated for reparations.

Some lands did show a passing interest and even Australia sent a small team to look things over with an eye to the end of the reserve period but they realised VW was not likely to be offered even then and lost interest. France was more eager, due largely to Marcel Paul, their communist minister of industry, who fully intended to have the whole KdF plant moved to France. There he would use Professor Porsche, whom he had got jailed, to update it as a new Gallic automobile. The French motor industry was naturally united against this operation although Jean Pierre Peugeot had denounced Porsche for slave labour crimes at the Peugeot plant, only dropping that once any taint of his own possible collaboration—Peugeot made KdF parts during the war—was sufficiently obscured.

Paul and similar left-wing politicians dreamed of a national French 'peoples' car' with Porsche's help but the Peugeot attack sidetracked that threat to private builders in the land. In the end, certain machinery supposedly 'borrowed' from Peugeot during the war was returned to the French; 'to keep VW clean', as Hirst put it. Berryman claimed the British were somewhat more on the VW side than the French, if they took sides at all. In the end France received 50 cars for military service evaluation. When the 'ceiling' on German industrial activity was finally lifted in 1949 Volkswagen was not even on a short list for reparations and thus not attractive to any of the Allies anyway.

Hirst suggests the original British evaluation which returned a negative report was probably based on a *kuebel* captured from Rommel, in the belief this was the real 'volks' car. Personally he thought the Beetle a very modern design with its all-independent suspension and ability to run at top speed all day, 'mostly because the fan absorbed so much power at high revolutions it acted like a governor'.

Rough edges like cable brakes and a 'crash' gearbox could be smoothed away easily enough and until the suspension was softened and the power increased, Hirst even found the car reasonably safe to drive. Air cooling remained the chief item for debate. A unitary chassis/body would have been cheaper to build but once trim, chrome and ventilation were updated Hirst felt the car was more than viable and even suggests the VW did British industry a good turn in the long run by showing them an up-to-date design.

Apart from certain carry-over resistance to any product from the Third Reich, those who did shun the car usually claimed it lacked the basic technical requirements of a 'real' automobile, was too ugly and loud and 'couldn't possibly stay popular for more than two or three years'. The Rootes Commission concluded it would never be competition for British cars. Hirst does point out that the British did not actually turn down the Beetle or the plant for the simple reason neither were ever really offered to them. Sir William merely told Hirst, 'I would be a fool to think VW might ever produce cars again'. Apparently Berryman later tried to interest Rootes a second time, but without official sanction, and received no response.

Ford was another quoted by the Germans as saying that he would not have the car or rights to it as a gift. Hirst, again, explains a somewhat different case. Having production problems in common with German Ford of Cologne, he had contacts there as well as in Dagenham before Henry Ford II visited Germany in March 1948. Volkswagen heard Ford was vaguely interested in them although they were not on any reparations list by then, but Henry II dismissed the idea flatly when he saw a map. Wolfsburg was far too close to East Germany for his taste.

As for the Russians, they had not objected to the MilGov reserve on the factory, taking the official position that *Kraft durch Freude* had been a social project after all and they could only favour the whole idea of a car for the masses. Their only real function was providing a spectre to nudge production along during 1946, 'so the plant won't be shipped east'. Their 23 hp Moskvitch with modern pontoon shape and performance actually helped VW. If its tooling had remained at Opel, Wolfsburg would have faced far more modern competition in the crucial early years.

Despite all distractions the Anglo-German team even established a production run, reaching their first 1,000-car month by March 1946 and a proud year-end total of 10,200 cars produced, among spirited debates on the civilian price which turned out to be 5,000 Rmk for the standard saloon. Later VW totals would dwarf their figures—the dreamed-of 2,000-car month never quite happened—but the achievement was quite rightly called a miracle by 1946 standards. For one thing, their product had never been built in quantity before and a great deal of debugging was necessary, some of it basic. The steering box had a potentially lethal design flaw, oil coolers leaked due to improper solder, the crankshaft oil system too often was 'total loss' and leaking fuel pump seals passed petrol into the crankcase. German management then was only interested in completing cars so Hirst had to ask for an inspection team from the REME to do what amounted to customer inspection checks before any Beetle was delivered.

Many problems came from suppliers, of course—such as steering arms with hidden cracks, caught before the cars were sold. Certain officers who crashed Beetles tried to blame it on the steering arm rumour but unfamiliarity with the car's handling proved the real reason. The supplier was making do with exceptionally tight steel rations. When he found a crack he would simply reheat and shrink the arm to cover it over. He was corrected.

An ex-Ford man named Paulsen handled these purchasing headaches although Hirst had to certify each order as essential for MilGov purposes. When that did not secure deliveries in all cases, so that some cars might leave the line without tyres, for instance, they decided to rally local MilGov support in each area behind local suppliers.

Whether it might be ball races, a prime problem, sheet steel, ferrous or non-ferrous castings, tyres, batteries, electrics, glass or cloth—the shopping list would be broken down by areas within the British Zone and a man sent out to help the component firm solve its problems. In the end Hirst had an entire British network behind his German car. Even then hardcore shortages remained. Rolling mills were in such bad shape VW could not find sheet large enough for the roof panel. First they spot-welded a lap joint, then turned to butt-welding two pieces together, once the tool room built a welder capable of the task.

On another occasion a MilGov branch shut down their source of crankcase and transmission housings because the supplying plant had been part of the aircraft industry and thus came under the mandatory dismantlement rule. VW had a foundry building which never had been put to any use so they 'rescued' the dies and opened their own non-ferrous casting operation.

Carburettors were a more complicated problem when they found the Solex licence-holder in Berlin simply could not deliver any in 1946. Brörmann and Hirst took a carburettor to pieces on the latter's desk top and decided VW might manage gravity-cast housings but internals would be far more of a problem. So they visited Voightlander Cameras in Braunschweig and found their source of floats, jets and other minute parts. Hirst recalls Solex of Paris was 'very understanding' when informed later of these copies.

Anything to build cars—yet 1947 sales of 8,987 were below the previous year since the whole plant had been shut down during the 1946/47 winter when coal was simply unobtainable. Nonetheless, when Professor Porsche was released from French confinement in August of 1947 and driven through Germany by his long-time secretary and nephew, Ghislaine Kaes, he was astounded by the number of Beetles on the road, so many he lost count. He was deeply gratified to find six of every ten cars they met were his child.

Production reached 2,500 per month by the end of 1947, a corner turned, and they could even take a stand at the Hannover Trade Fair, a move which brought a flood of export inquiries, even before national currency reform.

British policy then encouraged all German exports as a means of reducing the tax burden on Britons still supporting the occupied land. Since the Reichsmark had no foreign standing at all, potential exports had to be funnelled through the Anglo-American Joint Export-Import Agency. At least VW could appoint foreign agents, starting with 56 Beetles for the Pon brothers of Amersfoort, Holland. Ben Pon had to hire five drivers to take his first Beetles home. He had ordered six cars but one got stuck on the shaky assembly line. Before long the Officers' Mess in Wolfsburg had become a kind of international hotel.

German civilian demand was increasing even faster while Allied needs had largely been met, so Hirst instituted the first moves towards having the British step back to become, eventually, just another VW customer. The rebuilding line was merged into a VW service department. Prior to the currency reform in June 1948, however, most locals could only obtain a reconditioned Beetle, and even that required a priority number proving they performed some service the occupying forces deemed necessary.

The embryonic sales-service network then, with its quasi-dealer system initiated by MilGov, was gradually converted into a proper dealer network with Hirst insisting dogmatically that there must be spares before sales, a policy VW would soon embrace as its finest feature. As Ivan Hirst recalls, the early German management was lax about such things, into 1947, although there had been at least some sort of technical back up right from 1945. The first bulletin from the Wolfsburg Motor Works—in two languages—sent out in June 1946, explained how to file those which would follow. The scant interest in service may have come from the fact that they had never been forced to operate in an open market.

The British had an early driver's handbook written; a successor to the KdF book printed with great pride and thoroughness before the war, even before the cars. Hirst's team also produced a spares catalogue with exploded view diagrams which seemed new to the Germans there. They initiated defect investigations while a new service department designed special tools and opened a training school for mechanics. Wolfsburg soon realised that spares must have priority equal to new cars and that after-sales service had real value.

Towards the end of 1947 Hirst felt it was time to restructure the entire operation with the goal of easing Britain entirely out of management. Enlisting the aid of Leslie Barber, described as a quiet but deep-thinking economist, and Colonel Radclyffe, officer in charge of all German light industry matters, Hirst set up a board to represent MilGov interests and advise the Germans if asked.

Since the workers' front had been abolished by decree, neither town nor plant actually had an owner but there were still absent interests to be protected so that VW remained a British trust up to the moment it was turned over to Bonn. The three key board members were supported by Berryman, 'a splendid back up to the German production manager', and a good solver of on-the-spot problems, and by an accountant from Barber's staff, resident in Wolfsburg.

The Germans included Brörmann in 1946, then Steinmeier as works manager although there was no general manager in 1947. Another of the one-time Americans, Höhne, would follow Steinmeier, while Orlich, an ex-Opel man, headed the vital inspection department as of 1947. When the plant passed to German management, virtually all those put into key jobs by Hirst remained.

There was no design department then, nor did they even have a chief engineer, so Hirst made an offer to Rudolf Uhlenhaut, still waiting for the revival of Daimler Benz. The legendary race car tester and development engineer did not feel VW had a future, however, so we can only speculate on Beetle handling if he had taken the post.

The British property control side soon proposed a Dr Münch of Berlin to be General Manager although he was basically a banker with no deep understanding of, or experience in, the car industry. He did take care of finances for the time being and the search continued for a director from the car branch.

At this juncture Hirst probably made the most telling of his many contributions to the Volkswagen future, although it began as no more than a man to interview. A MilGov friend asked Hirst to speak to 'an unemployed Opel man' who had been awarded the honour of 'economic leader' during the war, when he headed Opel truck operations. This title made him ineligible to hold any executive position in the US zone, where Opel's remaining plants in the west were located. Since British rules were more lenient, Hirst asked him to Wolfsburg for an extended talk about a possible deputy position for production, under Münch. After two days Hirst was sure this was no deputy but the man who should be their General Director so he sent one Heinz Nordhoff to Radclyffe, who agreed completely. He was hired, with effect from January 1 1948.

Frank Novotny, another Hirst appointee who became PR chief in 1947, and Nordhoff soon took total control of the firm and Nordhoff became a legend in his own lifetime for his business acumen, technical knowledge and globe-girdling vision. If he was also, 'something of an enigma to ordinary mortals', as Hirst adds, his aloofness may have been only restraint. The British board agreed Nordhoff needed a free hand and gradually phased out internal and external signs of their occupation, from parking facility markers to the demobilisation of Hirst himself during the winter of 1947/48. He was immediately appointed to the same job as a civilian. He remained at Wolfsburg, providing advice if called upon, until August 1949 when he completed the four years which had firmly established a one-time Hitler dream as a free-world phenomenon.

Ivan Hirst turned down positions with the British motor industry, both before and after he left Volkswagen, to remain in the field of international co-operation. His role at Wolfsburg was publicly recognised in 1977 when Hirst was formally welcomed back to the city by the mayor of that now-thriving metropolis. In 1948, however, the barely-ten year old town was just on the verge of its boom period under the reign of Heinz Nordhoff, the next key figure at Volkswagen. Soon expansion would overflow Wolfsburg itself, turning the dream into a permanent legend.

Chapter 5

The boom begins

Heinz Nordhoff ruled over Wolfsburg for a full 20 years, but it was the first decade of that span which ensured his place in the Volkswagen pantheon. In a very real sense, he and the economic wonder were inseparable. Nordhoff lived for VW and eventually he even distributed gold coins as the firm's Christmas present—one side showed a Beetle, the other his own profile. And after he died, this man who had made a personal crusade out of popularising Beetles on every continent of the earth, was quite properly made the first honorary citizen of Wolfsburg.

Nordhoff had not invented the Volkswagen, it's true, but he was most certainly the man directly responsible for its proliferation. He took over a design he had once described as being, 'as full of faults as a dog of fleas', and applied post-war production methods to turn it into a true car for the masses. He constructed a town where this might happen and established a motoring monolith on Hirst's foundations, 'once he got the place to himself'. Later historians might comment it was this same Heinz Nordhoff who controlled Volkswagen too long, who counted over-much on a one-model policy, but that was only saying that the sort of manager capable of turning a bomb-site car shop into a worldwide concern might also be prone to heed very little of what originated outside his own office door. Nordhoff had been right in the early days when he resisted considerable internal and external pressure to abandon the Beetle for some 'better design', so it would seem only natural later to continue urging his team to think of nothing else but Beetles.

Whatever counsels of cautious status quo Nordhoff may have embraced towards the end of his incredible reign, if stands beyond all dispute that without his energy, enthusiasm and vision from the first day of January 1948, there very probably would not have *been* any Volkswagens 20 years later for those with hindsight to debate. He was thus the fourth of those vital figures behind the Beetle and arguably the most important, ultimately. He certainly held the world VW stage the longest, through the toughest period any of them had experienced.

Heinz Nordhoff was born in Hildesheim in 1899 as second among three sons of a private banker. Thus he was as much a Saxon as the VW, although the family moved to Berlin in 1911 when his father's bank failed. Young Nordhoff survived a leg wound in World War 1 to study mechanical engineering in Berlin. His first love was ships but he quickly decided a man has far more personal contact with the car and moved to BMW as a trainee—on aeroplane engines. He already realised that Germans might design fine cars but it was Americans who designed products. When a chance to work at Nash in the US was foiled by the 1929 Depression Nordhoff joined Opel, writing service manuals and spending his holidays on the assembly line to gain a deeper view.

One reward for such ambition was a trip to America where he studied production and sales at General Motors. He even found time to marry in 1931, while moving steadily towards a position on the Opel board which came in the late 30s. By 1940 Nordhoff was

Left *Heinz Nordhoff.*

Below right *First German-built Beetle, after Nordhoff took over running operation from Hirst and the British—a 1949 deluxe.*

head of Opel's new truck plant in Brandenburg, the finest in the world then.

As a pre-war Opel man he was loyally bitter about 'cheap competition' from the KdF, only deciding later that Porsche had produced a rough diamond which might well be worth the polishing. The change began when Nordhoff found himself barred from any job higher than labourer in the US zone. Instead he would build VW along 'American lines', an orientation he shared with Porsche.

He accepted the British job offer on the condition he would have sole word. There was little to lose and a camp bed in the rat-infested, derelict works to gain, as he recalled that first month of 1948 when the new director faced a car which had 'a personality, a will of its own, an unusual aura'. It was a real match for his own missionary zeal and wide range of interests. This was his unique chance to build a car empire from the ground up and the man who arrived in Wolfsburg, underfed and white faced, did just that with a willingness to make any and all decisions from day one.

He bound a new team close although many—including politicians who would soon trumpet his praises for pacing their recovery miracle—laughed at first. Nordhoff's laugh proved the most enduring. He would raise output from only 19,244 cars in 1948 to well over half a million yearly in a decade, and be turning out 3,000 per day for the first time by 1959, all from a brand new town which soon boasted the most cars—and kids—per family of any in Germany.

The pivotal year was 1948, 'the first in VW history when the plant must stand entirely on its own'. Nordhoff arrived to find it took 700 hours to build one car. He announced that would soon be down to 100 hours per car, but first they all had to face June 20 1948 when Bonn decreed an overnight currency reform which wiped out the Reichsmark and replaced it with the new Deutschmark, at only 40 per person.

Volkswagen did not have a *pfennig* in the till and no credit but Nordhoff called every dealer in the land and told them to hasten up to Wolfsburg with suitcases full of every DM they might scrape together. A standard VW was going to cost 5,300 new marks and people were clamouring for them. By November VW had 15,000 domestic orders and another 7,000 from abroad so his dealers listened. As the only working car factory at first, VW had enjoyed a headstart in lining up dealers who had once handled rival lines.

In saving the plant he rescued the town too. VW took a paternal approach to Wolfsburg from the beginning, already planning a better workers' life in 1948. They soon had the cleanest, brightest—and most neatly aligned—industrial city in Europe. The factory poured in money for school lunches as well as schools themselves, for churches, pools, skating rinks and cultural treats. Yet they were careful from the first to avoid 'competing' with the town. VW would support the city library, for instance, rather than start its own.

By 1949 they were rebuilding, with 228 new dwellings, and by the end of that year could claim nearly 25,000 inhabitants who built 46,000 cars on the eve of a vast expansion, fuelled by the Korean war. With cars pouring out and people streaming in to build them, Wolfsburg remained the most crowded of all German cities despite its building boom. As late as 1951 they counted five heads per dwelling compared to four in Frankfurt or three in Berlin and both of these were heavily-bombed cities. Population doubled between 1945 and 1951, quadrupled by 1958. This one firm would draw 150,000 new people to the area.

When MilGov order 202 finally relinquished all Allied control over German properties ownership of the factory passed to the state of Lower Saxony for the time being whereas the town across the canal was based on an English municipal structure with ground rights invested in the community to discourage speculation. Births soon outran deaths by 3:1

and the first of five city planners was hired from Berlin. Deciding such a town would never need to house 90,000, as grandiose pre-war plans had projected, he dropped the ring road in favour of a small town parallel to the plant, one which might absorb 35,000— a figure exceeded only two years later.

In the end, the city fathers decided the man to recall was Peter Koller, the original architect who returned from a Russian prison camp to build Wolfsburg after all; including the churches from his original plan. He placed a hospital and school atop the one small hill rather than a party acropolis and did his first housing in a solid, late-30s style of mixed pastel colours. As a matter of early pride, there was no 'better' or 'worker' section. All early flats had double-glazed windows, tiled baths and central heating from the factory, a feature still true today for homes, offices and hotel alike, explaining the largely smokeless air over an industrial city. Environmental concerns were part of Wolfsburg planning from the first since they lie in a river lowland where wastes would be hard to handle.

VW provides the tax money which makes Wolfsburg one of the best-financed communities in the Common Market, a city carefully composed of homes, green belts and artificial lakes. By April 1951 they were ready to break away from status as a nominal suburb of nearby Grifhorn and assume ownership of onetime DAF properties. That came shortly after the town fathers named their new main road after Ferdinand Porsche.

This is the wide shopping mall running south from the canal, past city hall and out to 'Germany', the route taken by 90 per cent of the work force on its annual August vacation. Ignoring all extension schemes the German railway has left Wolfsburg totally dependent on automobiles, yet their planned *autobahn* spur never appeared either. The 30 km/18 miles of two-lane road from city limits to the nearest motorway interchange have become the longest no-passing slow lane in Germany. It was only a little less jammed when the father of the Beetle finally visited post-war Wolfsburg to see his dream at work.

The grey, somewhat stooped man in a long, dark overcoat watched peoples' cars gushing off the assembly lines and politely returned the nods of the many floor workers who may not have quite realised just who this was, only that his picture hung in almost every office. Finally Ferdinand Porsche turned to the director and said, 'you know, Herr Nordhoff, I always pictured it this way. But I wasn't sure I'd been right until you proved it'.

Today Porsche Strasse points at the heart of the plant in a town of 135,000 where the social rule is 'no car talk at parties'. Every population projection proved too modest but they still managed to expand without losing the feel for grass and parks, incorporating instead several nearby villages in the 70s. By then the plant had grown to three times the most optimistic pre-war dream and the town had to keep pace although it was sited at a narrow point of the Aller River valley and could only stretch north-west without impinging on old established urban interest spheres. In fact, Wolfsburg gradually became the major hub itself.

Only recently has a 'Wolfsburg species' begun to show. For many years the inhabitants considered themselves emigrants in their own land, an inner-German melting pot. Psychologists dubbed this the gold-rush town, the coldly perfect paradise where materialism ran stronger than even that in other rebuilding German areas.

It began as Nordhoff and his people versus all those 'others', with each worker from teenager to top boss pressured to be more, earn more, learn more and produce more. Those 'others' were any misguided souls who did not at least drive a Beetle. 'When we began', Nordhoff would recall, 'and needed help badly, no man, no bank and no government body helped'. Then the boom got rolling and the boss discovered it was a blessing to have neither owner nor overseer to argue when he cut prices, raised wages or denied both, as he liked. By the 70s, of course, Wolfsburg had attracted a more aware generation, even mellowed without losing all of its early, easy swing as the town with few class distinctions. What it could never escape was the fact that three-quarters of the townspeople (versus roughtly half in Dearborn) worked for one company which carried some 70 per cent of the local tax burden.

This could easily lead to over-dependence in less-affluent car years but all efforts to attract other industry foundered on the simple fact that VW set wages too high for others to match. The city fathers could only trust Nordhoff was right when he proclaimed, 'even if cars do disappear from this world, the last one sold will be a Volkswagen'. Not necessarily one built in Wolfsburg, however. By the 80s only one VW employee in four worked at the mother plant. VW builds or assembles cars in every corner of the world, an expansion which began in the 50s when they were turning out a Beetle every 30 seconds and still had a six month waiting list (longer in Wolfsburg than America, thanks to Nordhoff policies).

When it became evident a second German plant would be vital, and that it could not crowd into Wolfsburg, they picked fully-industrialised Hannover as the place to build Transporters, the first model not directly descended from Porsche and thus an apt one for the first non-Wolfsburg plant.

Heinz Nordhoff was well-described as a gambler—a man who loved the risks, once he had calculated them carefully. When he doubled daily production at a stroke in 1949 his Bonn watchdogs were aghast. He was embracing sure bankruptcy. Nordhoff replied that good cars, of top quality, at a bottom price, backed by first-class service, would always sell. Typically, he would always insist miracles played no part in their boom, only work, thought and knowledge. He ran a one-man show yet was at his best with people and eventually built up one of the largest design staffs of any European firm, only to have them all labour over detailing.

By the time VW men had added ten years of fine tuning to Porsche's decade of design their boss could boast there was not one part left on the car in its original shape. Nordhoff remained true to the one basic idea for the first six years, hardly changing engine dimensions at any time, but he clearly meant to build his own (better) car. A team of 4,000 inspectors would see to that.

At the very start of his era the engine ran but materials to build it were short and constant watchfulness the price for quality. As late as 1951, raw materials bottlenecks could still halt production although they topped the quarter-million mark that year, raffling off the anniversary car among the workers.

Up to roughly the end of 1952 they were firming up the foundations and brooding over future directions. Many self-styled advisers—Nordhoff never lacked for those—now insisted the VW was too fancy and its backers should seriously consider fours of much smaller capacity or even half-litre twins. (Porsche might have told them how that would work.) There was even modest support for a diesel flat twin around 1949. All this was aimed at still-cheaper motorisation along the lines of the Russian Communard, a Beetle imitation of only 750 cc and 20 hp. Nordhoff sensed his market would prefer a second-hand Beetle to such a lame new machine. On the other hand, the luxury class—where he personally would rather have liked to offer a model—was not really VW territory either. He was tempted, however, and let one likely prototype get very close to pre-production status before casting the decisive 'nein' by telegram from Africa. He could not quite manage to axe the project on the scene.

So VW built only Beetles, a name which probably appeared for the first time in the *New York Times* for July 1 1942, although another source notes that Porsche himself had specified a shape, 'streamlined as a May beetle'. The tale is uncertified. We do know the

VW drag figure was 0.49, unbelievable for the 30s and only some 10 per cent worse than the European small car average 40 years later.

When they focused on the basic VW, Wolfsburg engineers realised its engine might be a wonder on paper but also close to unproducible in the general car sense since it required ultra-precise tolerances and critical alloys. Many of the first ones died within 50,000 km/ 30,000 miles, prompting Nordhoff to offer those famous 100,000 km watches for any driver who reached that figure on one engine—while he upgraded works standards. By 1954 he could welcome 35,000 guests to a 100,000-club meeting and, four years later, had the engine so tamed the incentive watch could be dropped.

They concentrated first on detail improvements—thermostatically-controlled cooling air for faster warm-up, better cooling ribs, stiffer or thermically better heads—but no deviation from what already worked. Higher phosphor content in 1949 cylinders extended life, intakes were partly jacketed in 1950, bi-metal pistons and armoured exhaust valves came with an electron crankcase in 1951 and plastic cam drive wheels cut noise. Oil consumption was reduced in small, steady increments but all this left them with the inherent quality of an unstressed four. This was really version two, dating back to 1943, and remained their sole (1.1 litre) model until 1953.

During this same period, gearing and rear axle ratios were largely left alone, apart from slight variations to first and second gears. Chassis and suspension likewise remained the same in design until telescopic shock absorbers were fitted to the front only in 1949, although 1950 models did have five-leaf front torsion bar packs top and bottom while the round rear bar was reduced from 25 to 24 mm (1 inch to 0.95).

The most-praised 1950 change was hydraulic brakes in April for the so-called Export model, ten months after its introduction, along with more drum area as car weight increased. Pedal pressures were reduced by a third as well. Such new options as paint or trim never changed the basic bubble. Fans could identify 1948 cars, for instance, by large VW emblems on the hub-caps, flat bumpers with banana-shaped guards and L-type handles for both lids. These had round tail-lights but no outside mouldings. A year later the hub-cap emblems were smaller, bumpers covered with flanged guards and a cable release for the front lid allowed a fixed handle. Such were VW model changes.

Or 1949 would be known for clock space on the dashboard and optional ashtray below the centre of the panel. In January rear foot wells were deepened into the floorpan for increased legroom. The de luxe model even boasted a two-spoke wheel and ivory-coloured knobs. The driver had a sun visor, the rear passengers grab handles and the front seats were adjustable on rails—the left one was raised in October, to aid the driver in fast bends. Cigar lighter, locking glove compartment and sliding roof, not to mention a fuel gauge, were options through 1950, while owners in 1951 found a Wolfsburg crest on their front lid. It remained until 1963 when thefts to make amulets got out of hand in the US. Such a list indicates headquarters thinking—touch up any points which come to notice.

Nordhoff stole his march on most competitors by putting prime effort into proper service, right down to handbooks of manners and dress for each dealer and a list of 41 potential Beetle-buyer types. 'We expect the dealer net to maintain any sales tempo we dictate', he said; meaning, sell your quota or we'll find a new dealer.

In Wolfsburg the spirit was twice as pervasive although Nordhoff was neither 'capital' nor 'manager' at first. He benefited in those crucial years from having no board to peer over his shoulder. Neither nationalised nor private, he had more freedom than any comparable company boss. As early as 1949 he had faced the first shop-floor demands for more money. Nordhoff told them flatly that higher wages so soon after the currency reform were impossible. But if the men would be content with their average DM 1.11 per hour, he would promise they received a special share when there was some pie to slice

Above *1950 news—a sun roof.* **Below** *A side/rear view of a 1951 Beetle.*

at last. 'The General', as their Director was called, was as good as his word. Once the factory showed success there were extra pensions, health or life insurance beyond contract minimums, even a 4 per cent yearly bonus on top of the gross wage packet.

Authoritarian Nordhoff certainly was, but during his first decade there was simply no reason for a union to come in since the boss watched over worker interests better than they could themselves. When he eventually became the Honorary Professor, recipient of the Grand Cross with Star, lover of exquisite wines, antique furniture and impressionist paintings—the men merely assumed he had worked hard enough, as they had, to earn some pleasures. This rapport paid dividends through all the years of record production.

However, this unceasing drive to produce soon meant VW must export to justify unit costs. Nordhoff realised earlier than most that if Germany could not absorb all his cars, neither could Europe. The obvious step was world-wide sales.

Within a very few years this Beetle was the power behind Germany's overall recovery, the most-exported automobile in the world under Feureissen, a one-time Porsche colleague and Auto Union race boss, who now set up the globe-girdling Volkswagen network. In every week of 1958, to quote one instance, VW filled five car-freight ships (350-1,000 Beetles each) for 123 countries, but chiefly for America which took half of all

An early dashboard (1948 here but unchanged during first Nordhoff years), with optional clock and white steering wheel.

Beetles in the late 50s. It was this flood which pushed Detroit into smaller models and turned the United States from automobile exporter to net importer of cars. Of course, the fact that Americans were soon buying more Volkswagens than all US firms combined sent abroad could quickly turn from the unparalleled success story of the 50s into the spectre of Wolfsburg's next brush with extinction.

In 1947, when one Dutchman named Pon realised a vision he had carried all through the war, since Porsche personally promised him the first Dutch dealership, nobody foresaw possible export problems—except the one of having some exports. Holland received the first VWs sent abroad but Nordhoff was an instinctive exporter anyway, one who would visit Spain in person to launch operations. His first coup was a pact with Chrysler to use their European sales outlets which gained dealers without paying a penny. He quickly added Cadillac and Jaguar dealers since neither had a competing product.

Switzerland was the first true test since it built no cars, but once the canny Swiss buyer embraced his Beetle for its wintry properties, Nordhoff was off and exporting. Nearly a quarter of all sales were made outside Germany as early as 1948. He soon moved VW into the southern hemisphere to balance seasonal sales swings up north, earning early spurs with solid successes in the East African and Round Australia rallies where Beetle durability was visible to every buyer.

Trade barriers were endemic then and often CKD packets were the only way around local quotas. These made his cars costlier but they sold anyway, moving the French and Italians to set exceptionally low quotas as the only means of protecting their own small-car makers. When Sweden tried to slow the VW flood Nordhoff called on state support from Bonn where the threat of reconsidering a pending trade treaty proved sufficient.

But the US remained his wheel horse. Starting with two cars, late in 1949, that market rose to 400 in 1951, testing a field which importer Hoffmann in New York swore would never top 800 per year. Nordhoff responded by launching Volkswagen of America; eager young American managers backed by VW-drilled technicians. No car was allowed off the boat until it could be serviced properly. By 1955 36,000 Beetles a year were making Detroit nervous but VW doubled that figure a year later, and again in 1957, to capture 2 per cent of the richest car market anywhere.

An early extra seldom seen, the rear seat bolsters, 1949.

VW had either timed the general swing away from bloated transport precisely right or at least offered the proper product just as it was wanted. Some said Porsches helped pave this path—Beetle owners believed they were driving the 'everyman Porsche'. Soon a VW was not just cheap extra transport but the ideal inverted snob machine, 'the second car even if you don't have a first one'. Psychologists and sociologists rushed to issue learned papers on this phenomenon and car writers waxed euphoric. VW simply sold Beetles.

With the whole world wanting one it seems hardly surprising that all those pre-war savers who still had their stamp books, filled or otherwise, would want a Beetle too. Wolfsburg's problem was that they still wanted one for the rather subsidised 1940 price. This launched the longest and strangest court battle in post-war German history. The claimant was really a group, calling itself the Self-Help Association of One-time Volkswagen Savers. They asked, 'who is sitting at the wheel of this car of the people?' and found the answer quite clear: 'not the Volkswagen saver who was once godfather to this factory'.

The real drive which carried their suit up and down the court ladder for a dozen years came from one Saxon named Karl Stolz, from a town at the foot of the old Germanic Marsberg, seat of the teutonic war gods. Karl der Grosser (Charlemagne) had rampaged up there around 772 so the press naturally applied his title to this new Karl who founded his association on October 7 1948, shortly after the official seat of the firm was finally moved from Berlin to Wolfsburg. By 1949 he had a thousand members at half a mark each, peaking at 3,000 in 1951 when he added a second 'partner', Meischner, to broaden the claim. The suit was then filed in their two names with the other members as interested parties.

Meischner of Berlin had paid for a KdF in full, Stolz had only 875 Rmk in his own stamp books, so they now demanded a standard saloon for Stolz who should pay another Dm 365 by his own reckoning, and a sun-roof saloon for the Berlin claimant. Each man asked for the promised two full years of insurance as well. The pair soon dropped their claim to cars at the original 1,000 Rmk price, realising that had gone down with the Thousand Year Reich, but they pressed for delivery at Wolfsburg cost with prices converted from Reichs- to Deutschmarks at 1:1. After all, this car was based on the idea of minimum-cost transport for the little man, wasn't it? The Association further asked the courts to set aside 50,000 cars per year at a price they claimed should be DM 2,475 when VW put a price of DM 5,450 on the Export through a dealer. Volkswagen replied they had no connection with any pre-war savings plan, they were not a legal partner to this contract, and could not be expected to honour such altered conditions—particularly since they had not received a penny of the savings fund.

The case first came to trial on January 19 1950 when a local court rejected the savers' claim on the grounds that a contract no longer existed—that had been nothing but Third Reich propaganda. The state supreme court turned down an appeal but reversed the lower court and ruled that VW might or might not be a contract partner—this one factor kept the case in litigation another decade. The German supreme court now returned the case with instructions to decide who the partners might really be.

Volkswagen was plagued by the uncertainty of withholding investment funds in case they might have to deliver cars below cost so Nordhoff took the offensive and asked for a clear ruling on the partner question. He got the last answer he wanted or expected: yes, VW was a partner and now the factory had to pay the costs of appeal.

By late 1954, when the German supreme court heard new arguments, the entire country was caught up in this poker game for as many as 300,000 new cars. The next judgement held that VW was not a partner after all but Stolz could still sue them. When his state court turned back that suit in the autumn of 1955 Stolz was about ready to consider a settlement and VW proposed 'the best deal ever offered any one group': DM 250 in cash or 500 credit against a Beetle.

The Self-Helpers turned that down and went back to the supreme court, seven years after first appearing there, only to be bounced back to the state level yet again. By now even the press was beginning to swing away from the savers, feeling VW had done its best. Volkswagen pointed out it was not a welfare organisation, as both parties made their fourth supreme court appearance in October 1961. That bench finally ruled for a price cut of DM 150-600 on a new car, depending on the stamps in each saver's book, or a cash rebate of DM 25-100 on the same grounds. It was the end of 1970 before Wolfsburg sorted it all out, recognizing 120,573 valid pre-war 'contracts' with 67,164 of them settling for cash and the rest taking a new VW. The company eventually paid out DM 6.3 million in cash, another 26.9 million in rebates. Nearly 93 per cent could claim the maximum slice.

While it took 13 years to settle the last DAF lien against Hitler's dream, barely a year sufficed for Volkswagen and Nordhoff to realise it might be wise to retain the same Porsche design offices which had founded their fortunes. In 1949 Ferry Porsche met Nordhoff on neutral ground and his firm was appointed consultant to VW with a royalty on every Beetle built.

This pact did prevent Porsche taking on offers which came later from England and Japan for a small car but also assured them of early capital and parts for their 356 sports machine. And while Ferry turned down a personal offer to become head of VW development in 1953, his firm would provide a steady stream of prototypes for VW consideration, starting with a unitary chassis/body model using MacPherson front struts, ready the year Professor Porsche died, although this suspension system was not applied to a Beetle until much later.

Porsche functioned as a captive 'think tank' for Wolfsburg right through the 60s but the Beetle was doing so well in that era that none of their ideas reached the public. The first suggestion arrived in 1951-52 just as stage one of the Nordhoff era was peaking with production topping the 100,000 mark for the first time. That was only 17 per cent better than 1950, of course, following three straight years of production doubled annually, but any small worries were buried in export figures of nearly 36,000 cars for 1951 even before they invaded the US. Wolfsburg frankly saw no reason for a Beetle replacement although Nordhoff was later stung into displaying his secret garage of prototypes to prove he had not been asleep.

★   ★   ★

Heinz Nordhoff was far more interested in launching the first VW which had not been part of the original Porsche line-up, the Type 2 or Transporter. German dealers might cry for enough Beetles to feed buyer queues in a nation-wide boom, but Nordhoff decreed they must make do with roughly half his production within Germany while he introduced the one model Porsche missed.

There had always been haulers of one sort or another grafted on to the Beetle or *kuebel* but the boxy van shape was new at least. The British had played this game with great glee, making pick-up trucks or the closed-box Post Office truck numbered 28 but these were all based on the war-time Type 82. Later they built an ultra-short 'road tractor' with three feet chopped out of its wheelbase and a platform to carry loads you could not stuff through the doors of a Beetle. Hirst even sketched a flatbed factory shuttle transporter one day when they could not get fork-lift trucks. He put the platform in front where it could be lower and perched his driver above the engine in the back. This was little more than a tube frame with power but Ben Pon Senior saw one and decided there was a market for a light carrier with flat-four engine.

By this time (1949-50), numbering had settled down for the time being with the Beetle as Type 1, so a Transporter logically became Type 2—or 'bully' in popular German jargon in honour of its bulldog stance. Eventually this mobile brick would become very nearly as world-famous and a good deal more versatile than even the Beetle. This

Prototype of the first body style not laid down by Porsche, the original Type 2 or bully, as early as 1949.

specialised machine is still built in quantity and third-generation form 30 years later. Tucking the engine in the back (Beetle floorpan), driving the rear wheels with *kuebel*-like drop gears, and seating the driver over the front wheels left ample space for cargo, eight to nine seats or even full camper layouts on a short wheelbase. Volkswagen even laid claim to launching Germany's economic recovery with their delivery van, only a mild case of hyperbole.

It is at least beyond dispute that no other firm ever built more machines of this class— over 5.5 million world-wide by the end of the 70s. As early as the mid-50s Nordhoff already needed a new factory to keep up with Type 2 demand and put it in Hannover, the first vehicle plant outside Wolfsburg although Transporters would later be built in other lands as well. The bully would sell to 140 countries and be more widely copied by far more firms than the Beetle.

The very first Type 2 came off a Wolfsburg line in February 1950 with production up to ten daily by March 8. This 1,045 kg/2,300 lb machine, propelled by a standard 25 hp boxer engine in the rear cupboard, was rated for a payload of 750 kg/1,650 lb, but most owners simply carried everything they could cram into 4.6 m^3/162 ft^3. Within five years the bully got their 30 hp saloon engine to cope with this buyer habit, plus better heat distribution since passengers in the bus version (as of 1951) had been most vocal about drivers getting all the meagre warmth.

The Transporter was updated regularly and by the time they reached the first million in 1960 the tireless machine had 34 hp and a synchronised gearbox. Ruggedness was always their goal: wider main bearings (steel-backed for colder climes) or more cooling fins appeared first on the van, then in the Beetle. As a rule VW applied its latest technology to Type 2s first.

Through the years they produced an amazing number of variations using doors of every description, a wide variety of interior heights and special beds for every conceivable application. Unlike the Beetle, the bully came in any shape a buyer wanted. For Americans who found it hard to clear a motorway ramp with the wind against them, VW first offered their 1.5 litre, 42 hp engine in the Type 2, noting that such power was 'completely unnecessary' for a Beetle. A year later the 0.8 ton model received a mate capable of hauling a full ton but it would be the 1968 model year before the slogger finally received a fresh face, 17$\frac{1}{2}$ years and 2 million Transporters after the debut. Bully production alone roughly equalled that of all post-war Mercedes. The first million took 12 years to produce, the second, five and a half years. Extra shifts continued at Hannover when they were dropped at the saloon plants.

The first facelift included a curved, one-piece front window, and sliding doors became standard, but the real news was double-jointed half shafts in the back for greater comfort and notably better handling. This was the first Wolfsburg model to admit swing axles might not be the sole answer.

The 50 hp level was reached by 1971 with dual intake passages in new heads for their 1.6 litre Type 2 engine. Disc brakes were added as production passed the three million mark. Another year brought the Type 4 (VW 411 or Porsche 914) engine with fan on the crankshaft nose for a lower silhouette and 66 hp from 1.7 litres as an option. They could not make full use of this lower engine, however, since their basic 1.6 retained the taller (Beetle) fan housing.

VW was on the threshold of its front-drive, water-cooled saloon changeover by this time so many pundits hastened to write the Type 2 off as a dinosaur doomed to fade away. Wolfsburg fanned such rumours by producing a new range of larger Transporters called the LT line with no type numbers. These had a payload of 1.25 to 1.75 tons and liquid-cooled four-cylinder engines at first (75 hp on petrol or a Perkins diesel of 65 hp) mounted

Above *Popular early model for ski resorts and airport taxis—the eight-seat bus, here 1954-6 version.*

Right *The so-called 'hunting car' with opening front windows and wrap-around bars to fend off wild beasts.*

Opposite page *Variations on the Type 2 theme: Flat-bed or pick-up with two to three seat cab; Tall-box version with load area over cab as well; Dump truck version with additional storage beneath bed.*

Above *Cutaway of second generation Type 2 bus model. Maximum use is made of space, and later models had more window area.*

under a box in the driver's cabin. These quickly captured over 40 per cent of the German market in their class but were meant to complement, not replace, the bully and give them a vehicle in the next-larger division.

In 1969 the VW-designed six-cylinder diesel engine became an option when this LT 28/31/35 range was extended by the LT 40/45 models for two to two and a half ton payloads. A five speed gearbox and three final drive ratios were options for the diesel version, the gearbox alone for the smaller LT vans, which came with four final drive options. Various closed and open bodies were offered, with single or double cabins as well as an eight-seat bus unit, on 250 cm/98.5 in or 295 cm/116.2 in wheelbases. For the 80s these were refined with more sound dampening mats and new driver seats.

Volkswagen passed the 100,000 mark in LT production during April 1979, just four years after the debut, and offered 57 different varieties in their Type 2/LT programme. They had also signed a co-operative agreement with the MAN heavy truck firm. VW would build haulers up to six tons with MAN help while the latter would continue to nine tons, using VW aid as needed. It was an obvious way to even the peaks and troughs of a more volatile saloon world. Meanwhile the faithful bully had received an optional automatic gearbox for 1973, a front crush zone and better trim. They could hardly drop a line which only reached its record daily production of 1,200 in 1974, shortly before Hannover celebrated its fourth million. Enlarging engines to 2 litres permitted a 1,200 kg/2,650 lb payload and required helper coils in front.

Real proof that Type 2 burial was premature came in 1979 when an all-new third-generation Type 2 appeared in late August, to control the 1 ton class below their own LT line-up. Production still ran at 700 per day on new, automatic body lines as the 80s opened. Known as the Type 24/25 (passengers/goods), this vehicle was more saloon-like

The larger or LT line of VW carry-alls using front-mounted, water-cooled petrol or diesel engines in a wide variety of body styles.

in its comforts and offered 5.7 m³/201 ft³ of load area, up from 5 m³/177 ft³ in the immediate predecessor. It had even been 'styled' and was probably the greatest Transporter advance in 30 VW years, even though engines remained air-cooled and rear-mounted. The boxer did feature hydraulic valve lifters and sodium filled exhaust valve stems, however, to reduce maintenance. An inline, liquid-cooled diesel four, lying flat in the tail, was not far behind as an option.

Wolfsburg insisted this was a clean sheet that had only happened to come out as rear-engined again because this proved the best-balanced design for smaller vans. This no longer used the Beetle platform. Spare wheel and tank were moved up front to achieve 50/50 weight distribution, whether run empty or fully laden. It also lowered the centre of gravity to reduce oversteer and side wind sensitivity. Longer wheelbase and wider track improved the ride. Combined with all-new suspension by wishbones in front and coil springs all round they achieved a Transporter which handles like a tall car in the curves and offers fine traction for slippery starts—at the price of a suspension with very few VW features.

Once again a Transporter had received the new features first. Apart from suspension, VW converted both engines to crank-mounted fans which lowered the rear floor by 20 cm/8 in and tripled the size of the rear hatch. These van engines were also first to be fitted with digital idle stabilisation and service-free electronic ignition. This offers optimum city emissions by retarding the spark and making the mixture lean whenever possible.

Old-line VW van people would scarcely recognise a fully-trimmed cabin 12.5 cm/5 in wider and 10 cm/4 in taller thanks to a lowered floor. All mechanical parts and wires are tucked out of sight, the wheel is now half-way to the vertical position and attached to rack and pinion steering, and gear shifting is more precise. This new van, with 6 cm/2.4 in more wheelbase, even meets US frontal crash standards although it would be exempt, while the full frame, including rails in the roof, functions as a roll cage. Such technology, developed over six full years, naturally cost money but no VW van was ever really cheap transport except in the load-price sense. Instead they stress ruggedness, durability and 'go-anywhere' ability and even offer an optional limited slip differential in keeping the Type 2 image as a technological leader.

Nor does this mark the limit to VW ingenuity on the subject. In the early 70s their van division turned to the electric vehicle, based on a pick-up bodied Type 2. The key was rapid battery swaps by pushing new units in one side, under the load bed, and discharged batteries out the other. Lead batteries took up the normal payload but that could be increased with stiffer springs. Tests of the first 20 indicated an Electro-Transporter would do 45 km/28 miles in stop-go use or 85 km/53 miles at a steady 50 kph/30 mph.

Since existing motors then were either too large or too small, VW and the Rhine-Westphalia electricity works developed their own, giving 32 peak kW or 16 kW in steady use. This could be flanged directly to the four-speed VW gearbox where only second was used. A driver had only a 'forward' pedal (previously the throttle) and brake which first gave regenerative charging, then mechanical braking. A second test stage for 1974 put 200

A special option in the LT, Volkswagen's own six-cylinder diesel engine, based on their fours but used in no VW passenger car (Volvo buys them, however). (The most cylinders with a VW badge, only in LT.)

Volkswagen **LT**

Above *Cutaway of 1979, third generation bully.*

Below *Three generations together: Original bully left rear, second generation right rear and 1979 third generation, with sloping nose and entirely new chassis, in front.*

Above right *Wolfsburg wondered if enough people would buy a Type 2 with four-wheel drive so they allowed two young truck engineers to build one which ignored all terrain.*

such pick-ups into use and, following one of the longer VW gestation periods, the E-Pickup became available in limited ('a few hundred') numbers at the start of 1979, some 80 years after Ferdinand Porsche built his first electric vehicle.

72 batteries, weighing 860 kg/1,895 lb, provide 144 volts and require stiffer torsion bars while leaving the payload of only 800 kg/1,765 lb, about what the first Type 2 had. Top speed is a scant 70 kph/43 mph and 0 to 50 kph/30 mph takes 12 seconds but the pick-up had a city range of 50 km/30 miles. With a full half-million test kilometres (over 300,000 miles) on just one of its prototypes VW felt ready to enter the limited-use electric age.

In a completely different van mode, the late 70s also found two truck-division engineers who were passionate Sahara buffs building a hand-made Type 2 with four-wheel drive. They proved it would work and the VW board built several more for evaluation, with 80s production in view. This off-road solution was aimed at inexperienced hands. The four-wheel drive bully rivalled Jeep-type machines without the need for special driving skills. Using something very like the war-time Type 166 solution, the VW pair ran a drive shaft forward from their regular gearbox to turn the front wheels when a driver wanted that.

They bypassed the usual high-low transfer case by fitting a torque converter between gearbox and drive shafts. This 4×4 Van cannot get bogged down through careless driving—if it slows down the driver merely floors his throttle pedal and lets that converter apply as much power as necessary to creep out of trouble without spinning the wheels.

Compared to the Beetle, where we left it in 1951 form, such advanced technology and willingness to spawn new methods is a considerable turnaround in Wolfsburg terms. By the 80s their van division in particular had led a move away from the philosophy of 'any shape you want so long as it is Beetle-like'.

This technological splurge was tacit acceptance of the fact that many small operations outside the Wolfsburg walls had long-since shown the way to both special bodywork and advanced tuning, to engine sizes VW itself would only appropriate much later. These different Volkswagens ranged from a recognised 'special' which lasted 30 years to a great many which hardly survived that many days.

Chapter 6

'Improving' the product

The full variety of Volkswagen specials built in the three decades since the basic car appeared in public would approach infinity so we can only show the trends of such thinking by means of the more enduring or different ones.

Most successful of all was certainly Karmann's four-seat Beetle with folding roof although it really is not an outside special in the true sense since Porsche himself specified such a shape as one of his three original bodies and Wolfsburg took the post-war version completely under its own works wing. It was also Ferdinand Porsche who designed the very first trio of VW specials, in 1938, to enter a proposed race from Berlin to Rome scheduled for late 1939. They were Porsche Type 64, fourth variation of the Beetle, also known as 60 K10, meaning tenth body design.

Well before KdF town got anywhere near production Porsche was trying to arrange a supply of engines and chassis which he would turn into air-cooled sport cars. This project foundered on a law forbidding the sale of national products to a private enterprise. Ley also felt a two-seater was too élite for the workers' front. Not a man to give up easily, Porsche next promoted the idea of this Berlin-Rome race as ideal publicity for VW durability and thus received sanction for three such specials. Engines were only modestly

Left *First 'special' of them all, the Porsche-built Berlin-Rome racer. (Three were made, this is the sole survivor, for a race never held, in 1939.) Porsche always wanted to do a sports car on the VW chassis, these were as close as he got until his own 356 after the war.*

Right *Two-seater Hebmüller convertible built by that firm after the war, then by Karmann after the Hebmüller factory burned down. This is the rarest of the open Beetles.*

uprated by adding a second carburettor and raising compression to produce 32 (or 40) hp, depending on your source.

The necessary speed would come from extreme streamlining, while retaining as many KdF grilles and fittings as possible for popular identification. Weight would be held to 545 kg/1,200 lb. Specifications called for such thin sheet that his usual Stuttgart body shop declined the job. This trio was thus built by Rupflin of Munich, known for working wonders in light aluminium for racing motorcycle fairings.

When war cancelled that race the three cars became rapid transport for high officials, including Porsche himself who used one right through the war and even recorded a Fallersleben-Berlin run, over normal highways and through towns, at an average of 135 kph/85 mph. Another was run by Lafferentz and wrecked during the war, the last was liberated by US troops immediately afterwards and run into the ground. The sole survivor, apparently Porsche's own car, passed to an Austrian competitor who both raced and rallied it with great success in the early 50s. It reappeared at late-70s veteran meetings complete with wheel covers, a narrow-shouldered turret and pointed tail.

Such cars first established the building-block concept for VW offshoots, even before there was a Beetle as a cornerstone, but real 'specials' could not flourish until 1950, when the Porsche firm arranged to power its 356 with VW engines, thus building the ultimate VW special and launching a separate empire. Early Porsche catalogues even noted, 'any item not mentioned in this spares list may be assumed to be a VW part'.

While Porsche was turning VWs into road sports cars a Frankfurt VW (and later Porsche) dealer named Glöckler was building forerunners of the Porsche racing Spyders, powered by wildly-tuned VW engines. Interaction between Ferdinand Porsche, Volkswagen and Porsche cars will never be entirely disentwined.

Wolfsburg was never that pleased at the proliferating specials tacked on to its sacred floorpan (lack of unitary construction was the key) and only 'recognised' five outside firms so that their products might carry model numbers integrated with the Beetle list. In three main cases the end products looked like Volkswagens but in only one did these close ties

Hebmüller contemplated a coupé on the same basis but built only this prototype before a factory fire ended all VW work there.

survive the entire post-war period.

That firm is Karmann, builder of the four-seat Beetle cabriolet, the Karmann-Ghia in 1200 coupé and convertible forms as well as in 1,500 coupé guise, and later the Golf cabriolet and 2 + 2 Scirocco. The last is a pure VW project farmed out because Karmann has the capacity for relatively small-volume projects. It was also Karmann which introduced further confusion to early-50s model numbers, although it was not entirely their fault.

It all came about when Hebmüller, builder of the 'other' recognised cabriolet, a two-seater, suffered a massive fire. Karmann took over their design alongside its own four-seaters. By 1950 the Beetle carried number 1, making a standard saloon 11, the export car 13. But Major Hirst had already sponsored the idea of a convertible—Colonel Radclyffe had a one-off open Beetle—'so we would have something to drive in the summer'. More seriously, Hirst felt there were good commercial prospects for an expanded body line-up.

Hebmüller, a turn of the century Ruhr coach-builder, had been producing special car bodies for over 30 years, including Humber staff cars for the British, so they received a chassis and project number 14. The first three 2 + 2 Beetles with soft tops were completed by December 1948 and the next two years saw all but 15 of an eventual 695 such cars built. However, most of those were put together by Karmann after the mid-1949 Hebmüller fire even if the entire series is popularly called Hebmüllers today, since the top which folded completely out of sight was their idea. It could be stowed in seconds but the vestigial rear seats were only useful when the top was up. Apart from its extra weight the car was pure late-40s VW.

One-off two-seater made for Colonel Radclyffe and obviously kin to the Hebmüller although the rear deck is different.

Josef Hebmüller also tried a coupé, using the long rear deck of his cabriolet plus a metal turret and non-VW rear window but this project ended with the fire and only one car built. However, there was another open Hebmüller, usually dated 1949 although some of the first ones had 1947 VW chassis numbers. This was a four-door, open Beetle for police duty. A few of the eventual 281 (other sources go as high as 385) had half-doors in metal for parade duty but most made to with canvas curtains across the cutouts. Numbered 18A, this series began with Hebmüller but the last ones were built by Papler, also because of the fire.

That 'A' brings us back to the small confusion in numbering. When Karmann took over the two-seaters they found a problem. Their own cabriolet was number 15 but meanwhile plans were afoot for the Karmann Ghia coupé to be built on a Beetle floorpan to an Italian design. It had been assigned number 14 by somebody who forgot the Hebmüller. It is also possible some soul decided to apply 14 to all 2+2 cars. In any event, the K-Hebmüller was now dubbed 14A and 15 left to the open four-seater although that was later called 15A and even 151 as well.

Karmann as a firm goes back even further than Hebmüller, having built its first horse coach in 1874 and first car in 1902, but their decisive move came in 1923 when the owner visited America and realised that precision tooling and all-steel bodies were the future path for any firm building limited series of specials for the car industry.

In 1948, when Germans still needed an official chit to even buy a Volkswagen, Wilhelm Karmann obtained one and carried it to Wolfsburg to buy the car he intended to turn into a convertible. VW delivered number 10,000 to him, liked the resulting conversion and

Hebmüller Police 'cabriolet' with either side curtains or half-doors for parade use.

ordered 1,000 units, an unheard-of number so soon after the currency reform. By the time production finally came to a halt—amid anguished screams and mock funerals on the part of Karmann convertible owners—the firm had built over 330,000 open, four-seater Beetles with the last of them at the end of 1979 going to US buyers.

Priced originally at DM 7,500 (just like the Hebmüller), Type 15 production climbed from 364 in the last half of 1949 to a peak of over 24,000 for 1971. By the 70s this was the most highly-developed appliance of our time. It had received every functional Beetle update, often before these were offered in saloon form. Weighing some 70 kg/150 lb more than the Beetle a Karmann naturally needed more power, thus it had the 1.5 litre engine first and up to 60 hp at its best, fading to 48 with all emission controls in force by 1979. At that time it was the last bastion of their later MacPherson front suspension since Mexican-built Beetles had reverted to pre-war trailing arms once Beetle production ended in Germany.

With the numbers involved Karmann found it cheaper to chop Wolfsburg pressings off at the waistline so that doors, glass and window hardware were not interchangeable. Despite the price such methods required, they found it hard to pension off this famous car. When production hit a low of 5,500 in 1975 VW and Karmann got obituary notices ready—a move which promptly gave the car fresh status. Only the arrival of a completely new open VW for the 80s—the Golf Cabriolet also built by Karmann—finally ended three decades of a machine as wondrous in its own realm as the basic Beetle.

Not all VW-Karmann ventures were quite so successful although the Karmann Ghia coupé did very well, particularly in its early versions when annual sales climbed from 500 to 6,000 in the first four seasons. The first, boat-nosed Karmann Ghia coupé was introduced in 1955. It was longer and wider as well as a full 15 cm/6 in lower, yet

125 kg/275 lb heavier than the saloon and not quite identical in chassis since Karmann pressed slightly wider panels and sent them to VW where they were married to VW platforms on the normal assembly line. Then it all went back to Karmann for finishing.

Since the car was really a two-seater—an 'economy Porsche' in the popular mind—a convertible seemed logical too and it followed in 1957. Engines and brakes were improved in tandem with the Beetle which meant that any Karmann Ghia had to be compared with cars powered by a class-smaller engine to hold its own. A 1300 KG, for instance, was slower and yet thirstier than 850-1,100 cc sporty cars of its day. Front brake discs and a 53 hp, Type 2 engine for 1967 were KG milestones but most of them were purchased for VW quality, not performance. And a large number received superchargers.

When Volkswagen then released its Type 3 or 1500 at the 1961 Frankfurt motor show, Karmann was there with a four-seat cabriolet on this new/old chassis although it was not quite the form Herr Karmann had wanted. A year later they still spoke of production 'shortly' but the car was never produced, apparently for reasons of chassis flex. Instead Karmann revised the original coupé by creasing its nose metal and fitting it on to a Type 3 chassis with pancake engine as the KG 1500, not to be confused with the first KG coupé using a 1.5 litre engine. It was their least-successful venture, in large part because the car never went to America. This KG 1500 also looked stolid and lacked the peppy feel of their original effort. At first nearly half their 100 per day production went to this 1500 with two thin boots, front and rear, but it was only to survive a mere six years after the 1962 introduction.

Once their Golf was established VW naturally turned all thoughts for a successor to the most successful four-seat cabriolet of all time to this new saloon with its modern chassis and engine range. They did realise the problem would be competing with a legend, no matter how often they explained that noise and emission rules for the 80s doomed a Beetle-based car.

VW and Karmann debated both Golf and Scirocco convertibles but preferred Golf stiffness with the top off. Even then they settled, after an agonising debate, on a thin roll bar behind the front seats. They again chose a 'soft' but five-layer, padded top which folds in seconds but offers wind and rain sealing comparable to the saloon version. To retain

The longest-running cabriolet of all and the last Beetle built on German soil was the Karmann four-seater with its top folded into a bustle at the back. The open car (shown here) is 1949, the closed one slightly later. Karmann always paralleled updates to Beetle chassis and continued the 1303/Super Beetle suspension system after the saloon was dropped by Wolfsburg. The last ones were built in late 1979.

Above *The next Karmann project was the Karmann Ghia coupé on Beetle 1200 (later 1300 and 1500) chassis, a car with sleek lines but standard engine.*

Below *When the VW Type 3 was announced in 1961, however, VW showed an intended open four-seater cabriolet on this chassis, also by Karmann. This was still being mentioned well over a year later but never proved stiff enough to suit VW and was never actually produced. It was obviously intended at one time to replace the Type 1 cabriolet.* **Above right** *Instead Karmann altered the lines considerably and built the Karmann Ghia 1500 with a flat engine from the Type 3 and a boot at either end. The coupé (shown here) was produced but never caught on in real numbers. The convertible remained a prototype.* **Right** *When the faithful Beetle cabriolet was finally replaced it took an open version of the Golf to do it (in 1979). (To meet the safety standards of the 80s VW also used a minimal roll bar behind the seats, as much to anchor belts as to stiffen the body, which had several extra braces under the skin anyway.)*

the rear seat and a reasonable, although reduced, boot VW again chose to leave the folded top in a 'bustle' on the rear deck.

Indicative of newer safety rules, wheel arches, sills, dashboard, windscreen surround, boot and roll bar were made stiffer than any Beetle. It is also heavier than the Golf saloon, thus only sold with their larger 70 and 110 hp engines. Slower than a Golf saloon in acceleration it remains half-again as fast from 0 to 100 km (62 mph) as any Beetle cabriolet, with better drag coefficient than the Beetle model. VW admits this model with its market-basket handle is not the prettiest car around but they believe it has character and initiated Karmann production at 60-70 per day.

While Hebmüller was first and Karmann by far the most prolific builder of VW specials, another firm enjoyed Wolfsburg blessing and thus a model number. The Westfalia post office van, first mooted in 1962, carried VW type number 147.

German postal authorities had long sought an economical delivery vehicle easier to hop in to or out of than a Beetle. First talks with VW in 1962 suggested up to 8,000 units with a minimum of 1,000 in each of the first three years of any contract. The project was too small for Wolfsburg who engaged Westfalia, another coach-builder dating back to horse-drawn days and more recently prime builder of Type 2 camper conversions—over 200,000 of them.

Westfalia had the first PO prototype ready by November 1963. It featured upright seating like the Transporter, wider Karmann Ghia chassis and walk-through convenience. This baby van handled and parked like a Beetle but carried nearly half the cargo on its duckboard floor of a Type 2. In theory such mini-vans were available to all since German law only permitted the PO to buy commonly-offered vehicles, but the vast majority of the nearly 10,000 built before Westfalia found the costs too high in early 1971, went to German or Swiss mailmen and the German national airline as a ramp runabout. Later many of these appeared with flower-power decoration. This Westfalia was considerably more successful than a Matador delivery van which Tempo tried in 1949, using the VW engine, but never recognised by Wolfsburg.

The key feature of the Golf by Karmann was proper air flow, even with a roof rack in place—the top remained in a bustle but the folding mechanism reduced the boot somewhat anyway.

Apart from many such unapproved variants, some of which achieved high local prominence, at least two other models had semi-works numbers. One was the Miesen-built model 17, an ambulance conversion of the Beetle along Porsche's own lines. Another was the Austro Tatra 114. Conscious of its Austrian roots, VW provided chassis in 1950 when Vienna police wanted an open escort vehicle similar to the Hebmüller four-door. Austro Tatra had first tried Czech-based cars in 1948 but found few westerners interested so they revived a coachwork section and built the open four-door Beetle for some 14 months, importing chassis through Porsche-Austria—run by Ferry's sister Louise Piëch. Approximately 150 went to the Vienna police, another 53 to their state counterparts.

Porsche had also used VW parts to hammer out their first aluminium 356 sports cars in Gmünd, Austria but they were not the only firm in that land with like ambitions. Wolfgang Denzel of Vienna built fewer cars but his lighter, stubbier specials were at least as likely to win.

Denzel began in 1948 with a low, streamlined 'tub' on a *kuebel* chassis and won the Austrian Alpine Rally with hardly any engine tuning, prompting demand for a small series. He fitted a similar steel body to a modified Beetle pan, powered by a 1.1 litre engine with dual carburettors very like Porsche's. By 1952 he was reaching higher with a short-wheelbase steel chassis covered by an aluminium body in the Denzel shape and fitted with various VW components. He was as much involved with engine tuning as with whole cars by then, eventually extracting 64 hp from his 1,300 with Denzel heads to win the International Alpine Rally outright in 1954. He even claimed 85 hp from 1.5 litres when a 1.6 S Porsche had only 75 but could not maintain the pace and ended production in 1959 after selling some 300 open, coupé and 'sport' Denzels.

Most of these early Beetle-based sports cars had a slightly Porsche look although the Dannhauer & Stauss from Stuttgart in the early 50s looked more like a Denzel. And

Westphalia (or Westfalia, the German spelling) built the Type 147 Post Office van on a Beetle chassis to fill the niche between the saloon and Type 2. Some reached private hands and it was a rarity for carrying a VW type number.

Römetsch managed to give its VW specials (between 250 and 500) an elongated, banana-like appearance which set them apart—particularly from Wolfsburg.

In 1959 Römetsch .could look back on four decades of coach-building. Their hand-made aluminium car was rarer than a Karmann Ghia but cheaper than a Porsche. It took 2,000 man hours to build one so real VW fans cared deeply, at least until chrome trim and white-wall tyres fixed them too firmly into the middle-50s. The immediate cause for production ending, however, was the Berlin Wall, cutting the firm off from its work force. During 1953 this Berlin firm also built around 20 four-door taxi Beetles with rear doors hinged at the back and wheelbase stretched by 36 cm/14 in. When Trautman and Barnes in the US stretched just one Beetle in 1969, to produce a four-door special, they priced it at \$35,000.

Meanwhile, three Swiss firms were showing Wolfsburg what a Beetle might become in the late 50s—this was virtually a world-wide sport by then. Only one suggested both practical and sporting models and that was Beutler of Thun, the same firm which built Porsche's first cabriolet bodies. Beutler's first VW effort retained the nose, doors, seats and even rear wings, fitting a flawless, light-van box over them all. It came out much like Porsche's Type 88 proposal.

Using Beetle dimensions condemned them to a cramped cargo area and a ten-minute job of fitting pipes and panels together when making a load-carrying floor. Advantages were city compactness and maximum use of Beetle components but engine service required a contortionist. Built to order only, such a wagon cost half as much again as the saloon and never caught on although it appeared five years before VW built a similar 'squareback' estate. When it came to their coupé the Beutler brothers dropped all pretence of VW looks and produced a Porsche-price pair—European and US versions—often mistaken for Italian coachwork when displayed on their own Geneva motor show stand. These too missed the market niche between Karmann Ghia and Porsche.

Italsuisse, based in Geneva, wanted far more than a niche. They envisioned a production run for a 'new' VW shape, something all awaited in 1960. This shop decided a vaguely Corvair-like form by Frua would sell thousands if only Wolfsburg would furnish chassis. Mention was made of 5,000 orders from Israel alone. With flatter roof and nose the car did offer much more space plus four doors but VW was far too close to launching its own Type 3 to even consider such ventures.

Sporting specials using VW parts had always been the wiser path for small-scale builders, although there were not too many derelict Beetles to offer up their parts in the late 50s. The Enzmanns of Switzerland, father and son, had to scrap good Beetle bodies to fill orders for their glass fibre model 506 which found a small market by being totally different.

One of the earliest plastic cars from Europe this was a one-piece tub with an optional flip-up top. Steps in either side replaced doors and the passenger had a chest bolster moulded into the dashboard—early safety thinking. Despite its VW base the car looked so rapid many buyers added a tuning kit or supercharger.

Among the myriad glass fibre kits which followed the Enzmann in time if not theory was the very first car design by Luigi Colani, a hyperbolic industrial designer. It was unique for the anteater shape and sale on hire purchase through a German mail-order

Opposite page *Among body shops doing their own thing to a VW, the Beutler brothers of Thun, Switzerland, were most attuned to VW, although none were works-accepted. (The same firm did original Porsche 356 convertibles.) Beutler built both a 2+2 coupé on a Beetle base, and a small delivery van which only changed the top/rear body although it looked longer. Neither reached sufficient numbers to make the price interesting.*

house, although it was out of his hands by then. Colani later became internationally known in design and even produced a small-car styling study for Wolfsburg under contract but this was banished to the VW basement—in part because the always-forthright Luigi had announced that the Golf could not be replaced, only buried decently.

Outside Germany, Apal built a wide range of VW specials in plastic at Liège, Belgium before turning to Renault power, and Ascort of Australia noted Beetle mania down there to conceive a luxurious glass fibre car in the late 60s, only to find it could not be built at a competitive price.

Since Volkswagen has its most active overseas operation in Brazil, VW specials naturally flourished there as well. Puma was the most successful, opening in 1968 and turning out 300 cars a month by 1977, when they switched to the local Brasilia VW chassis. More than a kit car, this GT had less wheelbase and stood as high as the Beetle belt line, allowing a true 100 mph/160 kph speed in fastback, coupé or convertible form. A measure of Puma success is their export to Europe in the 70s.

The most outrageously styled VW special of them all was also the most international. Impetus came from England where the wild, wedged Nova was designed to be 'the best looking fibreglass special in the world'. Called Purvis in Australia, Stirling in America, and also sold in Holland, Canada, Venezuela, New Zealand and the Philippines, it was the ultimate response to a separate floor pan, selling a claimed 4,000 kits worldwide.

If that was the ultimate in dressing up, Southern Californians and then the world soon discovered a Beetle could equally well be stripped to the bare essentials—enter the so called dune buggy. Cars like the Empi Sportster and Meyers Manx evolved from bare-chassis sand racers and led straight to single-seat, VW-powered desert competition cars riding on 15 shock absorbers. The dune buggy idea caught German attention too, but strict licensing rules at home led to more enveloping bodywork, designed by a VW-oriented magazine which found itself swamped with orders once the bare idea was published. Coming full circle they had this Floh (flea) productionised by Karmann.

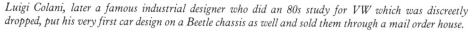

Luigi Colani, later a famous industrial designer who did an 80s study for VW which was discreetly dropped, put his very first car design on a Beetle chassis as well and sold them through a mail order house.

Dune buggies were a key VW conversion—so big in the US that they even returned to Germany where a bit more enclosure was required as on this Floh designed by a VW magazine and later produced by Karmann.

A similar case of time-repeated is the glass fibre Porsche Speedster replica kit made by Intermeccanica to fit a VW chassis—which is not all that different from what Porsche itself did in metal two decades earlier.

Through the years very few coach-builders even fitted motor show specials to the separate Beetle floor pan—but they were fewer than one might expect. Among those few was Delta Design of Stuttgart whose wedge with full-width front lights and integral roll bar was designed to promote Metzler sandwich plastics. All efforts to find a small-edition builder for this 1969 Delta V failed.

Giugiaro would have a direct hand in several later production Volkswagens but when he did a show machine himself, the 1973 As de Pique, it used Audi 80 mechanicals from a VW branch, not Wolfsburg. The water-cooled Volkswagens lacked that separate chassis but a few attempts have been made at specials, including a 2+2 Scirocco estate conversion by Nordstadt, the same Hamburg dealership which produces white Beetle convertibles with white leather interiors and white tops—for twice the price.

Americans were first to convert the Rabbit (Golf). One dealer added a full 66 cm/26 in to the wheelbase, put a partition behind the chauffeur, and created the mini-limousine. Volkswagen of American even stretched one 30 cm/12 in to show what a low-consumption taxi might be like.

Once VW of America had its own production plant it also developed a Brazil-like tendency to conceive body shapes not known from Wolfsburg, but keyed to the US market. Home builders had been fitting pick-up bodies to the Beetle for years but it was left to VW of America to do likewise with the Rabbit.

Eye-catching form was the key to all of these cars but that also caused owners of such specials to yearn for at least as much performance as the shape promised. Tuners have laboured to please them at least as long as the coach builders.

★   ★   ★

Ferdinand Porsche and son Ferry were really the first who wanted the faster VW but they were followed by an unbelievable range of power packs for the long-suffering economy engine. Count Alexis Argamkoff of the Polish Red Cross presented Wolfsburg with full technical data and drawings for converting their 1949 Type 11 to steam, for instance, with 36.5 hp guaranteed, but his was only the most amazing suggestion. When tuning got into full swing it became evident that the real secret lay in knowing which versions of the outwardly similar, air-cooled, flat fours were tuneable and which were more fragile.

Quite apart from normal production tolerances, there were both better and more doubtful VW years. Considering them from the tuner's vantage point helps to quantify the production powerplants too. During the first two years, when Nordhoff's men were smoothing out production complications, few were tuning anyway and the 1954-60 range of 1,192 cc fours was generally considered somewhat pushed by the factory, meaning less tuning potential left over despite outstanding workmanship and overall quality. Early fibre cam gears might soften in detergent oils or valve heads separate from their stems under duress but basically this was a good vintage, assuming critical spark timing was maintained.

A Transporter engine introduced in mid-1959 offered the same 36 hp and dimensions but was really a thoroughly reworked design and prototype for 40 hp saloon engines to follow in 1961. Bearing journals were enlarged, valve stems thickened, valve lash increased, piston crowns raised and more metal put into cylinder walls. Good tuning potential but perhaps the poorest quality record in VW history, due in at least three-quarters of the cases to head cracks. By 1962 the works offered new cam and tappets, then shorter rocker arm studs to relieve vibration fretting and, after 1965, new camshaft bearings and a higher-capacity oil pump.

The 1.3 litre 1966 engine had longer stroke plus the new rocket arm studs and stronger wrist pins for lengthened connecting rods. Cracks between plug and valve holes largely ceased to be a problem. The late-1963 to 1966 Transporter engine of 1.5 litres was really their susceptible 40 hp car engine with more bore and stroke as well as all the faults, until it received changes applied to the 1300.

For the 1967 model year both Beetle and Transporter received 1.5 litre engines with longer stroke from their 1.3 plus new bore of 83 mm. Compression was raised again, both inlet and exhaust valves enlarged, and electrics upgraded to 12 volts, making a much more feasible engine for race conversions.

Most tuners stayed ahead of the works in capacity, building 1.3 litre kits when the norm was still 1,200 and moving to 1.5 litres the day after a VW 1300 appeared. Many combined 1.2 and 1.5 components for a 1,438 cc engine with the shorter stroke, others fitted pistons and cylinders from the 1500 Transporter to the 1,300 Beetle engine. Among the later Type 3 (flat-fan) engines, the 1,600 size proved best suited to tuning while most drag Beetles and desert racers currently are of about 2.5 litres, based on the latest 2,000 cc Transporter powerplant. Well before that, most used stronger Transporter clutches and gearboxes.

While myriad firms, German and foreign, produced such kits the doyen was Oettinger, outside Frankfurt. As tuners of virtually the first post-war VW special they have been at it the longest and still offer anything from 50 hp in your Karmann convertible or Transporter up to a long-stroke 1,800 cc engine of 75 hp. Oettinger favoured elasticity via the longer stroke and special crankshaft—a favourite for Type 2 campers. Others, like S&S, used a roller-bearing crankshaft in the Porsche Super manner, slipper pistons and oil cooler to achieve as much as 6,000 rpm or even 6,500 'briefly'.

One of the more thorough projects came from Porsche Austria which produced a 160 kph/100 mph rally Beetle long after most serious rally drivers had written that car off. Using dual oil pumps and racing Porsche oil cooler with dry sump lubrication, special manifolds and heads for dual Weber carburettors, even 9:1 compression, VW Salzburg achieved at least 120 hp from 1.6 litres and won international events outright.

Although their Austrian importer was openly backing works-quality winners, Wolfsburg long decried all competition. When VW racers finally did reach Europe Wolfsburg was only concerned in a back-door manner. Formula V, an American single-seater racing car invention, gave each car an equal chance for a relatively small outlay. Original FV cars, around 1960, could be raced for no more than 20 cents a mile.

Five years later Porsche became the German outlet for both FormCar and Beach from the US, demonstrating the first cars at a national hillclimb late in 1964. All the 'team equipment' was painted in Porsche colours but most drivers believed VW had a hand in the original dozen racers and six Transporters, provided at a cost of DM 300,000 to launch this new class at home.

After initial juggling while Germanic race authorities took a hand for the sake of showing power, FV achieved European popularity too. Apal of Belgium built the first continental FVs, Fuchs the first German ones and soon VW dealers everywhere were backing this coming-driver division which led indirectly to later Wolfsburg 'racing involvement'. Within three years Austro Vee and Kaimann of Austria were the chassis for a cup aspirant to drive, even beating the Americans on their home turf. By mid-1966 a good FV could lap Nürburgring in 10 min 22 sec on 55 hp and German races drew 120-car training fields.

VW soon sponsored both national and international series for FV, as well as the later and more sophisticated Super V division whose cars got around the 21 km/14 mile Nürburgring in eight minutes, a good Grand Prix time in the late 60s. By the middle-70s Volkswagen had moved away from Super V, about the time these cars switched from air-cooled 411 engines to water-cooled ex-Passat powerplants. They were feeding DM 1.5 million yearly into motor racing through the Hannover-based VW Motorsport but concentrating more on machinery with the outlines of their road cars.

VW began with a series for Scirocco drivers, then a Golf Cup, a one-marque race series for cars close to standard technology. This gave their new youth-car image its proper boost. Cars were doled out at a price which could hardly have covered costs yet these 135 hp Golfs proved good value for spectators as well as new drivers.

Once Wolfsburg realised it had winning potential in open racing as well it moved on to the saloon circuit scene using various tuners as the VW racing arm, although international rally cars were prepared directly from Hannover as well. The Golf GTI of exceptionally low weight, with powerful brakes and an easy 120-plus hp in Group 1 form was a natural class winner in any event while the 180 hp Group 2 version harried the overall leaders. Similar engines in the Scirocco, with its lower profile, suited high-speed circuits best. The Golf Diesel even won a special class for compression-ignition entrants in the 1978 Monte Carlo Rally.

For the smallest class VW depended on its Polo whose cross-flow head was easier to tune for the 1,100 class, giving up to 150 hp. Some of Wolfsburg's stiffest competition came from its own Audi division, particularly in major rallies where the Ingolstadt team would make a direct international challenge by the early 80s. When it comes to even more esoteric VW performance, the Fittipaldi brothers' Beetle from 1969 takes a top position,

Left *Among the many who tuned VWs, Oettinger outside Frankfurt was the first and the longest-lived, as well as the most prolific. Alongside hot air-cooled engines and long-stroke versions for greater elasticity in VW campers, Oettinger took up the Golf and lifted its capacity to 2 litres with a 16-valve head (here), the ultimate for Wolfsburg's water-cooled era too.*

Porsche—obviously with VW acknowledgement if not direct support—first introduced VW racing to Germany at the 1965 Eberbach hill-climb **(below)** *when they brought US Formula V racers over and made them available to up-and-coming drivers. It was the start of all later VW involvement in motor sport. Except for this winning rally Beetle* **(right)** *built by VW Salzburg, run by Ferry Porsche's sister, and a terror to other works teams if the going got rough enough.*

after fitting two engines into the tail of a glass fibre Beetle shape. This 3.2 litre machine touched 200 kph/125 mph in top gear and was heading the likes of a Ford GT 40 when its gearbox broke in the car's only serious race.

More serious by a small margin and the ultimate road Beetle of all time was a Nordstadt VW fitted with a Porsche Carrera RS flat six, turned around to occupy the rear seat. With 210 hp it easily topped 210 kph/130 mph yet proved very stable at speed on nine inch tyres. Total cost: about eight normal Beetles.

Apart from power, various firms offered items ranging from ring-disc brakes by Maico before VW saw fit to convert those Beetle drums, to a Lukomat electro-magnetic clutch conversion from 1960, also rendered unnecessary when Nordhoff promised a semi-automatic factory Beetle 'very soon'.

It was far easier for small, outside firms to produce items vast numbers of VW drivers always wanted, but often these prodded the factory into a like response. By the time Volkswagen turned to water-cooled cars in the early 70s, however, Wolfsburg was far more tolerant of tuners generally. Germany alone boasted six to a dozen firms tuning Golfs at any one time although the works introduction of a 110 hp GTI cut into this business on one hand, while offering an approved and basically sporting chassis for all to build upon.

Extra capacity remained the obvious path to power with many tuners preferring 1.8 litres when the works reached 1.6 but most found it nearly impossible to take a Golf much past 1,840 cc. Those like Spiess who aimed at small-class monoposto racing engines had to use an Audi 100 or VW LT Transporter block and do without the rpm advantages of the short stroke and cross-flow head to touch two litres and 175-plus hp.

Oettinger and others matched the 110 works hp by using a long-stroke crankshaft for greater elasticity, once again. Later this senior tuner developed his own 2 litre car with

VW dealer Nordstadt in Hannover got its 150 mph Golf by taking a Porsche V8 928 chassis (up to 300 hp) and fitting a wider, longer replica of the Golf body which proved more aerodynamic than the Porsche original. After that—where could a Golf go?

twin-camshaft, 16-valve cylinder head, giving the Golf or Scirocco 150 hp with amazing tractability. The fact that Oettinger, among others, continued to do a thriving business in Transporter engines, now including 70 to 95 hp for the LT line as camper conversions, indicates VW tuning would not end with universal low speed limits.

A major late-70s power trick was turbocharging of course. VW tuners, mainly in the US, had first fitted mechanical blowers to Beetle engines with some success but the new, inline fours took to turbocharging with bravura. A 1.3 litre Turbo Polo produced 115 hp, a GTI Golf for general road use 140 hp. Costs were generally more reasonable than the same power from more classic methods, with reliability easily available from the latest Wolfsburg line.

In the end it was Nordstadt which trumped all sorts of tuning, including their own Carrera-Beetle, by shoe-horning a 240/300 hp Porsche 928 V8 engine into a car with specially-made Golf look-alike bodywork, proving there is no limit to fantasy. As a final note: their wider, lower 'Golf' on a pure Porsche 928 chassis proved 5 kph/3 mph faster than a proper Porsche, indicating the VW saloon excels for aerodyanics, even over fancy sports machinery.

Chapter 7

Building Beetle bastions

For Wolfsburg, the 50s which had opened with their introduction of Type 2, rapidly developed into that era when Heinz Nordhoff and his loyal team consolidated all teutonic technology in the Beetle, refined the world's most comprehensive service concept behind it, and based an entire nation's export viability on just one car design. They concentrated on a single-model policy with only the modest Transporter variation. In this way VW triumphed right through the 50s. Volkswagen produced its first million automobiles in the middle of this decade and its third million in August of 1959, about the time Transporter production passed the 500,000 level as well.

Taken together, all these positive signs helped to convince the man who mattered that he was not only firmly on the right track but that he could only remain there so long as he adhered to a policy of evolution, not revolution. At the end of the 50s Heinz Nordhoff could look out of his top-floor office in the brand new, 13-storey red brick headquarters tower and along a plant front which stretched a full mile beside the canal. He could know all this came from his single-minded devotion to certain ideals. Incidentally, a high-rise office complex, atop rather than alongside the main plant, had been part of the 1938 plan too.

Nordhoff's realm could be traced directly to total pre-occupation with improving the quality in every individual nut or bolt without touching the basic design concept. Only crass

Nordhoff surveys his domain.

Industrial engines were a key part of Porsche's original VW plan and a steady source of income for the firm in the post-war years.

outsiders who wanted to stir up a winning team dared question the VW path then. Mentions of the Model T fate were not appreciated in a one-car town where you seldom saw a competing make—in the car park or under evaluation. When asked if they had driven a new competitor VW could answer then; they did not need to test rival products, they already built the best car in the world.

Ensuring that this euphoric state might continue required a vast staff of inspectors. Such minute scrutiny doubtless served that particular model very well indeed but it made for a rather parochial atmosphere. On the other hand, such focused thinking got one hell of a lot of Beetles built. In 1951 slightly more than 14,000 workers, meaning just over half the town's inhabitants, built well over 105,000 automobiles. Only three years later the main plant would turn out three times as many cars in a year to pass the first-million milestone. They then employed 31,000 or 71 per cent of those living in Wolfsburg. If Transporters are counted, VW passed their million mark a good year sooner.

Their second million Beetles came before the end of 1957, when exports accounted for more than half of the nearly half-a-million cars built annually by 41,000 workers or better than 83 per cent of the town. As Nordhoff ended his first decade, exports were closing in on their first million and the Transporter plant had just registered its first 100,000 unit year. As a side light, the female proportion of their work force wavered either side of 10 per cent throughout the first decade.

Wolfsburg in these fabulous 50s was an automobile Midas, living for its record figures. On a technical note, car changes during 1951 included windscreen trim for the deluxe model, very important telescopic rear shock absorbers in April, and that ceramic Wolfsburg crest on the front lid. For 1952 such news centred on a rotary heater knob, pivoting front wind wings, self-parking wipers which swept a larger area, a door on the glove compartment and ashtray moved to the passenger side of the dashboard. A change in torsion bars gave a softer ride and a new gearbox for the Export and Cabriolet offered synchromesh on the top three gears. After several seasons of testing it was fitted to their familiar 1,131 cc engine with only slight ratio changes. Unsynchronised bottom gear remained 3.6, as it had been since 1945, second was higher (about what it had been in 1936, actually) and the top two gears were most-marginally higher.

Looking ahead, there would be two more such minor ratio changes, each to improve silence in the 'box, before VW finally decided on a fully-synchronised unit for 1961. The first such change, in December 1953, anticipated their first post-war engine enlargement the following month. A tunnel-housing gearbox was introduced with first and second unchanged but very slightly lower third and fourth, using the same final drive ratio. In November 1957 second gear was lowered, third changed back to its pre-1953 ratio and the final drive returned to 4.34.

Otherwise 1952 was notable for a widely-praised new stationary (industrial) engine. Volkswagen founded a sales outlet named VW Canada in 1952 as well, and a year later launched VW do Brazil which soon became their second-ranking producer.

In the popular view 1953 brought the most significant VW alteration up to that time when the divided rear window became a single pane of oval glass in March. This launched a brisk trade for body shops who would cut out your tell-tale, old-model divider for a small fee, to the much later dismay of the 'pretzel-window' club for classic Beetles. A switch to rust-free alloy trim at the same time was at least as far-sighted while eight-leaf front torsion bars extended suspension life.

At first it seemed a minor historical aberration to introduce a 'new' model in March. Common wisdom holds the majority of such changes were made when the works closed for its annual late-summer holiday. In fact, a good third of nearly 200 running changes made during the 50s fell in other months while their annual update was most likely to include sales-worthy items. An improved seal or bearing would be phased in whenever ready.

Around 1953 articles also began to appear asking whether that 'rear engine which left its noise behind' was the future thing after all. Most of the car world did nicely with front engines driving the rear wheels and more than one writer pontificated that 160,000 VWs a year must be close to the world's acceptance limit since they were so different. The most-praised features then seemed to be excellent gear change, light and positive steering plus fine brakes (meaning the writer had tested an Export with hydraulic brakes). Cables were used on their standard Beetle throughout the decade. Most road testers were also beginning to notice that 'swing axles want some watching'.

This was the peak of Wolfsburg's 'building block' era where engines remained outwardly similar, gearboxes were only altered in shop-manual terms, front axles only differed in number of torsion bar leaves and it took a VW fanatic to spot bodywork changes—yet each year was just a little better. Which is precisely why they attracted buyers who knew to the week when oval tail-lights with a heart-shaped lens came in. Then came 1954, the year exports first topped 100,000 and Volkswagen premiered its first promotional colour film.

Whereas the early 50s were a time of incremental changes, a one-time performance increase of 20 per cent, with more torque yet a reduction in overall consumption, had to be

Above left *The 1952 Beetle, still with split rear window.*

Left *In 1953 the first rear window without a cross-bar was a proper VW sensation. At the time it was the sort of change only VW owners could appreciate and a brisk trade in cutting bars out of older cars sprang up.*

Above *For the 1956 model year, introduced at the end of 1955 in their usual manner, VW enlarged the rear window ever further. In 1957 a steel sliding roof panel was now the option in place of the folding cloth, when the licence plate light holder was widened as well.*

Right *A Beetle engine of the 50s.*

major news. And it all came from a mere 63 additional cc. Retaining the 64 mm stroke, VW enlarged the bore by 2 mm to 77 for the 1,192 cc engine that January and extracted 30 hp at 3,400 rpm with a compression of 6:1, boosted to 6.6:1 that same August. Their first engine change came fully nine years after production resumed in 1945; it would be another six years before they did it again.

For once all Volkswagen buyers, and that included the 200,000th Australian customer in early 1954, had more engine to boast of, just like fans of other brands. Such beaming owners scarcely noticed the dynamically balanced fan although it reduced engine noise, just as a new oil-bath air filter increased engine life. For most 1954 buyers a three-way courtesy light was more important.

The reason behind this power rush was a plan to take speed limits off the autobahns. 100 kph/60 mph cruising which seemed so wonderful in 1938 could not keep up in 1954. Of course VW had to face the odd claim that their engine was now 'over tuned' and they must have faced it well because every second car on Germany's roads in the middle 50s was a Volkswagen. Workers there received the first of what became annual 'success bonuses' at the end of each year.

For 1955 they put the direction indicators at the corners like other cars, marking the end of the often-exasperating but always amusing semaphore arms. Since all other marques had dropped them much earlier the orange flippers had come to mean 'VW' to a whole post-war generation. As of August 1955 it was easier to change gear as well, thanks to a lever moved forward and bent back.

Nordhoff declared in 1955, 'we stand at the beginning of development without peer'. That August some 100,000 friends and admirers of the Volkswagen gathered in Wolfsburg stadium to celebrate the millionth VW, a golden Beetle posed beneath the flags of all nations, while entertainers from around the world took part in an extravaganza which could only culminate in the triumphal entrance of Heinz Nordhoff himself.

It was truly a golden era for Volkswagen and for Wolfsburg which made Norfhoff an honorary citizen to go with his grand order of merit from the Bonn government. Yet it was also obvious at this very peak in Wolfsburg's glory that production would have to be

At the end of the 50s the Beetles had reached this stage of indicator position and door handle.

decentralised. They could never build enough automobiles in just one town, certainly not in the year VW of America was launched, presaging expansion beyond any previous dream. Thus they put the new Transporter complex in Hannover while Braunschweig could provide tooling for both this new plant and for Wolfsburg where the work force had enjoyed its new, 45 hour week since February 1. South African assembly came under direct VW control in 1956 when they bought out local stock holders and Australasia followed in 1957.

Driver comfort dictated most 1956 model changes: a heater control moved forward on the tunnel where it could be reached more easily from wider front seats with three-position back rests, or a reshaped fuel tank to make space for a little more luggage. Tail-lights were also raised by 5 cm/2 in. On the other hand, several 1957 improvements, for 1958 models, were more technical; including stronger main bearing brackets and uprated exhaust valves. The clutch spring diameter was reduced for a lighter pedal and wheel brake cylinders enlarged front and rear with more work assigned to the rear brakes. Front brake shoes were wider and a reinforcing rib was added to the drum where it also served to keep out dust or water.

The throttle pedal became a treadle, tubeless tyres were fitted and VW emblems on the hub-caps were painted black. Finally, front heater outlets were moved rearwards and backed by large heat exchangers, all this following wool tuft experiments. In truth, the Beetle was never left alone but these were only minor notes alongside a booming Nordhoff challenge: 'we won't rest', he said. 'A daring move is planned for this year.' He meant no less than a full-scale invasion of America, home of the mass-production passenger car.

Such a direct and massive challenge to US cars on their own ground was effrontery indeed, compared to merely outselling all British makes combined in Sweden, the best VW export market in the pre-US middle-50s. But Nordhoff was completely right again—the US went Volkswagen-crazy with sales leaping from 75,000 in 1957 to 135,000 two years later when Volkswagen had to quote delivery delays up to six months.

This full-scale invasion was recognised at the end of 1958 when Ferdinand Porsche, Heinz Nordhoff and the latter's VW colleagues were awarded the Elmer A. Sperry Medal, one of America's most prestigious engineering honours. The presentation was all the more noteworthy since this medal had never gone before to either a foreign manufacturer nor to any automobile firm. For 1958 it was awarded to a foreign car builder, accompanied by a citation which read, in part: 'To Dr Ferdinand Porsche (in memoriam), Dr Heinz Nordhoff and the co-workers in the Volkswagenwerk for the development of the Volkswagen automobile which, in concept, engine design and production has made available to the world an automobile of small size for multiple uses with unique attributes of universality, of low initial and operating costs, of simplicity of design having ease of maintenance, comfort with adequate performance and suitability for rural and suburban use'.

In accepting this award, alongside Ferry Porsche who represented his late father, Nordhoff called it 'the happiest day of my life'. Then he took the occasion to note that the car industry itself was beginning to debate the question of buyer satiation—the end of the boom. Such car managers need only look at VW where Nordhoff's answer to cries of over-production would be even more automobiles—650,000 for 1959 and over three-quarters of a million the year after. Whereas it took 109 men to produce each VW in 1948, only 18 did the same job in 1958.

He suggested to the sceptics: 'don't try to sell what people don't really want'. Riding his crest, Nordhoff was convinced there would always be a car market because the world's economy depended on transport which offered honest performance and quality. In his view, millions would gladly exchange chrome-plated gadgetry and excess power for long, economical life and inexpensive maintenance. The lone ruler of Wolfsburg preached the familiar VW recipe but promised too, 'we have many irons in the fire still—we are ready'.

Building Beetle bastions

Interiors became slightly more chic—if you were a VW fan. Here is the 1952-3 model (**left**) which may be compared to the 1954-5 model (**below left**) when the gear lever was given a backward bend and the steering wheel crossbar changed.

Right The gear lever shown more clearly, plus heater knob on tunnel and typical seats (1955).

Below When Wolfsburg went to a half-ring for the horn for 1958-9 it caused violent debate.

The German press commented complacently, 'there is little doubt but that Nordhoff knows the way'.

Others of the motoring press were clearly getting Nordhoff annoyed in 1958, however. They asked the wrong questions, such as, 'too old a design?' Or, 'Must it always be built that way?' Actually Porsche had been building alternate 'peoples car' prototypes under VW contract for years but Nordhoff did not want to say none of those equalled the original. For instance, EA 48 from 1955 had an air-cooled opposed twin of 986 cc driving the front wheels, sprung by MacPherson struts. Apart from its noise level, this alternative for the Beetle price did no more than 80 kph/50 mph and offered less car in all dimensions.

Nordhoff could well retort that those seeking change at any price were mere hysterical stylists. 'You can't simply cut new metal on whim', he added. Furthermore, the Beetle was quite modern enough as it stood—hadn't a major German motor magazine called it 'up to date' as recently as 1957? One could drive a VW as fast and as safely as any car should travel. He even denied any Beetle needed that front anti-sway bar found on the Karmann Ghia where it certainly reduced oversteer. That would be 'too sporting'.

Shifting to his own ground, Nordhoff pointed out that the Beetle price had dropped from DM 5,450 in 1951 to only 4,600 by 1958, adding that was not simply amortisation and it would probably have to start up again shortly. This was reason enough to retain the detuned engine with its long life, elasticity and low consumption, not to mention the fact that a Type 1 was about the only car left with more tyre than it needed.

By this time, VW was already drawing on its new Kassel plant, a factory purchased late in 1957 because the area offered an untapped labour pool. Volkswagen cleared most of the existing buildings, some still rubble from the war, and produced its first reconditioned engines and transaxle units there by the middle of 1958 as one way to hold down service costs. Up to 150,000 units a year could be renewed in Kassel and sold for only 38 per cent of the price of a new engine or a third of what a rear axle and gearbox cost new. Soon every tenth German VW was powered by a reconditioned, exchange engine.

New engine output had been shifted to Hannover alongside the Transporter lines, while front axles and other sub-assemblies would be moved to an expanded Braunschweig plant, leaving Wolfsburg to bolt Beetles together. On the other hand, Nordhoff was quite sure opening an assembly plant in the US would be a mistake—'it wouldn't have that old-world quality'. Yet they did build or assemble cars then in Australia, Belgium, Brazil, Ireland, Mexico, New Zealand, the Philippines and South Africa while exporting 57 per cent of German production to some 100 other lands and financing all this expansion from their own profits.

Wolfsburg itself finally built a city hall in 1958 and threw pedestrian bridges over the Middleland Canal to facilitate worker access to the plant where considerable debate was raging over who owned Volkswagen after all. Nordhoff had done particularly well for ten years with no owner of record, of course—it may even have been a key to his success—and he now remained strictly aloof from this argument, promising only to protect his workers' interests as governments at all levels argued the control of VW with various financiers.

The options ranged from turning Volkswagen into a private, stock holder corporation— considered dangerous since big business or even other car firms might gain control—going private with a limitation to small share holders only; or turning the whole thing into a trust with any profits applied to good works. It would take some years to solve this puzzle. Meanwhile, rapid overseas expansion, particularly into America, indicated their quality was still admired but the age of the design questioned publicly and with greater frankness than most German magazines allowed themselves.

In 1959 Volkswagen was finally moved to open a proving ground, a relatively modest, carefully shielded, 60 acres just north of the main plant. They found room for a 1.8 km/ 1.12 mile oval which allowed speeds up to 150 kph/93 mph without side thrust, certainly adequate for cars they built then or even contemplated through the 60s. A steering pad offered radii of 10 m/33 ft up to 40 m/131 ft while a 600 m/1,960 ft skid pad was paved half in asphalt, half in basalt. Along with the usual sand traps, artificial rain and timing gear this remarkably compact area had asphalt grades of 6 and 12 per cent plus two of 20 and 30 per cent in concrete.

This proper proving site virtually within the perimeter fence marked a real initial acknowledgement by VW that there could and should be cars based on post-war parameters one day. It no longer bordered on heresy to ask what might be changed of a sacred design's basics. One of VW's new aerodynamicists even suggested openly that Wolfsburg engineers might be more aware of side-wind sensitivity than other Germans since the wind blows harder and more often in the north. They were truly evaluating the Beetle with new-found scepticism.

As for direct model changes for 1958—both windscreen and rear windows were enlarged. And even more thought was given to their quality control, one of Nordhoff's prides, with good reason. By 1959 VW employed one inspector for every 13 workers, grouping them in a department all their own with rank equal to the design or production staffs. These men reported only to a chief inspector, responsible solely to Nordhoff.

Set apart by their green coats such inspectors held every operation to very tough standards, starting with teams sent out to the main suppliers although Wolfsburg no longer kept men attached permanently to outside plants, if only because they might not view things through VW eyes. Long years of building one basic model aided their quality hunt, of course.

At the end of the 50s each individual engine and transaxle was checked briefly, with five per cent of all engines given a full dynomometer test and ten cars from each day's batch put through a full spot check. With production nearing 750,000 annually it had long-since become impossible to drive every car before delivery.

For the final year of the decade VW fitted a 'tropic' fan belt to their engine in July and reduced fan revs from 6,800 to 6,120 in August, to cut noise. They also fitted a stronger clutch spring but bodywork alterations after the works holiday were little more than new colours. Really relevant running changes would be applied during 1959. In August of that year VW engineers applied the so called 'Porsche cure' to their oversteer problem, ignoring the boss's comment of a year earlier. A 12 mm/0.5 in anti-sway bar was fitted. More basically, the gearbox mounts and thus the swing axle pivot were lowered by 15 mm/0.6 in so that engine and box tipped forward two degrees. Handling was improved while thinner, more progressive rear torsion bars maintained the ride quality.

Although Wolfsburg viewed its one pet as more of an economy device or ideal tool than an automobile, thus seeing little point to road test reports, magazines of the day remained interested and even alloted two paragraphs to new push-button door handles on the 1960 version while mentioning a steering wheel with recessed hub and half-circle horn ring which was less universally praised.

There were new colours yet again, a sales ploy previously ignored by Wolfsburg, and larger heater ducts in the unending battle to give this air-cooled car decent winter habits. Padded sun visors and a front passenger foot rest were added, along with a steering damper so that steering might seem a little firm for the first 10,000 km/6,000 miles.

The chief complaint in most tests of this era was a tendency for the engine to run on if the ignition was turned off when it was hot. VW eventually had to install an electro-magnetic cutoff for the carburettor idle jet to tame this problem, which hinted again that advances over the original engine were limited.

They faced an ambivalent public when it came to such changes. Magazines and some keen drivers pressed steadily for improvements while the automatic choke for 1960 (Renault had one) was promptly condemned by their mass market because it used more petrol. Anyway, many fancier cars still had a hand choke—'did Wolfsburg believe its buyers were less capable of thinking for themselves?'

Such debates were taken with deep seriousness throughout Germany where VW still quoted a four-month delivery wait as the 60s approached. With a turnover now exceeding DM 3 billion, VW was not only the land's best dollar earner by a clear margin, its success had become inseparable from Germany's own. VW had been the first foreign car to achieve annual US sales of 100,000, yet they still spent a reported $1 million on those famous, humorous American advertisements in 1959 alone, ignoring the five-month delivery delay there. 1959 was also the year Barbara Nordhoff, daughter of the Director, moved to a US public relations post, following similar work in Paris and Brussels.

Overall they were selling saloons or the bully to 120 countries as the 50s closed with Sweden, Canada, Australia, Holland and Switzerland following the US, in that order. Yet Nordhoff found time—and good reason—to deplore the lack of free trade within Europe, noting that any land could face up to his Beetles freely in Germany whereas France, for instance, only allowed 500 such cars in per year at 62 per cent duty while Italy permitted 1,600 German cars on to its market each year. If VW was a little smug, it was also too visibly successful. They were planning to be even more so—daily production of 3,000 during 1959 would be increased again, by 520 per day in 1960, and the payroll implemented by 8,000 new workers, to a total of 50,000 at VW as their 50s numbers game accelerated without any let up.

High productivity continued to be both the VW goal and trump card. Yet the company faced its first strike too, a 24 hour wildcat effort at the Hannover plant which immediately unleashed passionate national debate over whether this could be a simple wage matter as the burgeoning company inevitably became less personal, or whether it could be communist intrigue.

Volkswagen chose to appear at the Geneva motor show for the first time in two years, early in 1960, although their car had hardly changed since the last visit—apart from synchromesh for first gear in their Transporter, a feature the standard saloon still did not enjoy, incredibly enough.

In various ways, this first year of the 60s was the pause before VW lashed out in all directions, at least by Wolfsburg standards. At the plant 1960 was symbolised by tearing down the last war-time barracks building, eradicating the final trace of their bad years. Meanwhile, the VW ownership argument between the national government and state of Lower Saxony had continued into 1960 when they finally agreed to turn this prodigal into a share corporation with Bonn and the local authorities each owning 20 per cent of the stock while the remaining 60 per cent would be restricted to small holders. At the same time, a Volkswagen Foundation was established with its founding capital taken from the original stock sale. Its mission was to further economic and technological projects. By the end of 1972 this foundation would have spent DM 1.4 million on nearly 3,000 such operations.

VW capital of DM 300 million in 1959 was doubled in 1960. The new stock went on the market in 1961 at 350 per cent of par, reaching 1,100 per cent at its peak. The original issue was 3.6 million shares with a nominal value of DM 50 each and it was vastly over-subscribed throughout the land, quite apart from those shares reserved for VW employees. 7,000 share holders and visitors attended the first general meeting in July 1961 to hear management declare a dividend of 12 per cent.

1960 was also the year Nordhoff announced proudly that production had topped 4,000 per day. And it was still climbing. He was quickly reminded from several sides that only two years after the Model T set a one-day record of 9,109 it had collapsed.

Was a repetition of history inevitable at VW? The Wolfsburg wonder-worker replied, predictably, that the Beetle was not some primitive Model T so parallels could not be drawn. 'VW had kept up with all current standards, had improved right along, and would continue to do so.' While such decisions were Volkswagen's they were also a matter of national interest and widely debated. Wolfsburg replied by quoting German delivery delays then. A miniature car could be had in a week in mid-1960, it took a month to get a small Opel, one to six weeks for a Renault (the car pushing VW hard in America, briefly), the same for a Fiat—but dealers still said five months for a VW. Still—ads were beginning to appear in German newspapers offering to sell Beetle orders on short-term delivery.

By now nobody around Wolfsburg really denied there would be a new model, 'some day', nor that it would be very hard indeed for them to make a switch after so many years of single-minded devotion to one basic model. Somehow they did not seem worried yet— after all, their Beetle was still the car preferred by most German car thieves.

What Volkswagen really had in mind for the 60s became evident from a two-pronged attack launched in 1961. On one hand there would actually be a new model at last, albeit one closely related to familiar VW features. On the other, there would also be a very considerable Beetle revision indeed when considered in purely Wolfsburg terms: more cubic capacity and greater horsepower. This 'new' 1300 engine would come first by a few months. Not only that, it would be accompanied by a new gearbox as well. Volkswagen was truly facing up to a new decade.

Chapter 8

Technology pursued and a new model

There can be no doubt that Wolfsburg decision makers, with Heinz Nordhoff very much to the fore as always, viewed 1961 as their archway to a whole new Volkswagen era. They had the statistics to prove it—this would be the first calendar year in which VW produced a full one million cars. Furthermore, they were on the verge of making Beetle changes which could only rank as vast within the Wolfsburg framework. And they were actually planning to unveil the one motoring sensation never before tried by Volkswagen—a new saloon. There had been that Transporter of course, and the 'new' car owed almost everything to standard VW thinking, but it was still considered almost a revolution for the firm, which had become famous for one shape, to try another.

1961 proved more than the beginning of a fresh decade at Volkswagen, in many ways. It was the year of the greatest changes Wolfsburg had seen up to that time. After years of marketing strategy which considered that different hub-cap emblems constituted a model change, the 'power Beetle' alone would have startled true VW buffs. And VW launched this forward-looking Beetle first, despite all those breaths bated over a whole new car. This gave them time to establish its fresh features before Type 3 stole the show. Type 1 was very much the Volkswagen mainstay still, in 1961, and it would remain so for years thereafter, so it deserved a chance to parade its novelties without sibling rivalries. As Nordhoff had said, the one thing he was proud of was not changing a Porsche design.

Introduced after the 1960 August works holidays as was their habit, the new Beetle was improved not altered. Changes touched all parts of the car, from engine and transmission

Goaded by claims that he had never tried anything but Beetle updates, Nordhoff finally showed off the entire range of prototypes (largely Porsche projects) which VW had commissioned, and then decided it did not need, through his reign.

to trim and even boot capacity, all on top of various unmentioned 1960 updates like the Transporter steering damper or needle bearings for the top front axle arms.

About all VW left alone in the 1961 engine were bore and stroke. In what amounted to their Type 2 engine in a saloon they offered stronger crankshaft, larger rod and main bearings, new fuel pump drive, improved pushrods, rotating cup tappets, a Solex carburettor with temperature-regulated automatic choke and direct pre-warming for the mixture. Rather than seek more power through increased capacity (with their 1500 just below the horizon), Wolfsburg engineers redesigned their combustion chamber for the first time since 1954, using egg-shaped, well-radiused bowls with pronounced squish and better turbulence. Compression was raised and specific consumption reduced through improved efficiency. The result was 34 hp at 3,600 rpm, a 12 per cent gain, while torque climbed too.

VW proved that a Beetle could deliver the power to climb a 44 per cent grade in top gear, yet be quieter inside as well. They also took the opportunity to modernise less obvious items ranging from a smoother throttle cable to transparent fuse box and brake fluid reservoir. Push-on wiring connectors speeded workshop service. Many maintenance jobs could now be done in half the time.

Volkswagen proceeded to update the gearbox as well, offering synchromesh on all four forward ratios with constant-mesh gears in a stiffer tunnel housing. With beefier dimensions this gearbox was supposed to have twice the service life of its predecessor. Oil churning was reduced and the rear axle could be removed without disturbing the gearbox yet the new unit fitted in the old space and only weighed 3 kg/6.6 lb more. All ratios, as well as final drive, were raised slightly and the car credited with 115 kph/71 mph, a gain of 3/1.8, while a second came off their acceleration time from 0 to 100 kph/62 mph.

As a 'feminised' model the car came in seven 'softer' colours with colour-keyed mats and wheel on some models. A flat-top fuel tank held the same amount but allowed roughly two-thirds more luggage. In short, a very considerable alteration by VW standards and fan enthusiasm could hardly be dampened by motor journals which persisted in rating this obviously better Beetle last in comparison tests with cars of a good deal less engine capacity. In one such test the VW placed last of four in equipment, performance, consumption and comfort/handling yet was the most expensive. The magazine did admit it also sold best.

Nor did Wolfsburg rest on these laurels during the rest of the 60s. The 1962 Beetle, appearing in parallel with the Type 3 so that it attracted less notice, featured 'progressive refinements': screen washer pressurised by the spare wheel, larger tail-lights, a spring to hold the front lid up, petrol gauge and new heater slides. The saloon even benefited from Transporter worm and roller steering with adjustable tie rods. A year later their feature was the leatherette head liner.

A Beetle owner survey made during 1962 found that the car had lost its standing as the standard for space and performance in just five years. More disturbing to VW, even quality was less than buyers had expected. One car in eleven had roadside trouble, one in eight an engine failure, while 14 per cent needed new clutches, a prime weak point. The first ever German car with standard heater was now rated least-acceptable for winter driving. Yet 66 per cent of those surveyed expressed 'great pleasure' in driving their Beetle and nearly that many insisted they drove either 'flat out' or 'fast'. It was still a car to have, apparently.

Although VW had passed the 5 million mark late in 1961 and built 4,874 cars per day (56 per cent exported) in 1962, the world's third-largest factory and easily the largest consumer of magnesium anywhere, entered 1963 looking back on the first year ever in which it lost ground in home sales (down 8 per cent when overall registrations in

Germany were up by 11 per cent). They still had a third of the market, double the slice number-two Opel held, yet this had fallen further, to less than 28 per cent late in 1963, when overall sales were only rescued by foreign gains.

Suddenly VW realised it could even lose number one at home by concentrating on the Beetle—just as many Type 3 buyers were complaining of broken crankshafts or water leaks, two inspection slips VW men could not believe were as serious as headlines claimed. Little of this trouble was blamed on labour, although those first Italian workers in 1962 had since grown to a flood. Wolfsburg had to found a new department called 'VW Suburban Construction' to house them. Their percentage of women workers had also gone to 13 per cent, highest ever.

The 'Model T fate' inevitably came up again as everybody from Ferry Porsche to the janitor warned Nordhoff not to repeat Ford's mistake. Not even the ballyhoo of providing the first saloon to drive in Antarctica and similar promotions could paper over the breach caused by a full quarter drop in Beetle sales. The favourite German guessing game became; what will VW change next? Perhaps a steel sliding roof? Or that all-synchromesh gearbox for the standard model as well? Many of them were used by driving schools. Voices asked if VW should not build a 15 hp city car instead.

Volkswagen only admitted its car was somewhat cold in winter, curing that by offering a petrol-fired Eberspacher heater option for the Beetle as well as the Type 3. In Scandinavian lands and Canada it was even standard wear while others paid DM 200, installed at the works, or double that as an after-sales fitting. Plus DM 90 for the pre-set switch option. And it took up boot space. This heater lifted a Beetle from –5 degrees C/ 25 degrees F to just freezing in ten minutes of town driving or up to 15 degrees C/ 55 degrees F after ten highway minutes. These figures were roughly twice what rival cars required to achieve equal warmth—but still miraculous to VW owners.

Wolfsburg had already begun the planning for a new factory, when demand was still high, and settled on Emden where labour was available and overseas orders could be shipped directly, relieving Wolfsburg of the Type 1 export load while adding about 14 per cent to their overall production capacity after it went into production at the end of 1964. Output was later doubled to 1,100 cars per day by the mid-60s. Despite these ups and downs Volkswagen took three days to celebrate its 25th anniversary as a car builder in 1963.

On the world front, at the midpoint of the 60s Volkswagen was promising to build a plant in El Salvador capable of 5,000 cars a year while their Brazilian branch held over half its own market as the largest industrial plant in the land. South African expansion allowed them to build 1,200 cc engines as well as cars while the Australian plant was up to 95 per cent local content and Volkswagen de Mexico was just getting under way in Pueblo. At home VW now built 3,300 cars a day in two shifts, since 1963 exports were up 9.3 per cent, and exported nearly two-thirds of them, making Volkswagen the largest car exporter in the world.

In the US VW sales led the number-two imported model in that pre-Japanese era by a factor of 10:1, even if it meant Saturday shifts back home. A full million cars were built in the first eight months of 1964, up to the works' holiday, and a new series of chassis numbers was instituted for the next run, beginning on August 3. Nordhoff had turned over the 25,000th post office VW, a year before the special Westfalia 147 was ready. Within Germany Volkswagen now held 51 per cent of Auto Union—Mercedes had the rest—and would own it outright by 1965, using Ingolstadt capacity to build Beetles until 1969.

Virgil Exner did a 'proper' new VW in America which lacked all Wolfsburg character so the works had no doubts about opting instead for their 1200 A which cost a little more but offered the all-synchromesh gearbox to all. Steel sliding roofs did replace fabric at last, to go with new colours inside and out.

Certain other rumours came true as well by 1965. The windscreen was enlarged 15 per cent and bowed outward for better wiper clearance (and doubled replacement cost), while the rear window was enlarged by nearly 20 per cent too, its fourth increase since the war, and the waist-line lowered 3 cm/1.2 in. Even the outside mirror got larger. A folding rear-seat back allowed two travellers to carry a real load, defrosting was faster with four thermostatically-controlled flaps in the fan housing, the brakes required less pedal pressure and visors could be pivoted to the sides. As a road tester muttered, 'it wasn't easy to do yet another VW report'. Once you said, 'more glass and heat' and noted these both still trailed most rivals, you could only add a few words on the unbroken VW mystique: no change.

The works did not seem to notice that engine output and handling were slipping down the contemporary scale at an accelerating rate. Still, better vision was the most important move since the more powerful engine, in VW terms at least, and more noteworthy Beetle updates were only another year ahead, as Volkswagen founded its own high-seas shipping branch in 1965, to feed the export markets.

That very spring, as a US ad campaign was asking, 'how much longer can we hand you this line?'—only to answer, 'forever we hope'—a meeting was held to decide on the Beetle's successor. The group—Nordhoff chiefly—decided not to launch a replacement at the 1965 Frankfurt motor show after all. The reasoning went: sales of Type 1 had improved again in 1964. On the other hand, they had not given very serious consideration to a replacement one year earlier when sales were down, either. Either condition could be read as grounds for carrying on with the winner.

While the 60s were largely stamped by technological increments, they were also another decade of Nordhoff in control. He would hold the reigns until nearly the end of this decade and hold them just as firmly as he had 20 years earlier. If Heinz Nordhoff decided, 'no new model for Frankfurt', where German novelties traditionally bowed in, there would be no appeal. Instead the autumn 1965 VW press conference was treated to closed-circuit TV from Wolfsburg where car number 10,000,000 came off the line on schedule. 1966 would be a little different—a larger Beetle engine no less. Tuners had been first to build a 1.3 litre engine by lengthening stroke or fitting a Type 3 crankshaft to a Type 1 housing. This last was the path VW itself followed to build the VW 1300, a car 'so different' to VW watchers that people actually gathered to stare at the novelty.

By the time of the VW 1300 in 1961 changes from their original KdF car were considerable.

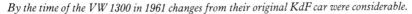

The minor model differences moved on—a 1961 VW 1300 with wider front indicators.

This new car with its 40 hp rating came about, in reality, because rivals were too much faster. And they chose to raise capacity as a means of retaining relatively low rpm figures. Torque also benefited, of course, with a true improvement immediately noticeable in top gear on the open road. Consumption did not suffer much, yet this VW 1300 would touch 120 kph/75 mph.

Along with its new crankshaft this 1300 engine had new heads with larger valves and ports, 19 cylinder fins instead of 14 and angled manifolds. The net gain worked out to 20 per cent more power from 8 per cent more capacity, plus a flatter torque curve. Fitted to their familiar shell it could only accentuate the oversteer—VW answered that buyers should drive more sedately. Despite ball-joint front suspension, inherited from the Type 3, the VW 1300 was about equally sensitive to side winds. Ride was better though, thanks to full-width torsion bars in the bottom front suspension tube while an anti-sway bar filled the top tube. Each side had dual rubber bump stops.

In mid-1966, VW did admit handling might be just fine, but improvable, and added a 'compensator' spring at the back too. This single, transverse leaf, in conjunction with softer spring rates, reduced oversteer. And finally, these 1966 Beetles featured wider rear brake drums which increased rear track by 1.5 cm/0.5 in. Higher tyre pressures were recommended.

Increasing production remained the VW idol but one of the most modern car factories of its day had to endure endless debates at this time over the idea that production was so large solely because there had been so few model changes, versus the contention that they held alterations to a minimum to keep production high. The fact was, VW was the prime

Above *The 1964-5 model with new rear lid and more glass was seen with domed and not flat hub-caps. Such disparities not only cause endless debate among VW fans but particularly between countries since home and foreign models did not always change at the same time.* **Below** *The hub-caps were settled by 1965.*

pragmatist of the car world. Only once had Wolfsburg extracted more power from unchanged capacity—and promptly suffered in engine longevity. In another case 1965 cars had drum-strengthening ribs, since 'disc brakes aren't needed on a Beetle'—while the next year, as production topped 12 million, buyers could have a disc-braked Beetle.

In truth, far more changes were initiated by VW competition for the market than most observers realised during the late 50s and most of the 60s. Many took VW at its word too easily when it came to the subject of building one model for ever. That autumn, when a new stock offer increased their capital, it was the first time proceeds went to the works not the Foundation. New models cost money.

When Wolfsburg then enlarged its engine for the second time in 12 months, the capacity shock was even greater. The new size was a full 1.5 litres, actually 1,493 cc for Type 1, although this was not the Type 3 1500 at all. Now VW had a model line-up to offer: 1300 and 1300 A with 40 hp/4,000 rpm and the new car producing 44 hp for Beetle, Karmann cabriolet or Karmann Ghia. They even had to design a new engine lid to fit over it all.

Once again engineers had combined a proven (1300) VW crankshaft with cylinder barrels from the family (Transporter). A new fan pulley raised its revs for more cooling while the new engine had a larger flywheel, 12 volts electrics to please the US and a new starter. The new disc brakes went with a wider track. Trim updates included door locks, flat dashboard knobs and more upright headlamps, all meant to prove the Beetle still had leeway for modernisation. Wolfsburg was still playing catch-up with *autobahn* traffic— although fleet owners could also order the old 1200 car with only 34 hp, not a model mentioned aloud.

Testers rhapsodised that the '1500 is a complete car once more and the best of Beetles'. Nader was given credit for nudging VW into better handling while Nordhoff's TV comment that no Beetle was particularly side-wind sensitive even drew a laugh from Germans. Top speed was now 128 kph/80 mph, a full 10 kph/6 mph above the 1.2 litre model and a higher third gear ratio aided overtaking. Meanwhile they still sold some 7,000 'outdated' 1300 Beetles daily around the world. Its chassis shortcomings were only

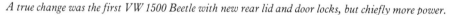

A true change was the first VW 1500 Beetle with new rear lid and door locks, but chiefly more power.

apparent alongside the 1500 and it was both one of the cheapest cars available in 1967 as well as a classless model. When figures were tallied at the end of 1967, however, it was clear most VW people wanted the 'new' 1.5 which sold over 400,000 or twice the 1300 total. Some of the latter doubtless went to Volkswagen's new captive rental department which had grown out of their leasing operation to become a handy sideline for dealers who rented Transporters as well as saloons.

For 1968 the Beetle had dashboard padding, integral or 'tombstone' headrests, higher and stronger bumpers, safety rims at last, larger tail-lights yet again, telescopic steering column, outside petrol filler and a brake warning light. World safety rules as well as emission standards were doing as much 'design work' as their engineers by now, as VW worked to keep a 30-year-old design current.

1967 had proved a mixed production year with 80,000 on short time in the early months but added shifts in August and September. It was a year of general recession in Germany although the economy picked up in the second half. VW's problem was a slump which fell below their industry's average.

Prices were going up now and buyers began to feel even a 1500 VW should offer more car for the money. When an increase cost them 20 per cent in sales the union chimed in: VW could easily drop prices rather than cutting working hours, in their opinion, and cast off excess cars that way. In Switzerland they called the top model a 1500 Sport to boost sales and in Germany publicly revived the 34 hp 1200 for individual buyers, to find it claiming a fifth of all output.

Nordhoff was still determined to increase daily Beetle production because that was what he had been hired for in 1948, yet some dealers actually had to sell 1967 models below list price, once a heresy. They still led all imports on the vital US market by a wide margin despite Nader's untargeted attacks. In fact, America took more Beetles than Germany then, never a healthy situation. When a professor there lost the crest off his Beetle he promptly mounted a full-scale research project and announced a million had been stolen, mostly by 13-14 year old boys who, he decided, found some sexual significance in a wolf and castle. The VW was more than a car, it was a myth.

At home, buyer dreams centred on a larger model which Nordhoff insisted was beyond the pale—some said he had made a deal with Mercedes to that effect. Thoughts turned instead to a possible heated rear window, new front axle for more boot space, even a semi-automatic gearbox which finally appeared in Germany following the 1967 holiday and captured half of all 1500 Beetle buyers up to the end of that year.

Bonn politicians seeking a cause now questioned Nordhoff policies, claiming the firm had dozed off and had a million unsold cars on its hands. They had not done a new thing since Porsche's project, in this view. To refute it Nordhoff lined up no less than 36 prototypes, largely Porsche suggestions, taken clear up to the pre-production stage but dropped. He could have brought in a viable alternative at any time, the message read, even if he had chosen to stop that Beetle successor in late 1965. One of the prototypes had been sent to Brazil after 500 were built for testing. Its tooling sank in the Channel but was raised and shipped on.

This collection of previously unsuspected machinery included everything from an air-cooled, four-wheel-drive baby twin to a rear-engined six of two litres. Later their secret car collection would even include the famous 266 only cancelled long after tooling was on order—and then by Nordhoff's second successor. VW wanted to prove it always had an eager technical team, merely no need to extend them. Yet development contracts still ran with Porsche on the technical side and Pininfarina for styling, tacit admissions that the home team might lack real fire when nothing they conceived had a chance of seeing daylight.

Volkswagen did realise they needed aerodynamic updating, however. Their Beetle with a C_d of 0.44 was no better than the brick-shaped Transporter while the supposedly sporting Karmann Ghia was no better than the three-box Type 3 at perhaps 0.40. Their answer was the industry's most modern and comprehensive wind tunnel with a properly wide throat, winds up to 175 kph/110 mph from any desired angle, a 5 to 95 per cent humidity range and temperature testing from −30 to +40 degrees C (−22 to +113 degrees F). With that on hand they could stoutly deny a rumour of joint stream-lining efforts with Citroën. Instead VW founded the 'German Automobile Corporation' with Daimler Benz in the middle of 1966, dedicated to intensified research and development. Yet as VW lost its number-one European production rating to Fiat, the first time since they began, it was not the cars which claimed all headlines out of Wolfsburg, but the man.

Heinz Nordhoff, 68 and thus already past the usual retirement age in 1967, had chosen his successor—who would only earn about half the Director's million-mark yearly salary, the firm was quick to point out. Nordhoff had been ill for some time but when Kurt Lotz arrived—officially on April 1—he was expected to serve under Nordhoff for an extended but unspecified time before taking over the troubled German showplace.

He would inherit a less than perfect world. Little NSU would clearly dominate the biennial Frankfurt motor show that year with its rotary-engined Ro80 while VW struggled to turn its Type 3, now a whole model range, into some kind of a success story. After all this was supposed to be the 'true Nordhoff VW', proof he was more than merely an administrator. Meant as an up-market adjunct to the Beetle when it was launched as star of the 1961 Frankfurt show, this line never sold more than a quarter as many cars per year as the 1500 Beetle. Where did its bright 1961 promise go astray?

★   ★   ★

The original premise behind the most stunning VW news in a quarter-century—an 'all new' model right in the middle of a world-wide car slump—was deceptively simple. But very hard to fulfill. Their Beetle had been an undisputed, resounding success so it seemed logical to apply as many of its principles as possible to a car which could both replace and complement the Beetle—Wolfsburg would use both formulations, singly and in tandem, during the 60s.

Dubbed Type 3, this car had the rear-engined layout, basic powerplant features and even the chassis dimensions of a Type 1, without being a copy. 'All new', referred to the shape and fans would debate endlessly whether they loved, hated or ignored its unassuming lines. At least it would never be confused with the Beetle and therein lay the problem: how to build a new car with the vital quality of its predecessor and peer both, yet set it apart without going so far that it would not be perceived as a proper VW. Competitors were crowding them badly in 1961 and a new model, whatever the service problems it must bring into their one-model shops, was inevitable.

The Beetle was really outdated in passenger packaging and vision. Everybody harped on that until they saw the VW solution which failed to excite. Furthermore, VW needed a model priced a little higher but close enough for Beetle owners to trade up comfortably. Without being too much larger or costlier, it had to stand comparison with cars of the lower-middle class. If it should become their main weapon—Volkswagen would later deny this was ever planned—it would badly need an eternal shape for the same classless image which made Beetles famous. This overlooked the fact that a Beetle was classless precisely because it was anything but unassuming or easy to overlook.

Carefully controlled leaks all through 1961 kept buyers panting for this new VW until the unveiling that September. Only the US market, which was saving their Beetle position, was told flatly there would be no Type 3 sales, 'for the time being'. When this VW 1500 did appear—its name caused some confusion later when there was a VW Beetle 1500 as well—it turned out to be a machine which did look larger and came out 16 cm/ 6.3 in longer, 7 cm/2.8 in wider, thanks to the nose and tail, yet it used a Type 1 wheelbase. This meant rear knee room would never live up to its price class although a few more inches of interior width were most welcome. The overall feel was VW but one you could see out of, and you still had to open a window to slam the door, seals were that good. Quality from the design standpoint remained.

As a nominal four-seater with shaped rear seats the 3 offered one clear advance over the Beetle—a boot at each end, both reasonably sized and shaped for a VW product. The front space would carry 180 dm³/6.3 ft³, that in the back, which was created by lowering the engine height and putting a floor over it, held 200 dm³/7 ft³. The sole secret to reducing engine height some 40 cm or 16 in was a cooling fan moved to the crankshaft nose, an idea Porsche had tried three decades earlier, than suggested again when this engine was laid down in 1959. The problem of moving enough air at crankshaft rpms was solved here by a fan of 30 blades set at an angle of 120 degrees.

VW would also use the Beetle engine housing but after that the 1500 was largely new with a longer stroke, larger bearings, new pistons, cylinders and heads. Only basic shape and materials were really carried over. The rest was detail work. Wolfsburg engineers found, for instance, they could not simply increase dimensions without the engine running on and wearing its cam lobes. Oval main bearing shells solved a thermal problem there and they finally achieved an asymmetric mount for the carburettor to feed all four cylinders evenly.

That rear boot got pretty hot initially, prompting several changes to its isolation but there was oil check provision without opening the engine compartment and handling was helped by better front/rear load balance. A 1500 still oversteered at the limits—but in less determined manner. Side wind sensitivity was reduced; by the shape but also by ball-joint front suspension with crossed, full-width torsion bars in the lower tube and an anti-sway bar above. Worm and roller steering was taken from the Type 2 but brakes were still all-drum when the new car was introduced although they were enlarged to take full

The original Type 3 was the notchback saloon on the familiar wheelbase but using the flat-fan engine to achieve boots at both ends and instant fame among hungry VW fans who finally had a new model—although they later became less enchanted with the car introduced in 1961 for 1962.

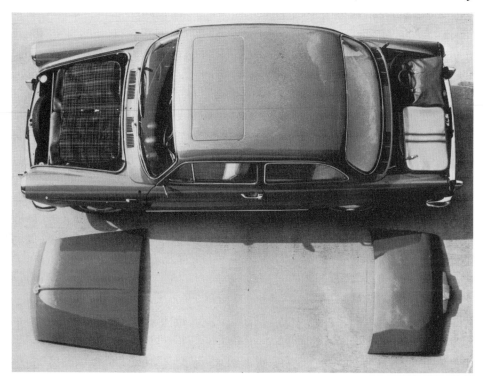

advantage of the 15 in wheels VW still favoured. What amounted to a semi-encapsulated engine in a subframe mounted to the body by six rubber bushings made this 1500 more civilised.

If 45 hp seems less than overwhelming, it was still a third more than the last Beetle and well-spaced gearing gave the 1500 100 kph/60 mph potential in third gear for passing while acceleration times were cut by a third versus the Beetle. A top speed of 132 kph/82 mph was significantly better. This 1500 could at least keep most competitors in sight on 10.5 1/100 km or 27 mpg, about equal to the Beetle.

Ventilation had been improved, although still poor at city speeds, and a petrol heater would be fitted for colder climes. VW treated 1500 owners to a complete new dashboard with speedometer, clock and fuel gauge, plus four push buttons and two knurled knobs for dashboard light intensity and wiper speed.

With a price about one fifth above the Beetle they had no trouble booking advance orders for the 300-per-day initial production, selling 10,000 between the introduction in September and 1962. An estate called the Variant was launched at the same time, going into production the following January for about 10 per cent more money, but the four-seat Karmann convertible which caused such a stir never appeared.

VW had been stung by the 'nothing new' charge and wondered itself how much longer the Beetle cabriolet might sell, so catalogues and ads were printed for this new, open VW with padded top which disappeared completely. There were even plans for a hard-top option to follow while the prototypes featured safety glass in the rear window. As late as 1963 the car was still rumoured but then Wolfsburg decided their shell could not be acceptably stiff without its steel turret—and that it would be too heavy for 45 hp if sufficient bracing were added.

Technology pursued and a new model

Left *Nobody from VW ranks complained much about the dual boots, however, made possible by the engine under the rear floor. The oil was checked and filled, if necessary, through a cap behind the lid, available without opening the hatch.*

Right *New seats and interior for Type 3, but still recognisable as VW.*

The Variant, however, became the most viable model in the entire 1500 line-up, carrying on through one six month period when the saloon was discontinued, then revived. Their flat-engine concept was ideal for an estate while the front boot gave the bonus of storing smaller items out of sight. Car testers generally praised the wagon, appeasing Wolfsburg which became rather sensitive to comparisons of their new saloon with its nominal competition, jousts the 1500 usually lost. Their Variant, on the other hand, did not drum when empty, had ample load capacity and even less side-wind sensitivity than the saloon. Heavier rear torsion bar, thicker front stabiliser and the optional heavy-duty suspension package gave this estate better handling than the saloon, not to mention a stronger clutch and better brakes. Lacking opening side windows at the back, it did have even less ventilation but many found it handsomer.

VW frankly needed such praise after the first two years, although production had doubled to 600 per day in the first year. Only 4 per cent of their first-year buyers could report no trouble at all and half the cars required work between regular sevice stops, all impossible conditions to the Volkswagen mind. Part of the trouble stemmed from the fact that it was a car which cost as much as those which carried more, faster, yet this admittedly ageing engine concept was not a leader in the thirst stakes either. More painful still, owner surveys began to rate foreign as well as domestic competitors ahead in reliability and quality.

VW quickly rectified most of these points, some due to their introduction of a new model which had to compete with a myth rather than a normal predecessor. When the carping did begin it was all too easy for it to include the shape and performance, items widely praised in the brand new car. 'Are hidden values enough', became the tenor of many reports.

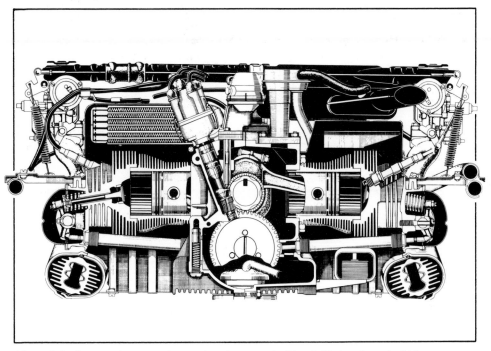

Above left *Announced at same time as the saloon was the Type 3 Variant (estate) which was an even better idea with a flat floor in the back yet small front boot for valuables. It became the favourite for this model range.* **Left** *Cutaway of Variant showing space utilisation.*
Above *The flat engine was familiar VW with a fan on the crankshaft nose (as Porsche had considered earlier but had not made work).*

None of this dampened overseas eagerness and when Canada received quotas before the US a thriving grey market sprang up, putting as many as 10,000 Type 3 cars on American roads so that dealers began to carry spares for an automobile they would not admit was in existence. Magazines sent their testers to Nova Scotia where they reported, 'it is hard to believe this is a VW'. Canadian owners insisted stoutly they had an all new car, not a rebodied Beetle, and VW of America finally gave in, to import the first thousands since Americans seemed to want them more than Germans.

They had waited long enough to offer the more powerful 1500 S, as it happened, giving the car more motorway panache from the beginning. Obvious attraction of the S, which came along two years after the original launch, was 54 hp from a dual-carburettor engine. Even keen VW tuners had not managed to crowd a carburettor on each side under the lid but VW managed it by angling intake passages. This S was no louder and at least as elastic, despite higher compression and a need for premium petrol. Its 54 hp still peaked at only 4,200 rpm and there was now a VW with claimed top speed of over 135 kph/nearly 85 mph. Even a Variant S, with the power to haul real loads.

Comparison tests against old foes began to rank this new VW as high as second instead of automatic last and without the continuing noise and side-wind problems, however reduced, this 1500 S might even have challenged popular hot saloons. A non-car consumer magazine did claim the car was unreliable and not recommended but that was settled when VW sued for DM 10 million.

Once the car had decent performance many found the gear change up to Porsche

A rare variation on the Type 3 was the delivery van, seldom seen but at least tried out.

standards and if the brakes were still not discs, at least they were very good drums. This was a car which even after comparison would rank ideal for average family needs. The Variant S was even more widely praised than that and called 'the car Volkswagen always needed in America', no small virtue since that market continued to support the firm. It reached there in 1966, the same year Volkswagen produced another bodywork variation called the TL. The final Type 3 would be built in 1973, the same year VW built its first water-cooled car.

For 1967 the 1500 received safety systems like the Beetle's that year and the following year brought Bosch fuel injection at nearly 10 per cent extra cost in Germany although it was standard in the US since it brought a decent reduction in CO emissions along with smoother acceleration and less baulking at hot starts. A computer in the left rear wing controlled the injection, making VW not only the first in Germany with electronic injection but still the only car to offer it in this class as late as 1970. Elasticity improved noticeably and there was a modest drop in consumption, thanks to development costs reckoned at close to a million marks. In some markets the model was called EL.

The one important bodywork change for 1500 saloons and estates came in 1970 with an extra 45 m³/1.6 ft³ of front boot thanks to a nose extension. Otherwise VW built its second million Type 3 cars with no more than trim or tail-light changes. Nearly 43 per cent of those cars were Variants.

When the fast-back TL also proved less than a full Beetle successor, VW increased engine capacity to 1.6 litres, making the 1600 TL. An automatic gearbox option appeared in 1967 but the automatic upshift points held engine revs too low for sufficient heat on cold days. The automatic also added about a third to fuel consumption. Of course most Americans loved it, when no more than 5 per cent of the Europeans might order one. The 1600 did have a good match of power curve with ratios and very smooth gear changes. VW had to change the rear axle geometry to suit the shaft angles of this automatic transmission and thereby achieved a two-pedal car which handled better, with less tuck-in of the inside rear wheel, than their manual model. Since side-wind problems were reduced as well, some bought the automatic just to get the newer axle.

Appearance of the slope-tailed TL in 1966 launched a round of model musical chairs. The 1500 S was dropped since the 1600 also gave 54 hp, then the TL added, although its nose and tail did not quite match stylistically. The car did have a taller rear boot by a

When three-box Type 3 proved less than a super hit VW tried a fast-back version, called 1600 TL, with larger engine and still two boots (rear now enlarged) but the proportions were never quite right.

third, giving this TL the total cargo capacity of most class rivals, although VW's was divided into two luggage compartments. A TL was now the most expensive Type 3. To confuse numbers further both the three-box 1500 and 1600 TL were called Type 31, ignoring the totally different shapes. They skipped 32 and assigned 33 to the right-hand drive 31, of either shape, while 34 became the Karmann Ghia 1500 coupé and 36 the Variant.

Germans called the TL a poor man's Porsche and it is true you could hardly miss one in a crowd, as you could the hatchback. Although the tail could now be overloaded, to the detriment of handling, the most expensive VW of its day did come with disc brakes at the front. When it ceased to be cheap transport, judgement became harsher, focusing on sparse instrumentation and sluggish performance for 1.6 litres. The public, curiously enough, decided this must be the greatest VW for 1970, although a 1500 Beetle could outrun it.

Wolfsburg tried hard to promote this TL as the 'sporting' shape in its range, perhaps a somewhat rueful admission that the original, saloon-style 1500 had been just a little too self-effacing. By the middle of its model run, as the 70s opened, this TL had become a sort of middle ground, sold in decent but not VW-like numbers, although their own Audi from the Bavarian branch usually came off better in comparison tests by then.

In sum, Volkswagen had expanded its range in its own way only to find—objectively—that they needed some truly new and exciting models badly by the late 60s. Several of that ilk were actually imminent during the final year of Nordhoff's reign but the biggest and most visible change by far in 1968 would not be a new car but rather the end of an era, the disappearance from the Wolfsburg scene of a man who had dominated it so totally, of a man whose VWs had done so much to change models everywhere, not to mention US car habits.

Heinz Nordhoff had presided over the most critical twenty years in Volkswagen history. In 1968 he was gone.

Chapter 9

Kurt Lotz: limited options

Nordhoff had been far more than an important name in Volkswagen annals, he was Mister Volkswagen in person, and the most famous manager in all Germany, by a wide margin; a man of worldwide reputation. In a land which appreciated achievement Nordhoff stood out for doing precisely what he set out to accomplish: build more Beetles than the car totals from any other maker, and export more cars than any other firm. In the course of managing that he also led Germany into second place among the world's automobile-producing lands and VW itself to fifth among producers with 1,352,000 cars turned out in 1967, a figure topped only by Fiat that year, but VW was determined to surge ahead once more.

In the year he died Volkswagen would complete its 15 millionth car of all kinds since the war, with no less than 11 million of those Beetles and 9 million exported. Nordhoff did not manage all that in two decades by playing the pliable man, of course. When sales fell in 1966 he told Bonn to remit registration tax for a year and he would not need to put his plants on short hours. Strauss, a regular sniper at VW and then in charge of finances for Bonn, said no. When a partial production shutdown did come, VW paid 60 per cent of basic salary to those laid off and reduced its force by offering six months severance pay. That cut their labour pool to 51,000 by the end of 1968, although it was back to 60,000 a year later.

The range of cars VW built in the 1967-9 period.

By January 1968, when Nordhoff had displayed his famous 36 unneeded prototypes, he could tell an interviewer, 'the Beetle star still shines with undiminished brightness and you can see for yourself, every single day, what vitality is hidden in this car which has been pronounced dead more often than all those rival designs nobody even remembers any more'. He added, in another interview, 'we're a poor land and the US is rich'. Therefore, 'Germany should follow where VW leads and not the other way around'. Over one million workers and their families lived on VW earnings. 'Germany needs its key industry', he said, never doubting the firm would always be there. If money got any tighter, and cars went out of style altogether, 'the last car purchased will be a Beetle'.

In answer to a question, Nordhoff said that he felt he was much too important at VW to contemplate a direct career in politics. He could always offer ample advice to the government from Wolfsburg—although that was not stated outright. Actually Heinz Nordhoff had been a sick man in varying degrees since an operation in 1958 for ulcers and by 1966 even admitted ruefully to limiting his love for German wines to a mild Mosel. But he still meant to pick his own moment to retire—and wanted to head the firm's supervisory board thereafter.

Such an overseer group was typical of any German corporation but Volkswagen's was a little different since it consisted of two members each from the Bonn government and state of Lower Saxony, seven worker representatives and ten car-management members. These 21 were technically empowered to pick the Managing Director. Nordhoff first meant that man to be Carl Hahn whom he called back from America to groom as direct successor, but Hahn fell out during various management shake-ups his US methods aroused, and when sales showed a lag during 1966-67 he quickly became the one man the board would not consider as new VW director. Instead they picked Dr Kurt Lotz in April 1967, with the intention that he would have ample time under Nordhoff to learn the car business, a new world to the towering new manager.

Then Nordhoff died suddenly at 69, suffering a heart attack in early 1968 before he could retire gracefully to the role of paternal advisor. The entire plant downed tools for a minute of tribute and the one man most responsible for the modern, workable Volkswagen was buried imperially, leaving Lotz in sole charge on April 12 1968, considerably earlier than he or anybody else had expected.

Lotz was a farm boy from north Germany whose robust early sports were motorcycle trials and the decathalon. He aimed originally at a career with the police, then joined the *Luftwaffe* when war came and quickly showed such talent for planning that he was advanced to the position of a general-staff officer. Escaping from a Czech prison camp at the end of the war Lotz made his perilous way home, then worked as a farm labourer until a sister who as a secretary at BBC found him a book-keeper's job with that electrical giant. Kurt Lotz was upward-mobile before Germans even knew the phrase. Working his way through night school the tall, ambitious young manager-to-be became a BBC director in less than ten years, General Director there in 1958 when he was the youngest ever to hold that post, at 45.

Inevitably, this boy wonder of Germany's economic miracle would not always be popular with unions or other managers yet Lotz regularly turned down offers of 'better' posts and spent eight years as the head of BBC in Germany before becoming Nordhoff's assistant director in 1967, the man in charge little more than a year later.

This director, who avoided interviews whenever possible, was careful not to criticise the previous management but he knew from the first that new impetus was badly needed and did tell the press to, 'wait and see what we will have for you shortly'. He had arrived in 1967 to find both turnover and exports down (by 7 and 16 per cent respectively), although those reliable Americans again bought more VWs than they had the previous

year, easing the overall slump. Retaining 'number two' in Europe was scant consolation with a 20 per cent production lag. Lotz did enjoy an early boost when 1968 turnover spurted ahead and 1969 proved even better. In his first year at the helm Volkswagen paid DM 10 on a 50 mark share and his board congratulated themselves on the choice. Three of that board were men of the Nordhoff era and the average age of this body was into its 60s when Lotz arrived—when he turned it into 'his' board the average age was middle-40s.

Outside car watchers were less sanguine anyway. VW had become too successful through the 60s to risk any sudden change, as Lotz himself realised. 'We had been immovable under a single director for twenty years. Now we had to move from monolith to a many-faceted product.' To him that meant a US management advisory firm and internal competition.

Calling himself an optimist, 'within limits—I'm always self-critical and avoid being utopian', Lotz informed his share holders, 'there is no recipe for success, only future plans and work towards a firm goal'. In his later autobiography Kurt Lotz would say, 'VW was often called the exception in German industry (of its day) and it used to be just that, in many ways. No other German firm grew so rapidly. No other had such disparity between larger and smaller production programmes. Thus no other had an equally high risk level'. He could add, 'VW provides such an exemplary model for the problems, goals and lessons of industrial politics that it would have had to be established as a text book if it hadn't already existed'.

Thrown into the deep end ahead of schedule, Lotz at least knew his problems. He probably tried to solve too many of them simultaneously, bringing out too many models before they were 100 per cent-plus ready in the VW manner, or buying up new technology whenever he could not find a quick solution within Wolfsburg. There was continuing pressure to produce—immediately.

He had arrived at VW to find the drawers of his development engineers empty and wrote later, 'it was bitter to discover that too little had been invested in the future during a period of high profits. Since we saw our only chance for survival in a new car, this raised the unavoidable question—where do we get the necessary money now? The old joke that we might have to go begging very nearly proved true'. Hardly the VW casual outsiders imagined—yet even Lotz never quite shook free of the inherited, one-model syndrome, hard as he tried. With the first 15 million Beetles looming he could only predict, 'Wolfsburg will never see the 20-million mark', insisting, 'we won't repeat Ford's mistake'.

By that point, of course, they had added a Type 4 to the line-up, purchased Audi and then taken over NSU, all proving his readiness to try new paths. One of these fresh routes was Professor Dr Werner Holste, second non-automobile man on the board besides Lotz, and one of the youngest at 40. With a background of general mechanical engineering, Holste took over the technical reigns at VW as Lotz cast around for aid with less of a pure VW orientation. He also called in Claus Borgward, blocky son of a famous north-German car empire, to establish a quality promotion department.

At least as pressing in that first year was their dependence on the single US market to absorb a third or more of all production, just as a revalued German *deutschmark* meant export prices should climb by 7 to 11 per cent. Lotz had only just nudged American sales up by a quarter and decided to restrict his US price boost to 2.5 per cent, absorbing the rest in the face of stiff new eastern competition.

VW's American image was quality service for useful cars, in Lotz's view, but he was also convinced that younger buyers were seeking more power with greater comfort for the 70s. His long-term answer was more co-operation with Porsche technically and Pininfarina in styling, not to mention Nissan for certain technology. At the same time, VW vehemently denied any merger rumours with the Japanese. For the short term Volkswagen could only improve the faithful Beetle—again—but this time the changes would run deep. Nothing less than new rear suspension was planned, appearing at first only on the model which also featured their new quasi-automatic gearbox. As a new 1968 model, introduced, of course, in late 1967, this considerable updating appeared just as Beetles topped the Swiss market lists for the 18th straight year and Austrian students claimed the Beetle-stuffing record: 57 bodies in the car which drove a full five metres/16 feet afterwards.

Hungary wanted Beetles badly enough then to pay part of the bill in car horns and the largest auto-carrying freighter in the world had just become the 64th ship in Wolfsburg's flotilla, one capable of carrying 2,500 cars on nine decks.

Despite their sales problems, production increases remained a dominant factor. 350 Beetles daily were built in their Ingolstadt plant, taken over with Audi, and now a new factory was planned for Salzgitter where 500 cars a day could be churned out not far south of Wolfsburg, and close to the East German border where Bonn wanted to encourage new facilities. A new north-south canal to the coast would go right by Salzgitter shortly as well.

The ill-kept secret of a truly revised Beetle fitted right into this atmosphere. Never before had there been so many changes at one time, some for US safety reasons, some to remain a VW. A collapsible steering column and dual-circuit brakes were long overdue while new fresh air intakes and two-speed wipers were a boom. Higher bumpers, upright headlamps and larger rear light clusters were added as well. But the real news remained that word 'automatic' on their rear lid. It was really a semi-automatic, with no clutch pedal but a normal box of ratios, plus a sensor in the gear knob to disconnect drive electrically when a gear had to be changed. A hydro-converter then took up the drive.

For something less than DM 500 they offered a car which would start from rest in any of its three gears—reverse occupied the slot of the now-redundant low—and proceed to 65 kph/40 mph, 105/65 and 125/77 in the three available ratios. Second was the universal ratio for all but the steepest grades or highway cruising, while the engine could not hunt between ratios like a full automatic, ideal for its small capacity.

The car was extremely easy to drive so long as you remembered not to rest a hand or knee on the gear lever. This 'automatic' Beetle could even be tow-started. In performance terms the 1.5 litre semi-automatic was about equal to their manual 1.3 aided by a lower, 4.375, final drive ratio. About 5 per cent higher fuel consumption went with the 10 per cent power penalty. With all that, the real reason most German buyers wanted one was the combination of new, two-joint half shafts at the rear with Porsche-style angled locating arms which kept the rear wheels more nearly vertical in a bend and made handling more neutral at the limits. This quickly became the 'status Beetle,' as the first true change in basic VW principles for over 30 years, after all.

Despite all these virtues, overshadowed somewhat by the 9 per cent surcharge, this semi-automatic VW only claimed about a tenth of Beetle sales initially, in 1968 when VW put 100,000 two-pedal cars on the road. The real surge in this field came from their Type 3 with a proper automatic gearbox. Even so, this 'automatic' Type 1 was soon known as the most modern and/or best buy among all Beetles. They had also given more thought to the integral seat/headrest units US law had seemed to require. Those 'tombstones' restricted rear vision badly and left rear passengers in a well. At the same time 'safe' but flat dashboard knobs were a problem to operate with gloves on.

Production reached 7,400 per day by the autumn of 1968 leading to a constant struggle with their Ingolstadt plant which needed its assembly lines to build Audi 100s by then, whatever the Beetle output. Bavarian or Saxon, these new Beetles also showed dismaying small flaws at first. A reader poll might give good marks to engine and gearbox as well as finish (poor heat was such an automatic complaint few noticed) but valves, ignition and brakes were questioned. VW even had to recall 160,000 cars, over half of them Beetles where the spare wheel could rub through vital lines. This was not the sort of problem they had faced before the annual model change.

Comparing the new cars with five contemporaries, German magazines had to mention widest door openings or best jack to find VW plus features. And while model constancy made it easier to stock spares, Wolfsburg was also in trouble there with the anti-trust office over fixed prices, a charge later restricted to their prices on engines and panels alone.

There were, quite naturally, fewer updates for 1970, barely a year after the longest one-year list in their history, but German buyers were turning nasty about Americans who could order that new back axle with a manual gearbox. Volkswagen claimed 'service problems' prevented its sale at home. An internal black market now developed as Germans bought cars through local American troops to obtain that newest VW status symbol—non-tuck-in.

The model-mix game was accelerated too. Their plainest 1200 could now be ordered with 1.3 litre engine or semi-automatic box, while the fancier 1300 also came with a 1.2 litre/34 hp engine. All cars came with extra horizontal engine lid slits for quick identification. The 1300 now held some 20 per cent of the German market with 40 hp and a 125 kph/78 mph top speed. For one thing it did not look 'small car' to the neighbours. Kommenda had obviously produced a very good classless shape, as intended, when it could be both the trendsetter in rear-engined days and solid last bastion of that design when the rivals turned to front-wheel drive. Once they got its rear suspension under control Volkswagen engineers turned to the front, along with another engine update.

The new badge read 1302 or 1302 S, meaning a 'Super Beetle' with works blessing and a considerable gain over their 44 hp/1.5 litre engine. In manual gearbox form a 50 hp, 1,600 cc (despite the name) S would touch 134 kph/83 mph and some tests even claimed another 6 kph/4 mph. As an automatic the 6 extra S hp made up for gearbox losses, yet it ran on normal petrol, with compression of only 7.5:1.

This engine featured a stronger magnesium crankcase, new cylinder heads, chrome exhaust valves and aluminium oil cooler but they had also cut a few price corners too: no

For 1970 the latest in bumpers and pierced steel wheels.

water trap for the engine lid, a carburettor which tended to ice easily, and removal of silencer boxes from the rear heater ducts, for example. The car was somewhat heavier with wheelbase stretched by 2 cm/0.8 in and length by 5 cm/1.6 in while the front track was nearly 7 cm/2.8 in wider and the overall car broader as well.

The added track dimension belied their real 1302 change—MacPherson strut front suspension, suggested by a Porsche development paper, which amounted to their second change in a principle in VW history. Handling improved considerably, the car was easier to control with its worm and roller steering giving 2.7 turns and the 9.6 m/31.5 foot turning circle was a real improvement. But the basic reason for a new front suspension was quite simply more space in the boot. Volkswagen took full advantage by laying their spare wheel flat and lowering the tank profile while increasing tank capacity slightly. They even claimed the new nose was more aerodynamic. As a final touch, this S had disc brakes at the front, the plain 1302 larger front drums.

Once the early euphoria over a 'super' Beetle wore off, however, most discovered the ride was a little choppier than torsion bars had offered and side wind sensitivity about the same. Even so, VW could properly call it their most important model to date, since there would be no true successor to the Beetle, as Lotz explained clearly to a stock holder meeting, where he also announced an increase in capitalisation to DM 900 million. They might be apprehensive about coming US regulations, he admitted, as the five millionth VW was sent to the States, but it would be too much to expect even Wolfsburg to produce any car which could replace a legend. As it turned out, the Beetle survived Kurt Lotz on the Wolfsburg scene and was still produced more than a decade after he left, although German construction did end about six years later.

Including the 1302 cabriolet, there were four Beetles available in 1971 but two-thirds of all buyers preferred the new ones. The following year many features filtered down to their lesser models and a plug-in diagnostic socket was considered their prime advance. US rules now consumed a disproportionate amount of their time but Wolfsburg found

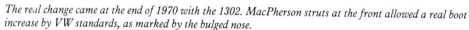

The real change came at the end of 1970 with the 1302. MacPherson struts at the front allowed a real boot increase by VW standards, as marked by the bulged nose.

breathing space to work on carburettor heating and to reduce consumption, a frantic project once the S acquired a reputation for excessive thirst.

Their Emden plant, where Beetle production would first be transferred to make way for the Golf, built a full quarter-million of the Type 1 in 1970, entirely for export and mostly for the US. That lifted Emden totals to a million in the year VW captured a quarter of the first two-million car year in German history.

Their new Salzgitter factory now became the final domestic VW plant put into production and with its output, non-Wolfsburg totals came within a whisker of matching the home factory production, effectively doubling Volkswagen plant area. The following year VW posted the highest production and turnover figures ever—but the lowest profits, which became a basic reason for Lotz's departure after only one term as leader. Costs had simply spurted far ahead of production. Furthermore, VW of America sold fewer cars in 1971, due in part to dollar/DM uncertainty. Home prices were up as well and the days of the sub-5,000 mark Beetle were gone forever. American colleges now gave courses in Volkswagen maintenance and repair while the manager of Chevrolet worried publicly that VW would move up a class (as promised by their Type 4 and Audi). VW of America announced that 35 babies had been born in their cars during 1971 alone, bringing the total to 218 since records had been kept. That included twins, born logically enough in a Type 2 Microbus.

During 1972 they were still building 5,800 Beetles every day around the world and discovered that only 2.2 out of any 13,000 in a week would be precisely alike, a growing headache, although not as pointed a problem as the need in the summer of 1972 to discount 1302 and 411 prices to clear stocks before 1973 models were announced.

The most famous car production mark of them all, the announced total for Ford's Model T, was passed on February 17 1972 when the 15,007,034th Beetle came off the assembly line. (Certain later re-counts put the T total slightly higher but the point was academic; VW beat any figure named by early that year.) A second milestone in the same year, twenty million VW vehicles of all kinds, was celebrated by a series of 15,000 cars with numbered dashboard plaques and extra trim.

As the mid-70s loomed VW itself felt the Beetle's days must be numbered but they would build such cars as long as anybody really wanted one. It was doubly hard to axe a winner when their Types 3 and 4 were not taking up any sales slack and the brand new, front-drive saloons were still so young. Since all Beetles built after that time were no more than variations on one apparently-ageless theme, however, we can complete their story here.

There was another body change for 1973 and a new number—1303—to underline their struggle to keep the product competitive. A 'panoramic' windscreen was introduced for the 1303, the roof flattened and a neater dashboard with improved heater/ventilation outlets installed. Seats were more firmly anchored and sound dampening slightly increased. Marketing even came up with a 'sporting' 1303 S at this point, in a limited edition: alloy wheels with low-profile tyres, black bumpers and front lid, leather steering wheel and untouched engine. VW life was becoming very like all other brands under the new management.

1974 was then a year for detail improvements and the dropping of several models with the original axle systems as they anticipated a complete phaseout in the face of water-cooled cars; but the 1303 L did have a quartz clock.

All production was now centered on Emden where the US Beetles had been made since December 1964 and it remained there up to that moment in 1977 when the last German-made Beetle, car number 16,255,500, left its assembly line some 43 years after the design was launched. This final teutonic Type 1 was reserved for the works museum. The

The new screen marks the 1303 in 1973.

occasion was celebrated with special-series Beetles for various lands, such as the silver-grey run of 300 for Great Britain.

That greatest rarity of all, the absolutely final Beetle, still lay far ahead. Brazil, Mexico, Nicaragua and South Africa were still building 1,100 per day when Emden ceased and the worldwide Type 1 total was some 19,300,000 so the 20-million bench mark could be foreseen. What is more, there was a sky blue, Mexican-built Beetle in attendance the day that last German model was celebrated. Emden would continue to process latin Beetles for those few die-hard Germans who would not give up their favourite car. Management did not expect this service would last much longer since they were selling barely 960 Beetles a month in January 1977, against ten times that number of the Golf; reason enough to wind down old faithful.

When they actually tried to do just that, however, German Beetle sales soared by 55 per cent for 1978 and they had a ready market right through 1979 for the car. Many felt 'buy safe' was synonymous with 'buy Beetle,' even at a price close to DM 9,000. It was still the cheapest full-value automobile offered and one of the best for resale. Every fourth used car bought in Germany as late as 1978 was a Beetle. The car was purchased despite—or perhaps because of—the fact that VW Mexico had dropped the fancy MacPherson front suspension, trailing-arm rear axle and upmarket engines. While the Karmann convertible continued with their best chassis to the end of 1979, Mexico reverted to swing axles at the back, front trailing arms, manual gearbox and 34 hp.

This cheeky overseas Beetle for Germany still offered space for four, the two up front enjoying comfortable seats and adjustable head rests, and did its 140 kph/85 mph down hill with a following wind. It did not have much luggage space unless you folded the rear seat down but had real pivoting wind wings in the doors and a proper wolf and castle on the steering wheel hub despite its Pueblo origins. Their Mexican model was as solidly built as any previous Beetle, and a perfect way to relive the dreaded side wind syndrome. You even had to wind a window down to slam the door.

In the early 80s nobody dared predict any more when the Beetle would finally go out of production after all. It had already outlived various Beetle-based variations VW prepared for launch more than a decade earlier. In 1969 they actually released three 'completely new' cars with Beetle backgrounds.

★   ★   ★

All three of these debutantes were carefully keyed to the original Type 1 but none would survive anywhere near as long. The first to appear was also the one based most closely on VW saloon thinking, although Wolfsburg did its best to present the 411, first model of their Type 4 range, as a bigger and better automobile. This car had long-since been the subject of sneak photos from their new Ehra test track so the 'leaked news' of its imminent arrival was somewhat suspect in May 1968. Strauss had been sniping from Bonn again and the new director wanted to prove he was really prepared.

Pininfarina had an advisory contract with Wolfsburg and was credited with 411 styling—German journals noted his Austin 1800—but there was evident VW retouching too. Looking better in photos than in the metal, the 411 was revolutionary by VW standards for four doors. It came with both standard and de luxe trim from the first and manual or automatic gearbox—almost like any new range from a rival manufacturer. The basic shape recalled their Type 3 TL, enlarged all ways and mounted on a 250 cm/98.5 in wheelbase. Obviously heavier, the 411 featured a 1.7 litre, flat four engine bearing dual carburettors. It had stiffer housings, redesigned cooling fins and a mild camshaft but a little more valve lift. It was the most oversquare of all VW engines, producing a modest 65 hp/4,500 rpm to retain longevity.

Technical progress came down to specific parts such as recirculating ball steering or disc front brakes, along with a standard petrol-fired auxiliary heater. Power went through a new gearbox and hypoid bevel drive while suspension was by MacPherson front legs,

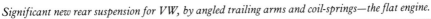

Significant new rear suspension for VW, by angled trailing arms and coil-springs—the flat engine.

Left *Overhead view of the new Wolfsburg model showing the number of doors and lids.*

Right *411E, the injected model which helped, and the wagon version which was better balanced in looks and (like the Type 3) the better car to have in this 4-range.*

along with rear semi-trailing arms in the then-current VW manner. It was the first coil-sprung VW and first with integral body-chassis replacing the separate floor pan.

It was also the first to come from the Wolfsburg development centre and Volkswagen felt it was really the first post-war, Wolfsburg automobile. They had avoided too new territory such as rear hatch or fold-down seat but extra glass aided parking, and made it feel larger, when taken in conjunction with better space utilisation and minimal wheel-arch intrusion.

Their only boot was up front but there was also a shallow recess behind the rear seats. By dropping the Type 3-style dual boot in the back they achieved 45/55 weight distribution unladen against 38/62 for the Beetle. Nearer-neutral handling and ride surpassed any previous VW in the eyes of early testers. As one magazine put it, those Beetles just grew and grew under the direction of a firm determined to build nothing but Volkswagens. The 411 was dubbed 'pure Nordhoff' although some began to ask why that same transaxle could not be fitted to the nose just as well. Production began at 160 per day against a potential of 500 daily and VW expected some 15-20 per cent would be ordered with the fully-automatic gearbox, about the same figure as their Type 3 achieved.

When it came to multi-car comparisons it was particularly noticeable that the 411 was the only car left with air cooling and rear engine, the most expensive VW as well as the largest. However an Audi from their own Bavarian branch offered more space on about the same wheelbase while a 411 could only score first in quality. It simply was not up to the contemplated class, particularly in performance, and Germans began to wonder aloud if VW could be trusted much longer as leader of their economic boom. Wolfsburg soon answered the power problem with a better 1.7 engine and the 411 E (*Einspritz* = injection) in line with their very early adoption of electronic injection, although it required premium fuel.

Power went clear to 80 hp with greater flexibility as well and compression was raised a fraction while altered engine mounts eased sticky gear changes and a change to the heater

reduced noise. Aluminium replaced old-favourite magnesium to stiffen the crankcase. The E also had new heads and pistons plus even more compression but it would cruise at 150 kph/90 mph, making first-year 411 buyers furious.

Their car was considered tall, thin and not too handsome anyway. Now it was obsolete in only a year. Sales never moved well after the first rush so Wolfsburg's latest problem child soon received a full 1.8 litres of engine and a new nose. Far more important was the eventual estate which had better styling balance and was even a fair bit quicker than the saloon. It remained pricey by VW standards and many rusted earlier than a VW fan expected but it was 2-3 decibels quieter. By 1970 quality was up to standard too as VW inspectors learned the new machine's quirks.

When quite a few of the E range had trouble doing the claimed 90 in top many doubted the rated 80 hp figure—that from a firm which had always tended to underrate performance before. Kurt Lotz, incidentally, assumed all responsibility for the 411.

By the time a 1974 model was announced, late in 1973, VW was into its second facelift in barely four years and using the new name of 412 to indicate improvements. Both three- and five-door estates were offered—they were the Type 4 sales leaders—and air conditioning became an option. Steering and brake loads were above the mid-70s norm, dials below expectations, and the 1.8 litre, basic engine of 72 hp meant that the gearbox had to be used a good deal to make much progress. The big VW was clearly lagging further and further behind their own Audi 100 and could not even match the K70, taken over when they acquired NSU.

By April 1974 this Type 4 range was near the end of its short life, aided by the fuel crisis. At the end they were only building a few Variants. Some 400,000 Type 4s were produced in a scant six years, a truly brief run for Wolfsburg. If the two litre engine from their 914 project was ever contemplated, it was dropped in the hard light of Arab realities and carless Sundays in Germany during 1974.

The second new car released during 1969, one planned long before Lotz reached

Wolfsburg of course, was the go-(almost)-anywhere Type 181, marketed in America as 'The Thing', which summed it up with great neatness. This model was also built in Mexico as the Safari and exported to warmer climes from there. At one point there was even serious discussion of including China in that category. Some considered it a sort of four-door sports car, meaning the young might appreciate its draughty progress. Forestry workers and airfield people were the main target. They loved its flat sides, quickly-dismounted doors and rugged interior simplicity. Almost everybody would have liked it even better with four-wheel drive but the 181 remained pure Beetle in that respect, a true *kuebel* successor. Its detuned, 44 hp engine of 1.5 litres powered the rear wheels and took The Thing to 110 kph/70 mph—with a tail wind.

Since it was based on a possible army contract, the 181 was not built with commercial price requirements in the foreground. Thus it was plain expensive for civilians at roughly the price of a 411 or two-thirds more than the cheapest Beetle, which would reach almost as many remote places anyway. It was more courier car than Jeep competitor. Sitting tall it looked bulkier than the Beetle but was really a good foot shorter and offered more space for four under the folding canvas roof. Rear axle drop gears to improve ground clearance recalled their war-time tricks. Overall gearing was much shorter than the 1.5 litre Beetle so that a 181 could climb 55 per cent grades in low gear. Their aim with this 'multi-purpose' machine was clear from its model number, used as a public name: Type 1, variation 81.

Another decade would pass before Volkswagen, with basic assistance from Audi engineers, finally built a true post-war off-road machine. This Iltis (ferret) was a proper army replacement for the two-stroke, DKW-designed Munga which was totally outdated long before 1979. Once again, building to a government-funded price made the vehicle exceptionally expensive in its two-tone civilian guise.

This time they did achieve outstanding off-road ability and refinement, however. While the chassis, with independent suspension by lower wishbones and transverse leaf springs, was modified Munga, the powerplant was based on their water-cooled, inline four, found

Above left *Wolfsburg attempting to recapture the Kuebel mystique. Their 181, called 'The Thing' in US, 'Safari' in Mexico where it was still built at the end of 70s. The slab-side vehicle had only rear-wheel drive and scant amenities yet cost as much as a sports car.*

Above *Designed by the Audi branch (and based in many chassis ways on their old DKW 2-stroke Munga) the Iltis returned VW to four-wheel drive, now with water-cooled four in front. The first model was for the German army.* **Below** *By 1980 they were building a civilian model as well, using VW badge despite Audi parentage. The catch was the elevated price as always when the original is built to army specifications.*

in the Golf. For the Iltis they used a 1.7 litre engine block, as sold to Chrysler in America, to ensure better torque.

The goal was military potential with saloon-like ride on the road, a machine which could shrug off wide extremes of temperature or environment and which offered complete driver control over the six various drive-line modes, ranging from normal front-wheel drive to all-wheel action in a special low range with both differential locks in action. Avoiding the complication of a high-low transfer case they fitted a normal VW/Audi transaxle in front with case extension for the low-range and reverse gears. A shaft runs back to virtually the same transaxle mounted backwards in the rear. Parts interchangeability was a key factor in Iltis design thinking. Cost-no-object attention was given to shaft and drum brake sealing, to an engine ducted to the base of the windscreen to ford 60 cm/24 in streams, even to a flame-resistant petrol tank of expanded plastic or the hard-chrome coating for hidden wear points such as wheel brake cylinder bores.

A full roll cage was fixed to the ladder frame to meet all 80s crash tests despite the basic open body with canvas top. An enclosed and carpeted civilian version with hinged rear door followed the army model almost immediately. Developed by Audi this Iltis sold with a VW badge on the nose, at well above the price of say a Porsche 924, powered by an engine from the same family.

The final VW debut, which arrived at the end of 1969 as a 1970 model, was their joint VW-Porsche 914, that mid-engined two-seater which Wolfsburg powered with a variation of its 411 flat four (while Porsche fitted fewer cars with its own flat six). The car was largely a Porsche design and key feature of a new VW-Porsche marketing arm launched at the same time. Car and sales organisation had roughly equal life spans. By the late summer of 1969 no car subject in Germany was more debated than this mid-engined model revealed in the press as early as the previous January. Porsche had to go to some lengths to insist it would remain independent.

It was the 914/4 from VW which set the sales pace with the Porsche 914/6, in an identical body, adding prestige to both lines. In America they tried to sell them all as Porsches but found old-line Porsche people resistant to the whole 914 idea, no matter how

VW and Porsche collaborated on the mid-engined 914, with Porsche doing the design work and VW furnishing the powerplant for the basic version of the 1.6, later 2.0, litres. The car was pure two-seater with no place to store a coat inside and no one could decide whether it was a cheap Porsche or an expensive VW.

much new image the car gave Volkswagen. The basic engine was the 1.7 litre four using injection to produce 80 hp from the very first. Actually the chassis was sturdy and balanced enough to accept any engine fey Porsche engineers later cared to try, including a 350 hp 908 on one occasion.

This close-coupled 914 with removable top panel was even more rigid a body than the Porsche 911 coupé, aided by its Targa-type roll bar behind the seats. Porsche's chief stylist then was Ferdinand Porsche's grandson and namesake, usually called Butzi, and he believed two seats were all any sports car should have. Thus there was hardly space in the cockpit to lay down your driving gloves, although they did furnish a thin pad to fit between the two seats and make a 'three seater' out of it.

Styling was self-willed to say the least, and not to all tastes, but it was certainly good in aerodynamics, allowing 175 kph/110 mph on modest power. And there were boots at both ends, along with a very narrow engine access hatch which allowed you to reach almost everything except the spark plugs. A VW 914 could never be confused with any other automobile, either.

Drivers had to come to terms with mid-engined handling which allowed very high cornering limits but gave little warning when the eventual borderline was reached. Significantly, all efforts to rally the car were defeated by the near-impossibility of achieving that instant oversteer so necessary around hairpins. A sheet metal frame in unit with the body was sprung by a long torsion bar in front, taken from Porsche, and rear coils by VW. Karmann built the bodies which came with a choice of five-speed manual gearbox (with an excessively vague change pattern) or Sportomatic as used by Porsche. This was a near-relative of the semi-automatic two-pedal Beetle arrangement.

The first 914 had a handbrake between driver's seat and sill which was supposed to flop flat when not needed. It proved difficult to adjust, while the original passenger seat did not adjust at all. Vision was better than most mid-engined cars offered—except for the very tall. Both heat and engine noise had short paths to the cockpit. Taking on the dubious fame of 'most expensive VW yet', this 914 fell somewhere between Wolfsburg's usual market segment and Porsche fans who did not like to be reminded their exclusive sport cars had always been more or less related to VW components. Despite the stumpy looks—the wheelbase was actually greater than a 911—an American magazine quickly voted it import of the year and Karmann looked towards 100 per day for 1970, 25,000 with the VW engine alone that year.

In the autumn of 1973 VW fitted a larger, 1.8 litre engine from the 412, giving the ton of sports car 85 hp and excellent economy with lazy gearing. Top speed came close to 180 kph/112 mph, contained easily by four-wheel disc brakes. An exciting car, it did best in comparisons with its peers when the subject was lateral g ratings rather than comfort or space. The 914 finally received a full two-litre engine which cut its 0-100 kph/62 mph time below the magic 10 second mark while adding 5 kph/3 mph to the top speed. Power was now up by a quarter over the original 914, to an even 100 hp.

Admired at its debut like few European sport cars since the war, this VW-Porsche only found its real value-for-money niche in 2 litre form when it cost less than the original 914/6 from Porsche and performed virtually as well. All the same problems were worked out and the 914 2.0 carried on until late 1975, by which time VW had built 115,646 of them with a Wolfsburg engine.

★   ★   ★

These were the days when Porsche was also developing an equally different Beetle-successor for VW, one which could be tied to the mid-engine virtues of the 914. Porsche flatly considered the car a demonstration of Ferry Porsche's conviction that front-wheel drive was only a fad. It was also considered a logical extension of the building-block system, again using a single floor pan to produce a sports car, a 2+2 coupé, a five-seater saloon and an eight-seater Transporter, just as Professor Porsche had done originally.

Ferdinand Piëch, grandson of old Porsche and Ferry's nephew (son of Louise), was the engineer for this project at Porsche and he simply did not believe the Volkswagen managers could be moved any further from their familiar pattern than one chassis and its engine under the rear seat of the saloon. If rear engines were inherently hard to tame when it came to handling, they might move it just forward of the front axle, but no further.

The rumours of this car continued in considerable detail, fuelled by the mid-engined 914 of course, right up to 1971 when young Piëch moved to the 'outside developments' department at Porsche. The story went that he was too dogmatic about mid-mounted saloon engines and not sufficiently market oriented but as Piëch himself pointed out: the project numbered EA 266 was based on the premise VW would go no further—they could not anticipate an entirely new director with sweeping new ideas. For all these reasons, EA 266 was destined to become the most famous unseen wonder in German car history.

The first hint of this revolutionary Beetle replacement surfaced about 1969 when VW took over NSU and put its own initials on the K70 which had front-wheel drive. It was then leaked that Porsche was doing something entirely different. The machine had also been spotted in Lapland with Super Beetles as outriders, confirming the parentage. It soon turned out that some of the Wolfsburg board did not want a new revolution but rather a totally conventional, front-engined, rear-drive car; the kind Opel was doing so well with. Reports also surfaced that the 266 was so complex it would cost more to build than the price-class could stand.

In the end EA 266 underlined general board dismay with Lotz. Profits were down by 42 per cent in his second year despite high production and Lotz was blamed, although international finance had played a large role. Planned new cars from his own era were still four years away in 1971 and the immediate replacement untenable. The firm was slipping

Few cars were as praised on introduction as the VW (née NSU) K70, but few had such a short life at VW. The original model (shown here) kept the rectangular headlights, by 1973 the K70 S had four round ones.

into actual red ink when their annual general meeting was held in June 1971 and while the board still denied all thoughts of a replacement director, they certainly were not going to take the heat of no profits. Actually the battle between director and board had been more or less constant—to the extent they even allowed a union man to be seated among them if it would spite the director.

Specific complaints included too-early release of the Super Beetle—forgetting their own pressures for a new model had been intense—and the K70 which was proving expensive to build rationally in the new Salzgitter plant—although all had agreed a 411 replacement was vital—even a claim that his NSU merger slowed Audi recovery. Lotz had been 'too authoritarian' and 'responsible for a poor model policy'. VW only held 24.3 per cent of the German market, down a tenth since he took over, although Audi-NSU which he had put together, were up 7.5 per cent for the same time span. The truth was that Kurt Lotz had gone into a no-win situation, following too soon upon a legend only to face a nation-wide crisis. When Flick, the monied eminence, said they would have to change either the figures on the books or the faces at the top, Lotz knew his five-year contract was not likely to be extended.

Barely ten weeks after an announcement that, 'there was no replacement in sight,' every tongue carried the name of Leiding who took over on October 1 1971. In his autobiography Lotz would sum it up this way: 'By 1976 VW reaped a good crop from our planting but no word of thanks was ever given for those cars.' The Audi/Passat/Golf which originated in Ingolstadt saved Volkswagen with his early approval, so it is small wonder that the three or four years which played such a small statistical part of his managerial life received so much space in his own book.

Another of his accomplishments was the little-known VW Management Academy, established in the one-time knightly seat of Rhode near Wolfsburg. It was largely ignored, almost even dismantled, by his successor but saved by the director after that and now serves as a key stop, 'halfway to the 13th floor', as young VW management men, eyeing the topmost level, put it.

Lotz had formed the necessary bridge between Nordhoff's reign and Leiding's shop-floor instinct—presiding over both the bloom which was Audi, although not responsible for acquiring that, and the bustle of NSU, very much a Lotz operation.

These two outside firms proved vital in finally reviving VW but they had a good deal of help from a new engineering face at Wolfsburg, one who started there under Lotz as a matter of fact, and inherited one of the finest new test facilities in the motor world, just as it was needed most.

Almost every management man at Volkswagen had realised at some point that the market for air-cooled, rear-engine cars was shrinking. Still, it would be the 70s before the right answer to that puzzle was found and then it was the Ehra test track which gave that move its technical base, and Professor Ernst Fiala who promoted it.

Fiala, born in 1928 as son of a Czech baker who soon moved the business and family to Vienna, became another of those vital engineering men from Austria who determined the technical history of VW in north Germany. Without the old Austro-Hungarian monarchy's engineers, from Porsche to the present, VW might not have survived in any form. Ernst Fiala studied mechanical engineering in Vienna, took his doctorate, in lateral forces on radial tyres, then joined Mercedes' test department where he learned practical car construction in the heady days of the 300 SL.

This man, who now holds over 150 patents, moved next to Berlin as a professor and director of the technical institute, where he fixed on safety as early as 1963, while seeking a core study programme. Fiala mobilised industry money and built a key team but he and the institute's directors came to a fork in the road by 1970 when Fiala decided it was a

Left *Professor Ernst Fiala, head of design and development for VW, another Austrian engineer.*

Below *VW's vast test facility at Ehra, opened in the 60s to put them in the forefront of technical development work.*

case of emigrate from Germany or join Volkswagen. He chose Wolfsburg and promptly developed there a practical safety car which met US specifications without being a monster. Begun in the autumn of 1970, and built in barely 18 months, ESVW 1 had a target weight of 900 kg/1,985 lb rather than the American limit of 4,000/8,800. It turned out to weigh 1,360 kg/3,000 lb at a cost of around DM 100 million. When a VW or Audi for the public then cost around DM 10,000, they estimated a production version of ESVW 1 would be at least DM 18,000. But at least it was within reason.

This Wolfsburg safety car, on a compact 280 cm/110 in wheelbase, was projected for an engine of 100 hp and a C_d factor of 0.34 if rear-engined, 0.36 with the engine in front. Well before their new front wheel drive generation appeared, VW acted as if either configuration was possible. People-space in the padded interior roughly equalled that in their Beetle.

When Leiding became the next director Fiala moved up to oversee all cars, vans and engines for the firm, although he was not basically a powerplant man. As technical man on the VW board by the late 70s he spent more time administrating 7,000 engineers (including the Audi and NSU teams) than designing, even keeping a sharp eye on styling as befits a hobby painter. His favourite reading is history.

A key part of this Fiala realm, alongside the most comprehensive wind tunnel in the car business, is the Ehra test track, 1,050 hectares/2,620 acres where work on the facility began in April 1967 and was up to the level of initial testing by the time Fiala moved to Wolfsburg. Chief features are a 20 km/13 mile, high-speed oval with 8 km/5 mile straights and banks where a car can travel at 190 kph/120 mph, hands off and reach as high as 350 kph/200 mph in the hands of a racing driver, on a dry day. The 240,000 m²/287,000 yd² 'lake', a perfectly level asphalt patch on one end, is used constantly. Ehra, built like Wolfsburg on the flat sands of north Germany, even has its man-made 'mountain' with various gradients up to a maximum of 30 per cent.

In all, this area which is being enlarged and improved without pause, contains 100 km/60 miles of road, offering every conceivable surface. Volkswagen has made a total turnaround from no interest in any other product to become a technological leader. They now carry out US emission tests as easily as they might put a Super V racing engine on the brake.

Throughout all the new years, safety has remained a key goal, one Fiala believes will protect their vital export business. VW was first to offer passive restraint suitable for everyday use and taken directly from their study cars. In the Golf this is an automatic belt which embraces the body as the door is closed, while a companion knee bolster prevents your sliding out from under. Fiala is on record as saying the first thing he would do to a car with air bags is disconnect the danger.

When Lotz took over in 1968 the new cars just ahead were traditional and Beetle-based. Today they are equally in the front-drive mainstream, a convention VW itself triggered.

This salvation, in the form of water-cooled engines driving the front wheels, came into being under a new director who moved up from their own Audi branch late in 1970. What is more, the true foundations for today's successful VW line were based in considerable measure on talent and products from Audi and NSU. These two companies had been added to the VW fold at the end of the 60s, only to contribute far more than their size and status than might have suggested.

Chapter 10

Outside enrichment: Audi and NSU

The Audi-NSU phase of Volkswagen history divides fairly neatly into the separate tales of these two marques, leading up to the financially necessary mergers which brought both under the Volkswagen umbrella. From the VW standpoint it came down to the relatively tame corporate assimilation of Audi, located in Bavarian Ingolstadt, from Mercedes in unhurried stages, a move which brought them plant capacity at first and, ultimately, their third post-war director plus the crusty and highly-talented engineer who laid the foundations for their success in the 70s.

No single man could have saved VW during its crisis of the middle 60s but Ludwig Kraus had more to do with the happy outcome of that rescue operation than any other one person. This well-focused Audi operation was balanced soon afterwards by the stormy takeover of NSU in Baden Wüttemburg, a merger managed by Kurt Lotz with an eye to acquiring a ready-made model overnight plus future rotary engine technology controlled by NSU. In the event, both prizes proved blessings for Wolfsburg, if ocasionally mixed ones.

Both of the firms which came under Volkswagen's wing then could look back on far longer histories than their new parent. And both had ties to Ferdinand Porsche which pre-dated VW. He had done the Auto Union racing cars for an Audi partner and the last pre-Beetle small car for NSU in the 30s. Technically, Audi had offered four-wheel hydraulic brakes some four decades before they graced the standard VW. And DKW, an earlier Audi partner, introduced the first front-drive car in 1931.

Modern Audi grew out of the post-war, two-stroke DKW factory but its history as a marque goes clear back to the 1873 knitting machines of a man named Schmidt, who was building bicycles by 1886. As a car firm, Audi was founded in 1910 although the Wanderer and Horch rings of what was then Auto Union date from 1885 and 1899 respectively. DKW became the fourth ring in 1932. It had been an independent car maker for 16 years at the time.

During the 20s DKW and Wanderer were the key segments of Auto Union, building cars in Saxony where they both resented the rise of state-backed VW. DKW later lost its main factories in the east and survived the war in the Rhineland and Ingolstadt where it built front-drive cars with two-stroke engines quite successfully in the first post-war years. But the two-cycle idea proved a dead end as car buyers became more sophisticated so DKW entered a joint venture with Daimler Benz in 1957. Flick, the money man behind them, unloaded Auto Union on Mercedes which was committed to sending in a life saver. And it was this man who proved the salvation of VW as well, although they did not seem to need that in 1963/64.

In any case, Ludwig Kraus, a tough-minded engineer with 26 years of saloon and racing car design to his credit, moved to Ingolstadt late in 1963—where his Bavarian-born soul was right at home—and decided they would have to turn out a new car overnight since the firm was really flat broke. 'It was a start from zero, really, but a task which comes seldom to any engineer, doing a whole programme for a major firm. That was very exciting.' The initial solution was an engine he brought along from Mercedes even before VW was part of the picture, and quickly fitted to a face-lifted DKW shell in place of a projected two-stroke V6 which the foundering firm couldn't afford to tool up anyway.

Introduced as 'the car which doesn't know about side winds', this Audi 70 had a longer nose to accommodate the 1.7 litre four (DKW engines had been triples), ample elasticity and a 150 kph/90 mph top speed, not to mention better looks. Buyers found it easily worth more than 15 per cent above the VW TL of the same class, for comfort and handling alone.

The director in Ingolstadt was Rudolf Leiding, a production man by training and passion, and as strong a personality as Kraus who said, 'at the start we were on a war footing and I even gave notice once. The demands were a proper new development centre, less interference from him and more money for me personally. After that there was a sort of armed truce'.

Leiding was soon transferred to VW do Brazil to rescue that branch, then returned to Ingolstadt to sort out their second round of chaos. 'When he came back from Brazil the atmosphere was quite friendly and today we are good friends', Kraus explains. 'When he went to Wolfsburg he wanted me to go up there as technical director too but I was already a head of the firm in Ingolstadt and that was higher than a manager in Wolfsburg. I hadn't finished the job here anyway. So he said, "If you won't come north, you'll have to do what Wolfsburg needs from Ingolstadt." '

The Kraus team in Ingolstadt was built around three engineers and a stylist he brought from Mercedes. 'There were only some 440 men at Audi, only half of those engineers and the quality wasn't good at all. I wrote to engineering professors to send us their good graduates and around 20 applied from Mercedes on their own.' Kraus would be first to admit he is authoritarian but he also believes that 'building an automobile is a

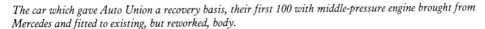

The car which gave Auto Union a recovery basis, their first 100 with middle-pressure engine brought from Mercedes and fitted to existing, but reworked, body.

psychological matter, not just business. It's all human taste. Your automobile must be accepted, it must speak to the customer'.

With that firmly in mind and with complete Leiding backing, Kraus and his revitalised new team completed their first 'own' car after the re-engined DKW-Audis in just 36 months, starting from scratch and spending a measly DM 33 million. 'The team was still small then, and not very clever, yet we had to get it right the first time. We would have liked to make the styling a little cooler, more refined, but the situation then was such that we couldn't embark on any experiments at all. This car *had* to succeed and be purchased by the everyday customer.' Which it was, immediately. The Audi 100 gave them a hot-selling middle-class machine, something VW had not managed on its own or through the NSU purchase, but it was only the warm-up for Kraus.

'For the Audi 80 which appeared in June 1972 we had three and a half years but it

Below *Soon Audi 100 had a coupé variant as well with minimal sheet metal change behind the doors and a shorter wheelbase to give the marque real style.*

Bottom *Their first own model and the start of the boom—the Audi 80 with Kraus' engine and compact body.*

The Audi 50 was meant to be a VW from the first but they made a fancier one for the Audi badge and launched it first, at almost the Beetle price.

wasn't parallel to the 100. There was no capacity for a second car until the 100 was well underway.

'We realised all along it might be a VW as well. Our suggestions was to do the notchback and they could do the same car with a fastback for VW. Then the whole mid-engined EA 266 story came up and our suggestion was shoved aside.

'Leiding was under terrific pressure when he first went up to Wolfsburg and he would fly down all the time to ask what I thought about this under-seat engine idea. I told him I wouldn't build it, for various reasons: the idea of smell and noise right underneath the passengers for one thing, and the construction height.

'Lotz had started that as something different, supported by Ferry Porsche and Piëch, but the first vehicle tests weren't satisfactory.

'I asked Leiding, when he took it over, what they had already spent and it was something like DM 250 million, a lot of money then. And what would it still cost? Another DM 350-400 million. I told him, for God's sake kill it now, that will be the cheapest thing. Knowing him, he would even save some of the 250 million by using the tooling elsewhere. He did manage to salvage 170 million of it. But we lost a lot of development time.

'So we revived the idea of reworking our 80 and that became the Passat. It went so fast that their Passat came out a year after the 80 and filled a hole VW badly needed.' It was this 80 which provided the engine, chassis and bodywork for a VW turnaround while its engine range also powered the best-selling Golf, a car otherwise designed by VW.

Next Leiding decided he needed a smaller car, below the Golf, and Kraus obliged with the Audi 50. 'That was ours from Ingolstadt but its engine could be used in the Golf as well. It was the last new engine we did in the 70s so it could benefit from the 80 range. And we did that 50 in the shortest time of all, just 35 months. We always had to do the next one very rapidly indeed to give Audi a programme.

'Actually the 50 was built as a VW from the first and they only decided to make it an Audi 50 afterwards and take in a little more money, even though ours appeared first.' As Kraus would say, 'if we weren't part of VW we'd be the biggest car builder in Bavaria', putting them in perspective compared to BMW just down the autobahn.

By the end of the 60s Audi as such was building 500 cars a day and exporting 40 per cent of them and soon found themselves so far behind on orders that the plant which had once used spare capacity to build Beetles turned around to have a portion of its Audi 100s built in Wolfsburg. It took them just seven years to build the first million cars after the take over in 1965.

Engines were the key to all this success, starting with the one Kraus brought from Mercedes and moving through two new lines he produced in record time at Ingolstadt, once he got the new development centre Leiding promised, in 1971. 'Before that it was just a barracks in the main plant. I made my wishes clear for this centre and it is very compact with each section backed right onto its own test beds.' The complex is popularly called 'Ludwigsburg', a pun on Kraus' first name and his imperial style. 'Burg' is German for a castle-fortress and the name was particularly apt for the domain of a man who loves Italian cathedrals, classic art and dachshunds.

Born in 1911 this true Bavarian studied in Munich, Stuttgart and Hannover, taking his masters degree in 1937 and joining Mercedes where he became head of racing car design in 1951, then boss of saloon pre-developments. The so-called 'middle-pressure' engine which gave Audi its first breathing space had been designed under Kraus' control at Mercedes and carried along to Ingolstadt where it promised near-diesel economy by using a cross-flow head with small, shaped intake passages which produced very strong swirl and allowed a compression ratio as high as 12:1, although they found noise excessive there and backed off to 11.2:1 for the first Audi 70.

Revolutions had to be held to 5,000 and it was a relatively heavy four with rods and pistons of near-diesel bulk but it produced a sturdy 72 hp and felt powerful, 'once we got it tamed', as Kraus put it. 'The drawback turned out to be an inherent limit on performance stemming from the strong swirl. Later we reduced compression to 10.3 and even 9.8 without giving up the idea entirely because it brought such very good consumption.' In the end it proved a technical side-step but it saved Audi at the time.

Once they knew Audi would be around for a while this candid man who once commented, 'nobody could design a proper car in a town atmosphere like Wolfsburg,' turned his cold eye on VW engine patterns in general. He decided the air-cooled boxer four was the best third-world engine of its day but the larger, Type 4, models were simply too expensive for the intended task.

Audi had been merged with NSU under VW by this time and Kraus recalled, 'we worked very intensively on developing the Wankel rotary engine too. We made it call-back safe with durability and consumption brought up to the point of matching a comparable six but we already doubted we would put the Wankel into all our cars. Production costs were high.

'Then we got the job of making it more powerful. There were two favoured paths on my team. One side wanted to add a third rotor while the others, whom I supported, said we could keep the Ro80 but enlarge the chambers by 50 per cent. When I retired it was still an open option.'

For the smaller, mass-production cars, however, Kraus turned instead to a long-stroke, water-cooled inline four of 1.3 and 1.5 litres, designated model 827 internally and eventually built in versions ranging from 55 to 110 hp plus a diesel, all with only minor changes. The most-used VW-Audi powerplant, it was extremely simple in layout with intake and exhaust valves on the same side and direct valve operation by cup tappets, but a lay shaft was needed to turn the alternator and oil pump. This later led directly to model 828 with five cylinders of the same design in a row, used as a petrol engine originally in both carburettor and injection modes, later as a diesel. Here the alternator was driven from the end of the overhead camshaft and the oil pump from the nose of the crankshaft, features of the second generation Kraus small engine as well.

This model 801, which only appeared after the higher numbers, was still-cheaper to build and simplified further as a clear culmination of his range. Designed for the area between 900 cc and 1.3 litres it first went into the Audi 50/VW Polo but was later the basis for a Golf/Passat base engine as well. Compactness was their prime consideration here since it was first used in a transverse position. Along with the crankshaft-driven oil pump and cam-driven alternator it used the camshaft belt to turn the water pump. 801 even had a cross-flow head, to the delight of tuners, and a smaller stroke than bore although rockers were used between cam and valve stem.

Finally, this engine family was expanded by the 831, used in fewest VW-Audi models but sold in short-block form to American Motors for their Gremlin. Originally AMC was to buy its tooling as well, for far less than designing a whole new engine would cost, while VW could have taken over excess US plant capacity, but this arrangement was never carried through. At home the 831 powers their LT 28 light van and is the basis for the Porsche 924 where it produces up to 170 hp with a new head and turbocharging. Another version goes into the Iltis.

Audi is clearly committed to turbocharging as well, with the Audi 200 for the 80s, a blown five in an extended, second-generation Audi 100 chassis. Both the firm's diesels and the 2+2 VW Scirocco using an Audi-based engine, were in line for supercharging as well.

Original model policy at Audi was a middle position between VW and Mercedes which paralleled their ownership situation at first. Then they took up the slack for VW although Wolfsburg originally kept the dealer networks apart to protect its 411/412 from the Audi 100. Soon the Audi branch was up to fourth in Germany, ahead of Mercedes in sales and right behind parent VW in 1973, when Wolfsburg had fallen behind Opel temporarily. Kraus explained, 'our philosophy was to build cars for people who liked to drive (he had tested the Mercedes racers himself). The high proportion of real-road testing here is part of that development objective, which always comes to a team from the philosophy of its boss'.

Given such feelings the original Audi 100—he refers to the middle-pressure models as his bastards—quite naturally became known for fine ride over bad roads and forgiving handling. It had more wheelbase than the interim model and 80, 90 or 100 hp, while the 100 S could even outrun a BMW, no small part of its reason for being, although the engine became raw when used that hard. In direct comparisons the 100 LS was usually second only to a Mercedes, justifiably claiming half of all Audi sales in its first year. They soon expanded the line with a two-door model and an engine using normal petrol, as well as an automatic option. The first 100 was a clear winner over either the K70 taken over from NSU or the Wolfsburg Type 4. Its final fling was a coupé achieved by removing 11.5 cm/4.5 in from the wheelbase and turning the tail into a fastback while the engine was enlarged to 1,871 cc and 115 hp. This machine would touch 185 kph/115 mph and gave them new panache with a minimum of body panel change.

Since the original Audi 100 had been such a clear middle-class favourite, its successor was among the most eagerly-awaited cars of 1976 and it fortunately lived up to most hopes, a worthwhile replacement for the 800,000 Audi sold of their first 100. Despite the same number, this second-generation 100 was longer, wider and lower and looked a class larger. Called the 5000 for America the new Audi 100 had a drag factor of only 0.39 just as aerodynamics became a key selling point.

The new 100 attracted even more attention for its optional, inline, five-cylinder petrol engine, once their new board member for technical development took over. Ferdinand

Above left *Without Kraus from Daimler Benz neither Audi nor VW would have been in nearly as good condition when they had to turn out top-selling new water-cooled models in a hurry.*

Above right *Kraus' successor as head of all Audi development is Ferdinand Piëch, grandson of Professor Porsche, son of Louise who is sister to Ferry. At Porsche he did the 917 racers and the under-seat-engine VW prototype killed by Leiding. Now he is key technical man at Audi.*

Piëch notes, 'the idea of a five didn't even exist when I arrived—in August 1972—but I had considered the possibility when I was a consultant to Mercedes and we did an investigation of truck engines for Algeria. A five came up which was superior to comparable fours where installation costs might dictate a compromise between low noise and cost on one hand, low consumption on the other.

'Acoustics were the greatest problem. Our Audi 5 ran up to 4,700 with no trouble from the first but was loud above that. For production we had to move the loud range beyond the rpm range to be used.

'It really is an engine of its own, not a four plus another cylinder. We had to stiffen the engine and gearbox case as a unit, ribbing them to a level not used before. The injection version came before the carburettor model because it took longer to work out the manifold balance.

'But we are completely happy with the five now. We sought more comfort than the four without getting into the consumption realms of a six. Today we have the quiet of the six and the thirst of a four—that was the basic premise of a five from the first.'

A year after the second 100 appeared the range was expanded by another Piëch idea, the Avant. There would be no coupé in the second generation. Instead the Avant was a hatchback saloon, 9 cm/3.6 in shorter and graced with special cargo-carrying touches including a bag which can be pulled out of the rear seat back to carry skis from the boot to between the front seats without losing its four-seater saloon qualities. The Avant was also a marketing surprise. Up to then VW built the fastbacks, Audi the three-box designs. Henceforth Ingolstadt would seek its own niche as the noble yet sporting marque with modest luxury pretensions. The 200 underlined that as the turbocharged 5T flagship at Audi.

Once the 100 had been moved slightly up-market, Audi brought out a second-generation 80 as well. It, too, was somewhat larger than either the previous car or the VW Passat and looked very much like their 100. In America this became the 4000 whereas the original Audi 80 had been called the Fox in the US. That perky fox-head emblem quickly became a favourite of Audi managers in Germany for their company cars.

Despite its solid appearance the new 80 weighed only 850 kg/1,875 lb. Kraus believed, and Piëch agrees, that practical front-drive cars should be held to around 1,200 kg/2,650 lb or less with weight distribution of approximately 60/40 for best handling. All the Audi designs since Kraus have been notable for meeting safety standards with a minimum of weight, thanks to finite element design. As for handling, Audi also became a proponent of negative scrub radius where the car remains stable even if one front wheel hits a slippery patch. As a bonus, this allows them to split the two brake circuits diagonally so that partial failure always leaves a braked wheel at either end.

The original Audi 80 sold 700,000 cars, including their 110 hp GTE which captured the attention of rally drivers since the works was willing to support them, and lasted four years with the new Audi 80—identified by an extra side window behind the C-pillar—appearing in 1977. It was larger but also quieter and better in aerodynamics which meant lower consumption.

While the 100 and 80 went through two generations each, the little 50 which did so well initially was allowed to fall behind VW's Polo. Styled by Kraus with Bertone help it was always more than a 'smaller Golf' and probably the best of the Audi line-up from a

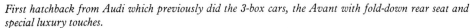

First hatchback from Audi which previously did the 3-box cars, the Avant with fold-down rear seat and special luxury touches.

The car of 1980—the Audi 200 Turbo. The turbo-charging enables the 2.2 litre five-cylinder fuel injection engine to develop considerably higher output. Acceleration is from 0 to 100 km/h (62 mph) in 8.7 seconds; the top speed is 202 km/h (125 mph).

technical standpoint. Car prices had soared before the Golf could appear so the 50/Polo actually became their two-door Beetle replacement. Shorter overall by 21.5 cm/8.5 in, it had far more interior room than the Beetle and a hatch at the back. It was also lightest in its class at 665 kg/1,460 lb. The 50 was phased out after a four-year run. Under Piëch the firm was not actually moving away from the 'building block' principle, but they were taking pains that the common parts would be less obvious.

The man who took over Audi development from Kraus is less effervescent but just as self-confident. Ferdinand Piëch does not feel personally that his engineering bent came directly from his famous grandfather but he is probably the one man of his Porsche/Piëch generation who shows the same initiative and originality in design. Born in Vienna, Piëch had an early interest in rockets and aeronautics. He received his Master's in engineering after eight semesters at the technical university in Zurich, before joining Porsche in 1963. His father had died when the boy was young, his mother not only built VW-Austria into a firm with greater turnover than her brother's Porsche plant, but was a director there as well.

Young Piëch was one of half a dozen from his generation who arrived in different departments of Porsche at more or less the same time. His talents ran from engine testing to racing design, right through that 12-cylinder 917 which swept the world's racing circuits as the 70s opened. He was also responsible for the EA 266 project at Porsche. By 1971, however, the crop of Porsche grandsons realised that there were too many cousins for any one firm and went their various ways. For Ferdinand Piëch this meant half a year as consultant to Mercedes then Audi in 1972, first as head of testing, then as development chief, including VW engines, and by 1975 he was the youngest member of a car-building board in Germany, joining Audi's at 38. His preferences continue to be black cars, motorcycles, American station wagons and a restored Austro Daimler from his grandfather's early era.

The Audi 80 engine which then powered the Passat and Golf at VW as well as the smaller Audi 100.

Like old Porsche, Piëch is a great fan of America as well, 'It pleases me, even after two-score trips. It is an unbelievably interesting car land and one of the world's test markets. America accepts and discards new things far more quickly than other lands so it is very important for Audi to see how the US takes to one of our new cars. Feelings of American customers have taught us many things about later reactions in Europe.'

While few believed that Fiala in Wolfsburg would ever permit a 'Ludwig II' to come out of Ingolstadt, Piëch can say, 'within the framework of a common marketing plan we have completely free design range for the given sum of money. I know of no case where a suggestion which fitted the cost requirements wasn't accepted'. To generate such suggestions he established a technical strategy committee which happens to be made up largely of men in their 40s and is spread into both the development and marketing realms—with the final word resting in its chairman, Ferdinand Piëch.

That is a key reason Audi still does a great deal of its product testing on the open road. Kraus could say 'we build cars which please us', and add that chassis tuning on them was performed in dashes through the nearby Bavarian woods, since Ingolstadt does not have a proper test facility like Ehra. Piëch does not even particularly want one, favouring tropic testing in the summer Sahara and winter runs through Lapland. 'My colleages say it is a disadvantage, not having a track, but I say it is an advantage. Hard-won results are the better ones.

'In my Porsche days we went to the Sahara or the alps but Audi must take far more cars and men. We can't depend on snow in the alps far enough ahead. We found a spot on the Arctic Circle that is always cold. My philosophy is that a car which functioned in the hottest and coldest spots we could find should give few problems to any customer.'

This dedication to winter tests led, in 1980, to a limited-edition Audi Quattro which solved problems that 99 per cent of their customers had not even recognised. Using a coupé body which would appear later with quite normal engines and chassis from their 80/100 line-up, this was a rally special with designs as well on anybody living near an alp.

Audi's technological breakthrough for the 80s, underlining their devotion to design and cars for keen drivers, was the Quattro Coupé which combined a turbocharged, five-cylinder engine from their largest saloon with the basic chassis of their 80 and the then-latest four-wheel drive system which actually reduced rolling resistance while greatly increasing traction on poor surfaces.

It combined the turbocharged five of their 200 T with a 1,290 kg/2,845 lb package trimmed with spoilers, bucket seats and fat tyres. The Quattro name tipped their key feature, however; full-time four-wheel drive with rear and/or central differential locks at the driver's command. Audi discovered from an American study that driven wheels have less rolling resistance than non-powered ones. Using four-wheel drive technology a step beyond their Iltis (differential fitted within the gearbox output shaft), they achieved four-wheel drive with a drag penalty of less than 3 per cent—to produce a sports car which can accelerate without spinning its summer tyres on an icy surface.

Ironically enough, these cars from keen drivers are now built in the first German city which closed its central area to private traffic. But their dedication has been widely honoured, Audi is the only three-time winner of Germany's prestigious Golden Steering Wheel award so they can look forward to continued semi-independence of VW. Yet they do not sell a single car directly to a buyer. Since 1979 Audis have been sold (on paper) to VAG, a new, common marketing combine which then handles retail sales. And their board chairman is also on the VW board.

By the end of the 70s Audi-NSU production had risen to some 350,000 special cars each year which gave them around 10 per cent of the German market. But their biggest headlines came when chairman Habbel announced there were no further plans to build a rotary-powered Audi or NSU despite long and only semi-private tests of the larger Wankel engine under both Kraus and Piëch.

They did not want to publicly discredit an engine which they still license—chiefly to Japan—but simply were not enthusiastic enough, despite a technical rating of 'superb' for the larger version. Piëch adds, 'we will continue development on the Wankel but decided not to put it into production at this time. It does have potential which hasn't been completely explored but there is a cost limit at the moment'. This revolutionary power plant came into the family as part of the NSU dowry, after all, and was not an Ingolstadt design.

⋆ ⋆ ⋆

Direct NSU contributions to Volkswagen, and thus to Audi, amounted to two models, one immediately appropriated by Wolfsburg, the other sold as an NSU for some time after the takeover. In addition, the Neckarsulm firm continued to sell its own previous line of small, sporty, rear-engined cars for several years. These enjoyed great success in countries like Italy.

NSU history traces back to the first production motorcycle, built in 1901, followed by records and racing fame for their (often-supercharged) two-wheel machines in the 30s. As the largest motorcycle builder in the world during the 50s, NSU had toyed with car production before; just before the first war, then with a Porsche prototype before the KdF and finally when they became Germany's smallest car builder in the late 50s.

Their uniquely symmetrical Prinz, powered by an air-cooled twin in its tail, sold 100,000, surprising even NSU. The Prinz 4, introduced in 1961, also sold well for over a decade and led to the Prinz 1000 with four cylinders in a row across the tail, the longer-wheelbase model 110, and the racey 1000 cc TT which ruled small-bore racing and hill-climbs. Funds never quite stretched to total development of any of them, however.

Meanwhile the rotary engine had fascinated them since 1954, well before Lotz became enamoured of the idea. The new VW manager was equally interested in acquiring in-house competition for Wolfsburg in 1969 and NSU was on the verge of releasing its first full-size, conventional car, the K70, so a stock battle was joined. NSU shares naturally climbed when VW interest became known although the picture was confused initially when Fiat bought 10 per cent of NSU from Citroën and tried for a full quarter of the stock.

Eventually the firm of Audi NSU Auto Union AG was put together with VW holding 59.5 per cent, NSU the rest. It nearly doubled NSU capitalisation yet share holders there fought bitterly to defeat this sale which marked the first merger of two 'healthy' firms in post-war Germany. NSU people argued this handed Volkswagen a car programme ranging from 0.6 to 1.7 litres worth even more than the Wankel access. VW replied that fresh capital would lift Audi-NSU to third rank in Germany. During a last-ditch, 12 hour meeting NSU bosses were roundly condemned for supporting this take over while a VW man, present unofficially behind a curtain, was not allowed to make any reply, not even when his 411 was called an unmitigated disaster. NSU clearly felt they were saving VW.

The deal was made anyway, in 1969, only to have resentment flare anew that Christmas when VW skipped the message to its NSU share holders and suggested a 5 per cent dividend rather than the expected 8 per cent. Wolfsburg was busily tying up loose shares including a block from one German bank to achieve three-quarter ownership of NSU in short order, squelching further debate. This did not quiet certain diehards who used phrases as strong as 'half-criminal' when they discovered a secret clause which would bill NSU for VW technology, via a previous VW-Audi agreement. Wolfsburg had attached NSU directly to Audi rather than VW. On the side, VW assured one and all that financial backing for the NSU-Citroën Comotor project to build Wankel engines would continue, at least into 1970. Much was said about a middle-class, rotary-powered car from the new Comotor plant for 1972.

All this uproar came just as NSU delivered the one millionth car built since 1958 and made sure it would be a Ro80 in honour of this Wankel-engined saloon passing the 1970 California emissions test. The Ro carried on as an NSU against a background of rumours that VW and Fiat would now collaborate through their common Citroën interests, but this was flatly denied.

Lotz did seem to have an idea he could build a VW-controlled car group first, then move on to an inner-German consortium based on his technical ties at that time with

Daimler Benz, through Audi. A 'General German Motors' may have been in the back of his mind. And Mercedes did hold a Wankel licence as well.

Actually that Ro80 which formed the pivot of so many such rumours was not the first Wankel-powered NSU. It had been their Spider, a small-scale, public test bed with single-rotor engine. The story went that NSU had hastened it on to a limited market to avoid having their Japanese licensee bring out the first Wankel car. Customers for the tiny, two-seat convertible were willing to play tester since the firm was extremely generous about replacements as they gathered road experience.

The baby Spider was light enough to make 50 hp seem ample without rotary consumption becoming obvious. Power was decent above 4,000 rpm from a totally smooth engine which gladly revved to 8,500, or even higher if wear was not a consideration. Top speed of 150 kph/90 mph was more than respectable for a one-litre machine, which was the class finally decided upon, although NSU insisted it was really only a 500. At that capacity the 11 l/100 km (25.6 mpg) fuel consumption was less impressive. It all depended on whether you counted only one of the three chambers, since only one had a spark plug and thus combustion, took all three for the engine size or compromised on two thirds of the overall housing volume which became the accepted standard.

Early Spiders used large amounts of oil and ran their one plug so hot they could hardly be restarted. The author only won an index trophy in a minor rally with one of the first Spiders to compete because his co-driving wife pushed the car for hundreds of yards when its hot engine happened to die. This was pioneer motoring once again but it caught the public fancy. NSU stock shot up 200 points in May 1966 on the basis of no more than Wankel rumours, before VW was officially involved.

NSU engineers under firm Wankel advocate Frohde—who had been one of the young engineer-observers for those 1936 Beetle tests incidentally—were already running the first dual-rotor engines with the trochoidal rotors offset 60 degrees to one-another. They claimed that two rotors equalled four cylinders and sought low-rpm torque from 110 hp development engines, using a front-drive DKW Munga jeep as their mobile test bed. This early engine would idle at 700 rpm without oiling its plug and produced maximum torque at 3,000 rpm, both considerable improvements over the Spider. Since their Munga only used low and top gears engineers did not bother to deny some sort of two-pedal operation was planned. The early engine with cast iron housings to put some weight on the wheels weighed all of 100 kg/245 lb, compared to 70 kg/155 lb for an all-alloy Wankel. They still favoured a single plug and side-draught carburettor, admitting consumption ran 10-15 per cent above a normal two litre engine—but so did output. Later Spiders used a one-rotor version of this engine to give dealers early training.

NSU now felt they had a mature engine, one which could safely carry the firm's reputation for adventurous engineering on to the public roads. The 1967 Frankfurt motor show was picked for the debut of the world's first automobile designed solely for rotary power, the immediately-legendary Ro80 which was uncannily quiet at 4,000 rpm, even quieter at 7,000, yet it would touch 160 kph/100 mph at only 5,500 rpm.

The original Ro came with selective-automatic gearbox with two pedals and the micro-

Top left *The end of the Wankel line for NSU was the short-lived co-operative venture with Citroën to make joint cars through the Comotor plant. Citroën first put an engine into the M35 which was merely another tail on the Ami 6, then into the GS Birotor, but with VW showing little interest and fuel economy a Wankel problem, this ended all interest.*

Centre left and left *Start of the whole Wankel rotary era—the NSU Spider with single rotor engine in the tail which led to two rotors, first tried secretly in the Munga.*

The famous NSU Ro80 which was everybody's car of the year on launch but not nearly as reliable as hoped despite very advanced body design as well as revolutionary engine.

sensor in the gear knob. A torque converter in the power train was vital to acceptably smooth operation at lower revs. 115 hp from twice-497.5 cc (nominal) gave the car a top speed of 180 kph/112 mph. The pronounced wedge of its body, designed by Claus Luthe of NSU, had an outstanding drag co-efficient of only 0.355 and would have been an excellent package with any engine. The chassis was sporting, right down to four-wheel disc brakes, and there was virtually no front-drive feedback in the steering. Inside space outdid all competitors. European motoring journalists promptly and near-unanimously named this Ro80 car of the year for 1967/68.

Felix Wankel, a cut-and-try engineering maverick, had been working on his rotary piston obsession since 1920 and first co-operated with NSU on a Wankel supercharger for that firm's record-breaking motorcycles. From there it seemed a logical, if highly courageous, step to a different looking automobile with a totally different power plant, but they simply lacked the development funds or capacity to finish maturing a fine idea.

It proved a sales disaster with first whispers of sealing problems already evident in 1968. The standing joke among Ro drivers was to hold up as many fingers as their car had consumed engines. NSU was extremely liberal about replacements again, two-thirds in the first 18 months, before they realised that many of these new engines were not even necessary. Dealers who simply did not understand it—their network then came largely from two-wheel and mini-car mechanics—simply swapped an engine when adjustment would have served, blackening the Ro80 name unnecessarily.

There was rapid tip seal and housing wear at first because it was the wrong car for the everyday driver. The Ro was fine for high-speed cruising but all wrong for many cold starts and short city trips. By 1970 they were using ferrotic seals which lasted longer—but tended to cause chatter marks in the housing. There was also carbon build-up if the engine was not revved up periodically like a sports car power unit, while others, too impressed by its effortless revving ability, also ruined engines by going thousands of rpm over the limit.

The first official changes came in 1970, after VW took over, while rumours were already thick about the 160 hp, three-rotor version. By this time licence holders like Mercedes were making no special secret of their disappointment with the concept, which naturally cast doubt on the Wankel as such. Most of the newer Ro80s would even potter around town without bother but the damage to their name had already been done. VW management never promised to continue forever, although their own board clearly preferred the Ro80 as a company car, one reason they built them in hand-work numbers as long as they did.

The Comotor project had peaked back in 1970 when the French side built 500 M35 test cars which amounted to a sloping tail on their Ami 6 chassis, with single-rotor engines of 49 hp. Selected everyday customers tested these further but they were actually the end of a line, not pre-production cars.

Early dreams of meeting new emission standards more easily with a Wankel gave way in the face of more stringent numbers and a 'gas-guzzler' image did the car no good during the 1973/74 fuel crisis. 1972 proved the last good Ro80 year with production up 14 per cent but they were still improving it as late as 1975. It turned out that VW had cancelled tooling for a new generation as early as 1973, since they would not actually have direct Wankel rights until the 80s and a rotary-engined Audi would only increase royalties to NSU share holders.

Project 871, funded by VW, was the larger-rotor engine Kraus favoured, in an Audi 100 body. NSU engineers were still testing all possible permutations of side and/or peripheral ports, pointing out it took 75 years to get a diesel accepted in the saloon world. Twenty such engines were fitted to Audis for long-term assessment, still using an automatic gearbox. These cars would touch 200 kph/125 mph with the consumption of a normal 3-litre engine and had passed 1981 California emission tests before the project was finally dropped. Cold economics killed it. Tooling for an entirely new sort of engine would have cost DM 100 million while they could have equal performance by turbocharging the existing, inline five and nearly the same smoothness for a third the price. Those outside the Wankel club had called this engine the answer to a question nobody asked and Nordhoff once dubbed it a stillborn child.

Daily production of six cars, versus the 70 once planned, could not meet such criticism. Habbel flew to Japan personally in 1979 to tell Mazda they would be going the rotary route alone, followed by a public announcement that Audi was finally ending direct model research. The Japanese, who had built over a million rotary-powered cars, were delighted to have the field to themselves.

The final gasp came from an association to further Wankel engines which announced its 150 members were furious. They insisted VW made only mistakes; in development, licensing and promotion, and called for the board to resign. That ignored the fact that VW now held 99 per cent of Audi-NSU shares and was headed by a pure money man in 1979. At that, the Ro80 survived longer as a VW product than Lotz's other reason for buying NSU back in 1969. Even then, many had questioned the business sense of acquiring the imminent K70 with its 1.7 litre engine so close to their own 411. Actually that was just what Lotz wanted, internal competition; which was a lot to expect of this K70, interesting as it first seemed.

NSU had spent three years on the model, announced pre-release press drives, and booked space at the 1969 Geneva motor show to present it to the world when VW took over. The K70 soon became the most publicised non-car in Europe. Its features were front-wheel drive, a 270 cm/106.4 in wheelbase, which gave more interior space than many larger models, plus a big boot and a sporting, single-cam, water-cooled four projected for 90 hp to give the car a true 160 kph/100 mph top speed. This engine was closer to their inline, air-cooled four than first appeared since NSU did not have the funds for a complete new powerplant. VW, on the other hand, spent twice the original NSU budget merely preparing the car further for large-number production in that new Salzgitter plant which could turn out up to 400 a day.

Lotz declared they had nothing against water cooling or driven front wheels and proved it by fitting a VW emblem to the grille while retaining the K70 name to cash in on all the publicity. VW also discovered the NSU claim of aerodynamics nearly as good as a Ro was dubious at best and the supposed C_d of 0.41 came out more like 0.51 in the Wolfsburg tunnel. The chassis was very like the Ro80 and NSU had certainly planned to fit a rotary to the K70 later as well, but VW preferred to apply fuel injection to the cross-flow four.

By the car's second debut, at Paris in the autumn of 1970, threats by NSU fans to rip off those VW badges had died down. A plain, 75 hp, model was added to the 90 hp version since they now knew it would be a costly car to build. Even at a price between the 411 and Audi 100, VW made no more than DM 33 per car. A K70 S was added in 1973 with 1,806 cc and an even 100 hp at a lower, 5,300 rpm, figure. Their claimed acceleration equalled the VW-Porsche 914 but top speed was only 4 kph/2.5 mph better.

No German car since the first Beetle had been so thoroughly praised before production—nor so quickly disparaged immediately afterwards. Probably no automobile could live up to a 'wonder car' title in the real world, particularly when early tests uncovered many small design flaws. Worst was the barn-door shape which pushed fuel consumption way up. K70 production remained so low it was never logical to use its engine elsewhere in the line-up and its production costs were a strong reason for Lotz's departure in 1971. Thereafter the Audi technological inputs which he exploited so well for VW were used even more thoroughly by his successor, as were many NSU lessons.

Rudolf Leiding was a production man with a known predilection for the Wankel and he moved into the top VW job directly from Audi-NSU, with a natural tendency to favour projects from his previous branch. It was this man who led VW into the 70s, their first decade of water-cooled powerplants and front-wheel drive which had both come from the branches. It was a near-total but necessary turnaround in Volkswagen engineering philosophy yet he too would be gone from the Wolfsburg stage before all these measures were fully accomplished.

Chapter 11

Rudolf Leiding: technical turnaround

The Rudolf Leiding era at Volkswagen had many features which paralleled the preceeding Lotz regime. Leiding also took over on relatively short notice and in the midst of a crisis. In fact, he was even further down the dead-end road of an obsolete model situation which had first faced Lotz, but due to the work already in progress, Leiding at least moved on to the 13th floor at Wolfsburg when fresh cars were in sight. He would receive popular credit for new cars which had actually originated under Lotz. And Leiding would also receive much of the blame for excessive investments—but neither of these factors were foreseen in October 1971 when his first and toughest decisions had to be made immediately.

At the last minute Lotz moved to retain his position by proposing Leiding as vice-chairman for new models and technology—and five years later, hindsight would suggest this might have been a very viable solution. In 1971, however, Rudolf Leiding declined to play number two. He got the top spot instead, along with a rise which left the director's salary about half way between Nordhoff's and Lotz's, plus headaches of equal size.

This new director had first joined VW immediately after the war and moved to second in command of their service department after 13 loyal years. Nordhoff then put him in charge of their Kassel plant in 1958. Leiding moved on to Auto Union for the first time in 1965 and put that faltering firm into the black by 1967, when VW do Brazil needed rescuing. Sales there had sunk to a mere two-thirds of the market, from over 80 per cent, and the first head, Schultz-Wenk a long-time Nordhoff friend, had died. Leiding accepted the South American post and soon produced their millionth Beetle.

His next 'fireman' assignment was Ingolstadt again. Designs were now fine but unit costs excessive, and Leiding was a production specialist above all. Aided by Kraus' new engines he turned Audi-NSU, as Auto Union was now called, around, then completed his accelerated climb through the VW ranks by taking the top job of all. By then he had a well-established reputation as a tough manager, a man without scruple when personnel failed to produce. At first he seemed tame as a lamb in Wolfsburg but it did not last and word went out that the only paper this new boss might sign was somebody's release—including two for a board which was not destined to get along much better with its third director than it had with the second. This one thrived on crisis, as a matter of fact, and benefited from a variety of new models which appeared in his years with a richness never before known around VW.

That first year was also marked by a startling DM 1.2 billion in investments for 1972, the very year Opel men would flaunt '1' pins symbolic of the first time VW had been toppled from the home-market throne. Wolfsburg products were down by 20 per cent although Audi-NSU sales were up and adding DM 100 to the price of each Beetle for advertising alone (triple the 1971 figure) was only a stopgap.

Leiding would literally pour money into his new generation throughout the first half of

Left *Rudolf Leiding.*

Below right *When soaring prices made the Golf far more expensive than a Beetle, VW brought in the Polo (Audi 50) as a pure two-three door model with the most basic trim. It remains their bottom-line model.*

the 70s, racing to break even before Beetle sales faded away entirely. It was now common knowledge that Volkswagen was truly deep into a 'make or break' crisis after 30 years of one model, but Leiding had plans. He was more than tough enough to deal with the trauma which came from following technical trends after three decades of leading them. Followers could benefit from all previous mistakes, after all, and set the new benchmark.

When the Audi 80 appeared in July 1972 it seemed that he might win the race, particularly when it was followed in less than a year by the Passat with VW badges. But that was also the year of the first oil shock, before VW had sufficient low-price, minimal-thirst models. 1974 sales were badly depressed—minus 20 per cent at home, down a third in the US—while Leiding pressed forward.

The Scirocco sports coupé came in March 1974 as a stalking horse for the key model of them all, the one new VW with no direct Audi chassis as forerunner, the Golf which came just two months after its own sports car variant. That same September there was a baby Audi 50 as well, with the Polo version out by June of 1975. He had indeed blanketed the VW market.

Leiding needed that Golf—Rabbit to the Americans—most of all because one of his very first moves on taking over had been to axe the Piëch-designed EA 266 with its under-seat engine. Today Porsche says the project was halted, literally on the verge of launch, because it did not fit into the Audi-powered building-block system. This is true in some measure. The most persistent tale at that time was simply that nobody could build a car of such sophistication for the price they would have to sell one for.

Porsche engineers, led by the same Ferdinand Piëch who later replaced Kraus as head of Audi technology, had not flinched in the face of futuristic design. The chassis was relatively standard with lower wishbones and spring legs at the front, angled trailing arms at the back and boots at both ends. But engine location was unique—a water-cooled four with chain-driven single-overhead cam and hydraulic tappets rode flat on its side under the rear seat. Its cool air would enter through one rear wheel arch and exit through the other. This was nothing less than the mid-engined ideal in a small, 4-5 seater saloon.

Spy photos showed a low waist-line and the centre of gravity was low but they had considerable styling trouble with the tall tail which came from passengers sitting above the engine. A necessarily quiet power plant with low service requirements was conceived in sizes ranging from 800 to 1,800 cc while initial models would fall in the 60-105 hp range, to be priced between the Beetle and Type 3. With low polar moment of inertia this saloon handled much like a boxer 914, while two-seater and 2+2 coupé versions were also on test, the latter looking rather like Leiding's Brazilian coupé.

Yet Leiding was the man who stopped five years of intensive work here within three weeks of moving to Wolfsburg. Porsche was ordered to scrap every single prototype and used most of them as victims of their tank-testing programme. However one, if not more, apparently escaped the military crusher-treads although the whole memory was still too raw at the end of the 70s for any of those to reappear. The net result was a rush to the Golf as their mass sales model, although soaring prices generally soon forced Leiding to deny this had ever been seen as a Beetle replacement.

By the spring of 1974 they had to admit that downsizing must continue (imminent Polo) to the sub-one litre class, to find a car of near-Beetle price. Leiding insisted, 'our cars *can't* get any more expensive', yet prices were increased twice in the first half of 1974 alone, and a third time that August, as VW shares tumbled. This would be the first year of an actual overall loss in VW history, due, of course, in part to the vast sums it cost to produce six new cars in barely two years.

Small wonder they hardly bothered to even discuss project 425 either. That would have replaced the 914 but sports cars were not his main problem any more. Leiding complained, with some justice, that the same people who insisted VW was far too stolid before, now told him it had become too mobile. He did not add that some of the carpers were on his own skittish board, answering only that the world demanded a wide choice. In fact they had just entered into a joint programme for electric-powered prototypes and had ample plans; merely little capital and no time.

As a production man Leiding also realised Germany was becoming prohibitively expensive in world wage terms, just as Nixon applied strictures which favoured US-built cars by some 6 per cent in price. VW carried most of that burden when every *pfennig* drop in the DM:dollar exchange rate cost Wolfsburg DM 25 million a year. German labour had received an 11 per cent rise in 1973 and now cost more than American, once holiday and social benefits were included. Before long representatives from half the states in America had visited VW, seeking the only-rumoured US Volkswagen plant for their own areas. Brazil now built 500 engine/gearbox units daily for German cars and Mexico shipped thousands of parts 'back home' every working day.

VW would discuss plants in any land 'where the people still go barefoot', as Leiding phrased it. CKD assembly reached Yugoslavia in the autumn of 1973 with a goal of 10,000 per year, Nigeria was on the verge of building VWs and the Rumanian premier made a quiet trip to Wolfsburg to discuss a 'car of the middle-70s' which meant the Polo. They even worked out the name Dja-Ko-Tschung (armoured shell insect) for possible Beetles for China, to be delivered from Mexico.

Some of these plans were later launched, others such as America fell foul of Leiding's less than cordial union relationships in an era when Germany's overall economic picture was bleaker than its workers liked. Production in pivotal 1974 ran roughly 54 per cent Beetle/46 per cent Passat in Wolfsburg for January, while the VW town would build its last of 11 million Beetles by July 1, only a year after taking three-page ads to push this model. By the end of 1974 production had swung to 69 per cent Golf and 20/11 per cent for the Audi 50/Passat plus the 1,200 Beetles Emden still built, and 300 cars from Hannover, 500 from Brussels.

Computer lines for the Golf replaced their Beetle merry-go-rounds, meaning VW was forced to borrow heavily to update at the very time Datsun snatched number one in San Diego, California. It had not helped when VW failed its first California emissions test (it was later reprieved) and those 10,000 Volkswagens sold in Japan hardly balanced their US losses to the eastern builders. One brief bright spot at this time was Great Britain where VW became the first import to reach 50,000 units, 60 per cent of those Beetles, shortly before they also lost this leading rank to Renault.

At home the economic decline was serious enough that some VW dealers even threatened to shift to Toyota and sales boss Hahn was out. In 1974-75 the firm had half a million unsold VWs on hand around the world and no guarantee they would even meet the payroll regularly in 1975. By the time Leiding retired losses were close to DM 807 million, horrendous for a firm accustomed to think profit was its divine right. They were now burdened by well over 200,000 employees, few of whom could be conveniently laid off although personnel were now watched closely for good performance and up to 49 dropped 'for cause' each month—50 or more would have meant a clash with the works council. As early as 1972 any worker willing to leave on his own received a month's pay, as well as his coming holiday and Christmas bonuses, but that had only appealed to about 4,000. Even foremen who retired—some up to two years early with full benefits—were not replaced at this time.

More was at stake at Volkswagen than was the case at Ford or Opel with their multi-national backing. Furthermore, Wolfsburg had to contend with state and national government on its own board, politically motivated members unable to face necessary manpower cuts. The unions were close to panic by late 1974 as some plants closed for weeks at a time in Germany, after all the boom years.

Leiding's *détente* with the union bosses had not improved when he went directly to the men on a wage matter. When a new chairman now took over the supervisory board in November 1974 the director's plans for an American plant were turned down flat. The argument went that US sales were up slightly and the 412 'doing very well there', despite the first major VW of America recall (for brakes). Nonetheless, their one-time 'saviour' now retired 'for reasons of health' at the end of 1974 just as he could predict, quite correctly, that 1975 sales would be up again, at last. By the time Leiding stepped down a third 'crown prince'—this time a man actually named Prinz—was out as well so the new director would again come from outside Wolfsburg.

At the mid-point of the 70s Volkswagen had been to the precipice and recovered. Total production of all types had just passed the 25-million mark only 20 years after they built the first million, and an awareness was growing that they would have to market more intensively, a field largely ignored in the classic sense for many years.

Nordhoff firmly believed customers were out there to buy what he chose to produce. The best descriptions marketing men could find for the Beetle were that it was a 'real' car in the 50s, a 'logical' one two decades later. The idea of a single car, 'because it is good for you' had suited Nordhoff's grey eminence perfectly—he was PR man Frank Novotny, who was on the board until 1969. Then came Lotz, a general merchandiser but not a car man, one who could only theorise what car fans might prefer.

Wolfsburg next tried Leiding, a pure production specialist with little time for the esoterics of marketing. He cut overheads, launched new models left in limbo far too long and even ignored that oft-rumoured 'deal' between Nordhoff and Flick (assuming it ever existed): VW would remain below two litres if Mercedes stayed above that size. Leiding left it to any marketing men around to try and sell outdated cars until he could get something new built.

This led to interim eruptions such as the black and yellow 'sports' Beetle which merely annoyed Bonn by pushing performance at the wrong time. Somebody did survey the VW family at least, finding that 80-90 per cent were male and averaged 42 years old. Only 10 per cent had university-level schooling and their interests were spread about evenly over all the cars VW then built. Rational purchase sold more Beetles than trends. Outside Germany there was even less idea of what constituted the typical VW fan so they could only wonder why their cars fell to third in Switzerland after 20 years in first place. Management reacted by blaming all directors, past or present, but not those projects the board had also approved.

Once the 266 project was dumped, Leiding was left with water cooling and front-wheel drive which turned out very well but the cars available to him in the early 70s meant *de facto* abandonment of the cheapest market segment to foreign competitors. These shifts and stutters in the planning were widely discussed around the company town, leaving workers suspended between real fear that their sole local industry would close—as it very nearly did—and the smug certainty they were still the chosen among car men.

Wolfsburg itself had passed the 130,000 population mark by absorbing surrounding villages when its own land ran out. There was a theatre for touring companies, a music school and even a 'proper hotel' by 1973. Through all the years before a VW Guest House next to the director's villa had been adequate for those few who stayed a night in town. Five years later the one general hotel was habitually booked solid. This overly-organised, somewhat dowdy town was slowly turning into a place one might be from after all. Original workers who still related Porsche stories after three decades and would have considered a strike against VW sacrilege, had given way to a generation which came to work, to buy new cars at the rate of one for every three inhabitants, and not to strike against a firm which hired almost everybody in town.

But these too were being replaced by the first true generation of born Wolfsburgers, leavened by the flood of 'guest workers,' largely Italian at first in an unconscious replay of the 30s. This second latin wave prompted the factory canteens to offer pasta and red wine for lunch—only to have it snapped up by their German workers while the Italians preferred most of the 1,100 km/680 miles of sausage consumed in 25 canteens each month, washed down by beer. Of course you might still find the odd city-owned dustbin marked 'Stadt der KdF' as late as the early 70s but that boss up on the 13th floor no longer monitored speeding on the main street or admonished a worker who might dare to buy another marque. Wolfsburg was slowly growing up, just as those new models, so incomprehensible to the original labour group, began to dominate its car parks.

Certain privilege had even begun to creep into housing with some of those identical

VW Passat, the Giugiaro fast-back tail on the Audi 80, with more changes than the common chassis/ engine would suggest. This was the first new-generation VW introduced, right after the 80.

suburbs becoming clearly more equal than others. Wolfsburg natives became somewhat less dedicated to 'group' recreation although they also tended to find their pleasures closer to the town. There was less of the five work days in Wolfsburg but 'home' for the weekend. The clearest outward sign of all this was the spate of new models with engine and driven wheels at the 'other' end and square rather than bubble shapes. It began with the Passat.

★   ★   ★

It was more than high time VW produced a good car for the lower middle class, of course. With their still-smaller model three years away in 1971 a VW version of the Audi 80, for the spring of 1973, became doubly important although Wolfsburg went to some initial pains to insist it was a pure VW, not an Ingolstadt fastback. From the first this Passat, which used a Giugiaro tail very similar to one he had done for the defunct project 272, was offered in more versions than the Audi with which it shared engines and drive trains.

Despite the lack of proper boot shape they were extremely careful to avoid all flavour of the carry-all for this saloon—estates have always been suspect to Germans who abhor the thought anybody might think they were in a trade. For those who actually were, however, VW also produced a Passat estate later in 1973. Since this led to relocating the spare, springs and shock absorbers, the Passat saloon also came with a flatter boot floor than the Audi. Their Variant was the first to use a plastic fuel tank as well, following seven years of joint development with BASF, the chemists. This held an extra 6 litres—1.6 gal but weighed 1.4kg/3 lb less. The estate was only expected to account for 7.5 per cent of their Passat market. In America it would be marketed with Audi badges although the Passat saloon was sold there too, as a Dasher.

At first the saloon had neither a rear hatch nor a fold-down rear seat under its sloping tail, only a normal boot. This was the era when policy left fastback designs to Wolfsburg. In weight the Passat was very light for its class but some 10 kg/22 lb heavier than the Audi 80, due to more glass.

Although an aerodynamicist named Emmenthal has been credited with promoting this water-cooled line, for reasons of decreased drag, his early efforts to give the Passat a

The Passat was carefully kept a saloon, as emphasised by the presence of the Variant version as well, an estate on the same chassis. Having this flat-bed model was the reason for minor rear suspension changes versus the Audi 80 (carried to the Passat saloon too).

surface radiator in the bonnet, thereby dispensing with a grille entirely, never quite worked out. Instead, technology was Audi with the negative scrub radius, diagonally split brake circuits and unusually light, precise steering for a front-drive car. It was neither cheaper nor costlier than the Audi 80, merely a little different.

The name came from a favourable fresh wind known to all sailors—and also the name of one of Germany's last great sailing ships. By the end of its first year this Passat was already fifth in German sales behind their Beetle which still held number one, the Audi 80 in third and two Opel rivals. When compared directly to its chief German or foreign peers the Passat was most costly and thirsty but best in bodywork quality and handiness as well as one of the quietest. Early updates were restricted to items such as low-compression pistons for a model which ran on regular petrol in 1974.

One good reason for rushing out this Passat was pacification for their US dealers who eyed the Audi Fox with envy. The US Dasher used Bosch K-Jetronic fuel injection for greater economy with no sacrifice in driveabilty, keeping the features which would attract Americans in the first place. By US standards, however, the car was rated noisy.

For 1975 the Dasher/Passat came with a proper hatch in the back and fold-down seats, alongside the boot-lid model. The interior had been 'Americanised' meaning new seats and extra carpeting, as well as extra sound dampening. A shift in the DM:dollar exchange rate had pushed this car into a class—outside Germany—where its trim levels were never meant to compete.

With the basic saloon established VW quickly turned to the smaller 4-5 seater, choosing to introduce it somewhat obliquely by launching its sporting, 2 + 2 variation first. Also named after a wind, this Scirocco carried project number 398, indicating it had been planned before the Passat. Called the same in America for a change this Giugiaro wedge was both an élite touch for their emblem and a handy means for breaking in the new chassis/engine assembly line since there was no Audi predecessor (engines apart).

This 'public prototype' character explains why the Scirocco appeared in mid-year rather than waiting for the traditional Frankfurt show debut. Actually VW even considered skipping the show entirely on cost grounds, but did attend in the end.

The key feature for the new model line was an engine mounted transversely. More

Scirocco was the first on a Golf chassis, with transverse engine and, while a variation on the Golf, was actually introduced first, in 1974.

compact than photos indicate the car carried two in ample comfort, four at a pinch, offered a rear hatch and was first released with engine options ranging from 1.1 litres/50 hp to 1.5/85 hp. Karman was programmed to build some 200 Sciroccos per day. They now had a smaller, lighter, roomier, faster, more economical but inevitably more expensive prestige car than the Karmann Ghia with the Scirocco more of less replaced. Leiding had brought out a coupé during his Brazil days too and was obviously fond of the 'youth image' model policy.

He was proven quite right, particularly after VW added a 110 hp GTI engine to this coupé range, quickly selling the first 200,000—half of those in Germany—despite months-long delivery delays. In the longer view such a special car was only justified because Scirocco was the image edge of a wedge which prepared the way for their massive VW Golf attack which followed in the middle of 1974.

Of all the factors which might be credited with 'saving' Volkswagen in the 70s, the car which played the most important role and even gave fair warning that it might inherit the Beetle's throne, was one named originally after a wind out of the Gulf Stream, spelled in German as 'golf'. But so many people thought Golf stood for the game that even VW capitulated gracefully by the time they launched the Polo. VW knew they had a hit by the time this Golf was a year old, and sold the first million in only 31 months, a record. An eminently practical car, its launch as the fuel crisis hit was fortunate timing as well.

Professor Werner Holste, director of Golf development, favoured the transverse engine for passive safety reasons and received initial approval from Lotz in 1970, about the time they revealed the Super Beetle to the public. Dr Hans-Georg Wenderoth came in next, from NSU, to expedite the car. He was used to tight timetables, yet Franz Hauk had its new engine running even before the shell was ready. All this activity convinced Leiding they had a real chance here—prompting him to place his full bet on the Golf.

Under Fiala Volkswagen realised they would have to avoid all 'unique' features to get a reliable, even comfortable, car out as soon as possible. If that meant a standard Giugiaro silhouette, so be it. They would only have one chance to rebound. Keeping the famous Beetle wheelbase, VW reduced overall length to 3.7 m/12.1 ft, a foot and a third less than the Beetle. The Golf was wider, of course, and only 10 cm/2.5 in lower so four could still sit in reasonably-upright comfort. A torsional beam rear axle contributed to low seating and they tested heavily to achieve a car weighing only 750 to 830 kg/1,655 to 1,830 lb with outstanding crush rigidity.

The U-section rear axle which twisted by predetermined amounts under the leverage of trailing arms to the wheel hubs as a second component of the springing system, gave all of these new Volkswagens their superior handling. Even so, prices had outstripped their plans before the Golf could be released and even a very basic model with marginal trim, plus many luxury and powerplant options above that, could never really make this a true Beetle successor for a similar buyer circle. On the other hand, the bottom-line, 1.1 litre Golf might cost more than a basic 1.3 litre Beetle—but it would out-perform old faithful as well.

Wolfsburg clearly aimed at another classless car for all levels of society—but they hedged that bet from the first with their option list. A bonus for younger drivers was an early reputation as the car you loved to drive. By the time they became the first anywhere to offer an automatic safety belt system you did not need to latch, this Golf was number one seller in Germany and a key factor in their 22 per cent of the market which regained the lead from Opel.

The Golf now accounted for 57 per cent of all VW sales while the Passat finally moved ahead of the Beetle. Within a year they were already making fairly basic changes to the Golf, however, including better gear change and steering action, plus new pedal pivots, things which indicated—along with an early rust problem—that these machines had been hurried on to the market.

In 1976 the top Golf engine was increased by 100 cc to 1.6 litres and 75 hp. Golf watchers rate this model the start of the most desirable Golf range. On the other hand, their Beetle had made its earliest mistakes before and during the war when few noticed so its successor would not have an easy time. Despite all this, it did triumph, even in

110 hp Golf GTI, the ultimate boy-racer machine.

countries like Australia where a Golf was car of the year in the face of their known scepticism about new models. A 110 GTI engine made this the fastest VW to date, a diesel version turned it into the most economical. First viewed abroad as a mere homologation special, this GTI soon proved reasonable on the road too and gave VW a whole new image. Built in considerable numbers the GTI would do 180 kph/112 mph on only 1.6 litres and even handle well at those speeds. It also gave VW tuners a first-rate chassis starting point.

Designed for a life span of at least 15 if not 20 years, the Golf quickly acquired a Beetle-like reputation for easy resale and low operating costs (the latter somewhat of a myth for the very earliest cars). Installation of the first totally automated body lines, producing 3,200 shells per day, was soon vindicated.

To make even a partially fair comparison with the last and most refined Beetle one had to match 1.6 litre oldie against the 1.1 litre minimum Golf. The two cost about the same in Germany and the lighter Golf could claim a modest victory over its fully-matured forebear, which says about as much for Beetle refinement over four decades as it does about the state of 70s' small cars.

The only other valid comparisons would be between a Golf and its French or Italian competitors—underscoring a prime VW ground for building this contender. Even in teutonic face-offs, the Golf might win on performance, lag a little in bad-road comfort, and come out a good median car with better features adapted from all sides. Compared later to the Audi 50, a smaller car, a basic Golf for about the same money was not really much roomier and lacked the plush fittings—but it looked more like a full-size automobile.

In America the Golf became a Rabbit—whose badge was soon as coveted in Germany as the Audi fox head. It was first imported, then 'Americanised', later built in the US. The first Rabbits reached America in 1975 and were immediately dubbed the cars which put those Beetles out to pasture at last. This was a car dealers wanted—once a 23 page list of alterations put early flaws right. By 1978 press and public in the US were convinced this was one of the finest small cars in the world. The key factor was an American willingness to accept the Rabbit despite its price increase as 'like a Beetle only different', bringing heartfelt sighs of relief from Wolfsburg. Soon those most fervid of Beetle supporters were even fonder of the Golf than most Germans. A great many US owners lavished options on their Golf, a sure sign they had bought for love as well as reason, and most expressed a willingness to have another, as did the United Nations staffs of almost every eastern-European land.

The most serious drawback was what inflation did to the 'small car' price. For Americans the answer was a car of their own from Pennsylvania. For Europe it was a still smaller Polo, perceived at first as only a stripped Audi 50 but later as an economical 3-door on its own. Eventually the public bought so many Polos they discontinued the Audi 50 option. In price the Polo was closer to being a Beetle successor, than it was for having only two side doors, plus the hatch. On the other hand, interior space nearly equalled a Golf. It soon recaptured much of the smallest class from French and Italian rivals. Once moving, VW sold as many Polos in their first 18 months as Audi 50s in two years (over 100,000) and while they never quite turned them out at base-line Beetle prices—not having the aid of fully amortised tooling—they did get close with paperboard door panels in the first Polo and better trim in later ones.

The hard-headed, pragmatic Leiding had spent a very great deal of Volkswagen's money between 1971 and 1974, taking the almost-bewildering variety of cornerstones left by Lotz and assembling them into a whole system of cars which had the firm clearly on its way to recovery when the 1974 oil crisis struck. He did all this, however, without bothering overmuch about charm towards his board or the uniquely delicate feelings of a traditional work force backed by political managers. Without wanting to over-simplify a complicated corporate structure we can still say that VW probably could not have survived the headlong but necessary charge from Nordhoff to Schmücker without Lotz and Leiding to sift the options and initiate the move from stone to aluminium age, almost overnight as the motor industry reckons time.

By 1975 VW was clearly one of the toughest managing director posts in all German industry, but it was no longer a sure, or even possible, loser. True, they had too many plants building too few cars but at least these were the right cars at last, out where the public could and did appreciate them.

In the middle 70s it came down to dividing the work among plants which ranged from their unique home base in a company town to NSU in Neckarsulm which Leiding wanted to close, provoking street marches at the end of his tenure. Not to forget the plant he wanted to put into America.

At the beginning of 1975 Volkswagen's inland empire consisted of: Wolfsburg, where 17,000 workers produced the latest Passat Variant, Golf, Audi 50—and soon Polo— models, with scant fear they would be closed down; Braunschweig, where 6,000 people turned out front axles, door hinges and steering for all the other plants which virtually ensured their future; Hannover, where 21,600 built Type 2 Transporters, the 181 or Thing, a few stray Beetles and all the air-cooled engines, so that there might be labour cutbacks as emphasis shifted to water cooling; Kassel, the rear axle and gearbox facility (both manual and automatic), plus spares and reconditioned units for all the rest, meaning its 16,400 workers were quite secure; Salzgitter, which still built a few K70s, as well as Passat saloons and all water-cooled engines, giving its 9,000 workers the most assured future of all 'new' VW operations; Ingolstadt, where more than 51,000 built the Audi 80 and some of the 100s, two key models with no fear of closings; and finally, those two plants in Neckarsulm and Emden which seemed most doubtful then, just as Leiding's health led to the choice of another new managing director for Volkswagen, the third in a decade.

Under Leiding VW had not only found salvation in its new line of cars but also reduced the work force from over 150,000 in 1971 to 133,000 at the end of 1974, with every cut a painful one. They still had 18,000 working in the two least-productive plants most often mentioned for closure. Neckarsulm also housed a third of their test capacity, all the Wankel expertise and production of the Audi 100 plus the few hand-made Ro80s, but it was sited in that 'other' German state of Baden Württemberg, one which openly feared the Saxons and Bavarians were about to gang up on them, particularly since the ex-NSU plant was far from the most modern in the VW-Audi realm. Emden's problem was more acute but less visible since it was in Saxony like Wolfsburg. This plant built Beetles and US Rabbits, two cars VW could, and soon would, move abroad where they could be produced more cheaply.

Rudolf Leiding realised all these facts and doubtless knew, too, that the degree of direct government involvement in his operation, with all its opportunities for political posing, must preclude vast lay offs. Yet his statements on such problems seemed somewhat less than diplomatic so he retired to make way for a new miracle man, a life-long Rhineland resident who had already made his name as saviour of endangered industrial species although he had never tackled one like this before.

Volkswagen's overseers, too, often thought in pure teutonic terms while their operation only flourished because it had branches on almost every continent of the world. Toni Schmücker would have to bring those two views into focus.

Chapter 12

Germany, around the world

Few products have been so totally identified with Germany as the ubiquitous Beetle, yet Volkswagen cars right up to the present have also been built, assembled, even 100 per cent-sourced in an amazing number of countries. It is popular knowledge that VWs have been exported from Wolfsburg to every conceivable location since the middle 50s. By the 80s it was equally true that Volkswagen had also become one of the most multi-national car producers of them all—even an importer of its own Beetles.

American-built VW cars received the greatest share of press attention simply because they came from the land which symbolised mass-production automobiles. Yet cars bearing the wolf and castle have come from many other countries, before and after the United States: from plants in places as widely scattered as Brazil, South Africa, Yugoslavia, Nigeria, Australia, Mexico and Indonesia, even from Ireland, the Philippines, Uruguay, New Zealand or Venezuela at various times, not to mention a long-time Belgian assembly operation on Germany's own border.

Some of these locales only bolted together CKD kits from Germany—occasionally even kits from a non-German VW factory. Others went so far as to initiate models all their own. Together they made the Volkswagen dream far more universal than even Porsche himself had ever contemplated, particularly in South America, a VW market enjoying two-digit growth right into the 80s.

★   ★   ★

One of the first, and always the most active, branches—from production numbers to special body styles or engines—was and remains VW do Brazil. It was nudged into being by North Americans plus a close Nordhoff colleague and managed on two occasions by later Wolfsburg director, Leiding.

Two Chrysler men brought Volkswagen and Brazil together. Ford had been Porsche's ideal but Chrysler proved the usual VW foil or aid, worldwide. José Thompson, Chrysler importer for Brazil, convinced C.T. Tomaz, the firm's president in 1949, that this Beetle car was predestined for Brazil. That prompted a call to Nordhoff who visited the country, accompanied by his close friend, Friedrich Schultz-Wenk. Capital was found in Rio from a group which backed 20 per cent of the firm, with Volkswagen holding the rest. Soon they had assembled the first Brazilian VW in a rented shed on the outskirts of Sao Paulo, rolling it out in March 1953. In the next four years some 200 workers put together 2,820 VWs before the Brazilian state provided support and VW do Brazil began its own plant in 1956.

A Transporter became the first Brazilian-built VW from a new factory near Sao Paulo in September 1957, a vehicle embracing 50 per cent local content. Four more years and

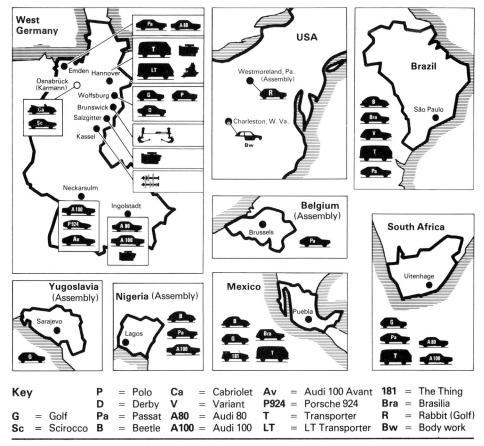

Key

		P	= Polo	**Ca**	= Cabriolet	**Av**	= Audi 100 Avant	**181**	= The Thing
		D	= Derby	**V**	= Variant	**P924**	= Porsche 924	**Bra**	= Brasilia
G	= Golf	**Pa**	= Passat	**A80**	= Audi 80	**T**	= Transporter	**R**	= Rabbit (Golf)
Sc	= Scirocco	**B**	= Beetle	**A100**	= Audi 100	**LT**	= LT Transporter	**Bw**	= Body work

What VW builds where, a good overview of their international efforts (Autopress).

the local portion of both Transporters and Beetles—whose production began in 1959—was up to 95 per cent. By the end of the 70s a Brazilian Passat was virtually all native-sourced, apart from the odd belt or carburettor. It went so far that Wolfsburg was ordering its chrome wheels from VW do Brazil.

The Brazilian plant became an exporter generally, sending car kits and whole vehicles to 50 countries, headed by Algeria, Germany itself, Nigeria, Venezuela, the Philippines, Mexico, Uruguay and Curaçao in that order. The Beetle was chief export product, followed by Brasilia and Passat, while over 300,000 Passat engines and half a million Passat and Beetle gearboxes have gone to Germany and Mexico as well.

In the 20 years since production began this has climbed from five to 2,100 per day. It took Brazil ten years to build its first half-million, four more to reach the million level, but only three further years to double that figure. During this period VW do Brazil held anywhere from over half to nearly three-quarters of its home market, ending the 70s at 53 per cent, the clear Latin American leader although VW also captured 39 per cent of the Peruvian market. Five million VWs were completed by the end of 1979, led by the Beetle but spread over ten other shapes and sizes too. Only the Brasilia and Passat have risen to challenge the Beetle for number one car in the land. Half their production were 1200s, later the 1300, 1500 and 1600 cc Beetles, while Transporters also moved from 1.2 to 1.6

litre engines. The Type 2 itself stands third on Volkswagen's Brazilian list of hits, with half a million sold.

Second, however, at well over 800,000 is their own Brasilia, introduced in mid-1973 as a home-styled model based on a Wolfsburg prototype and logical successor to the VW 1600 built with German tooling. That Type 3 eventually ran for seven years with a rather Type 4-like nose and sold reasonably well but Brazilian designers had a better idea. This Brasilia has a high, flat shelf over its engine and comes in either two- or four-door form plus a practical hatchback, powered by 1.6 litre engines of 48 or 54 hp (one or two carburettors). Modest top speeds of 132 or 138 kph/82-86 mph, testify to Brazil's octane problem. Compression ratio is only 7.2:1. Since only a fifth of the land's two million road kilometres (1.2 million miles) are paved, stronger torsion bars are a feature of all locally-built VWs.

The company also produces a Variant II (Type 3 estate) and even built the Karmann Ghia 1600 for a while, as well as two locally-designed but VW-powered sports cars. The first KG 1200 was built in 1962 and the line continued up to a 1600 TC in 1975, a car somewhat wider than its European cousin since it was mounted on the Brasilia chassis. The second sporty model, called SP, came from their own stylists under direct Leiding influence. His hobby was drawing automobiles. Starting in 1972 VW do Brazil built some 25 of them per day, powered by 1.7 litre engines of 65 hp and mounted on a largely 1600 chassis.

About the only other car one might expect to find in Brazil's VW range is the 181 but a project to build this utility Beetle was dropped on the grounds of complication, although they do turn out a four-wheel drive machine for the Brazilian army with a 1.6 litre boxer engine in the back, a torque converter and Passat axle. In addition, a wide range of local builders uses the most-available chassis in the land—but only Puma among them has posted truly respectable numbers. These plastic sports cars are even exported to Europe.

Since 1974 the locally-built Passat has rounded off their programme in versions with two, three or four doors, plus an even cheaper, youth-orientated version called the Surf. Once early quality problems were solved the Passat was on its way to the position of best-selling Brazilian VW. The Beetle will eventually be replaced by a Polo in the early 80s, to maintain their grip on the first-buyer market.

The unique rear lines of the Brasilia.

The Variant II has a nose all its own to identify with the rest of Brazilian cars.

VW do Brazil has given hearty backing to motor sport, ever since Formula V was launched in 1959. This received direct support until 1974, while backing was also extended to one-class racing for both Brasilia and Passat saloons as well as to rallying where Passats are only now edging ahead of Beetles in the longer events.

As another mark of their original thinking, or distance from Wolfsburg, VW do Brazil produced an improved air-cooled flat four with opposed valves and hydraulic tappets which came out at the end of 1979, offering great hope to both desert racers and Transporter fans—for whom it was actually designed. By 1980 all air-cooled engine development for Volkswagens in Germany and abroad had been shifted to their Brazilian branch.

Fuel is the land's overriding concern—their Algerian contract swaps cars for oil—so that Brazil has become a leader in alcohol fuels while VW engineers, largely Brazilian now although the first technicians were German, could market a car for 1980 using pure alcohol if the government provided a network of filling stations. Two Passats running on alcohol completed a 15 day marathon averaging 8.86 l/100 km or 31.8 mpg during 1979, which led directly to daily production of some 15 alcohol-powered cars (five Passats and ten Beetles) for taxi use, farmers and government agencies at first. Projections see a quarter of a million such cars in 1980, burgeoning to 350,000 by 1982. Their five-millionth car, at the end of 1979, was a methanol-powered Beetle. Brazil intended to be entirely free of oil dependance by 1984 and meanwhile restricted rare diesel supplies to trucks over one ton which move the nation's produce. Diesel-powered cars were not wanted.

The company runs three factories, turning out everything from magnesium castings to full cars in their original plant, the largest in South America. Works II, taken over from the DKW (Auto Union) licence holder in 1967, concentrates on research and development while body panels come from Works III. Many of over 41,000 workers came out of their own training schools but they also hire labour from 40 different countries, beating even Wolfsburg's 'guest worker' record.

Volkswagen's non-car interests in Brazil run the gamut from a joint moped plant near Rio designed to build 100,000 Steyr-Puch-powered pushbikes by 1980, with 51 per cent ownership by VW do Brazil, all the way to a 140,000 hectare/345,800 acre ranch where 400 VW farmers herd 25,000 head of Indian Nelore cattle. Founded in 1973 to use profits which had to be reinvested inside the country, this Rio Cristalino ranch will run over

Typical of third-world expansion by VW is their Nigerian assembly operation which trains its own people and occasionally builds models differing slightly from the Wolfsburg norm (VW badge on an Audi 100 for instance). The Passat is pure, however, but to the latest aerodynamic specifications.

100,000 head by the mid-80s. This arm of Volkswagen has turned heavy government restrictions—later a total ban—on imported cars into a thriving local operation which moved from importer to exporter, to a little of everything.

The Nigerian Itala, for instance, is a four-door Brasilia with 1.6 litre, air-cooled engine, while that same African country also assembles Beetles and Passats from Brazilian kits and even produced a version of the older Audi 100, bearing a VW badge on its grille, in its Lagos facility. Nigeria opened as an assembly plant in 1975 and receives its Audi kits from Germany, all else from Brazil, although Lagos was letting the Brasilia project run out in the early 80s as it approached an overall mark of 200,000 cars.

*   *   *

Historically the first VW sales to Africa go clear back to 1949 when an American selling a little of everything to Morocco added Beetles to his list and soon found he was delivering 1,500 a year. His operation never grew into anything like that which operates as Volkswagen of South Africa Ltd. At the southern tip of the continent they share one vital concern with Brazil, research into non-fossil fuels. Once again the vehicle is a Passat, here with both petrol and diesel engines converted to part-methanol power. VW sells only the Passat there in compression-ignition form while the diesel-methanol combination is a rare research project.

Not a large operation, the South African company is one of the oldest links in VW's overseas chain. The first two imported Beetles landed in 1950 with assembly on the south-east coast at Uitenhage by August 1951, on lines shared with Studebaker. By 1964, when a local content programme of 45 per cent by weight was initiated, VW built Transporters and micro-buses in the country. Their record year was 1969 when 34,000 cars were produced while the end of their first quarter-century in 1976 found them holding the land's one-car record of 250,000 VWs. This marque has always been in the South African top three. Today some 5,100 workers, including a design staff which adapts Volkswagens to local conditions and uprates specifications for the more luxury-orientated local market, turns out the Golf, Passat, Audi 80 and 100 models plus Transporters, with 66 per cent local content, at the rate of some 200 per day. This gives VW in South Africa some 15.5 per cent of their market, around 11 per cent for light commercials. Beetle production ended there on January 18 1979, at the 290,916 mark, while the plant has also produced Type 3 saloons, fastbacks and squarebacks (estates) as well as the 411 between 1969 and 1974, always for its home market only.

★   ★   ★

On the other side of the southern hemisphere, the problems faced by Volkswagen Australia have proved very similar: specialised market conditions plus a relatively small and geographically-isolated home market. The proper name of Volkswagen Australasia Ltd better indicates their scope. The Australians began as importers, of course, and soon moved to assembly, then launched a major construction and export drive which ran through the 60s until complicated and shifting local-content regulations brought them full circle. The firm first cut back to assembly only, then to merely importing the more specialised VW and Audi products for the 80s.

Strictly speaking, the very first VW in Australia was about as early a model as you could find anywhere, a 1946 Beetle brought to the country in 1951 as the baggage of a German lady joining her husband to make a new life. They drove the car, purchased originally from a British occupation officer in Germany, over 160,000 km/100,000 miles before trading their rarity to VW Australia for the 100,000th Aussie-built VW ten years later. Officially, however, Regent Motors was the first holder of Wolfsburg rights and imported its first cars in 1953 with first CKD kits arriving at a plant outside Melbourne the following June.

Beetles promptly took command of the car-breaking Round-Australia Trials, proving themselves easily the toughest machines in the land by winning five years running with a high point in 1957 when the first six cars to finish were VWs. Another famous Australian VW spent a year in the Antarctic, often at –45 degrees C/–50 degrees F, yet it always fired first time. Back home, Beetles were even purchased to herd sheep.

Starting with 1,385 cars assembled in the second half of 1954, Volkswagen had 7 per cent of the Australian market by 1957 and decided, following a Nordhoff visit in 1958, to build a giant plant for Beetles made of Australian materials. This went up in Clayton, a Melbourne suburb, which turned out its first car in late 1960. VW had passed 10 per cent of the local market for the first time a year earlier and reached what would prove their all-time peak of 12.5 per cent for saloons plus a 7-8 per cent share of the light commercial sales in 1960. Hopes and sales held up reasonably well through the middle 60s with 1500 Type 3 production added and local content climbing to 76 per cent by 1962. They even built a stark special called the Country Buggy, a sure mark of a VW branch in an expansive mood since it was all their own design.

An inflexible 95 per cent local content rule by 1966 put them in immense difficulties since it froze Beetle specifications just when imported or assembled cars could be updated. One solution was direct competition with the parent outside Australia, and Wolfsburg even approved the cars VW Australasia sent to New Zealand, Fiji, New Guinea, British Solomons, Malaysia and Indonesia, plus spares to Hong Kong, Noumea and New Caledonia—all places where Australian quality was then appreciated.

The Clayton plant, where a third of 2,600 employees came from 20 countries as far away as Russia and Malta, was one of only three in the middle 60s to have a master jig which kept locally-made dies up to standard—the other two were located in Wolfsburg and Sao Paulo. Despite new engine shops and a foundry which went into service in 1967, a year when Australian VW sales were about a tenth of those in Brazil, for instance, the firm decided to drop production, which had to be Wolfsburg-subsidised to survive, and assemble again. Their market share was down to 5 per cent. Assembly gave them more

The Country Buggy, a model unique to Australia in days when that land too had original VW production.

model diversity but did not prevent a further market slide to 2-3 per cent, not arrested by special introductions like the 1971 Super Bug. Clayton became an independent assembly plant turning out Datsuns and then Volvos, in addition to Volkswagens.

The facility was then sold to Nissan in 1975, shortly before VW Australia, an importer only, introduced a 1976 range of wholly-German cars. By the late 70s they concentrated on special models like the Passat, winner of a local car of the year award in 1975, the Audi 100 in top-line CD form, VW diesel models and the top of the Golf petrol range. Diesels are expected to account for half their import quota in the 80s.

Although VW managed to push the Beetle as high as second to Holden one year, even edging out local Ford, Australia remained a big-car market with too many state restrictions on too few total sales (barely a third of a million per year for all marques). Australia remains one of the more densely motorised lands of the world, relative to its population, but—since the Beetle at least—not a strongly VW-orientated one.

*   *   *

This became something of a Volkswagen pattern abroad: the successful arrival by Beetle which suited outback road conditions so well, and then the problem of promoting more sophisticated, water-cooled designs which they had to build for European demand before many other countries were ready for that step.

Going into the 80s Mexico seemed likely to prove an exception to all this. It all began with less than 500 Beetles there for 1954 but these launched a VW wave which led to a very successful assembly operation over the next eight years. Government rules on local content and integrated car production in 1962 prompted Volkswagen de Mexico to insert 60 per cent local content as required. By 1979 that figure was up to 71 per cent for the Beetle with all other models above the 60 per cent minimum easily, as they faced the 80s with just under 30 per cent of the Mexican market.

The 'all other models' refers to a range rivalling Brazil: their plant in Puebla builds Beetles, Brasilias, Transporters, Safaris and Caribes. That last pair are only local names for the 181 or Thing and the Golf, respectively. Chief changes for Mexican conditions—Puebla does no original design—are radial tyres and colonial-quality shock absorbers. Production of all models ran above 85,000 yearly in the late 70s, focused on the

A Mexican Beetle, looking just like the last German ones.

Caribe—20,000 each with petrol and diesel engines, the latter popular as taxis. The Brasilia (5,000) and various Type 2 models account for another 15,000 units, leaving no less than 30,000 Beetles being built in Puebla more than 40 years after the first were put together in Germany.

When Wolfsburg—Emden really—dropped Type 1 production to import the 'Escarabajo' instead, Mexican labour costs made a latin Beetle nearly an eighth cheaper although that also means a virtually-1961-engined model of 34 hp. At least the 1980 Beetle from Mexico is quieter, has chrome hubcaps and bumpers, boasts chequered upholstery on the latest seat forms, and even offers a glove compartment lid. The chassis is their faithful swing axle model, however, and the front boot has reverted to marginal due to the original transverse torsion bar suspension but at least the back seat folds down. The subjective feel is a late-40s time machine with full VW quality. Emden checks that.

When a new engine plant was needed for Volkswagens everywhere—up to 1,600 four-cylinder powerplants per day—it seemed only logical to put it into Mexico. When a German worker was earning DM 24 per hour, including all social benefits, and a VW of America worker the equivalent of DM 16.50, their counterparts in Brazil (DM 6) and Mexico (DM 4) could produce the parts far more economically.

In all, Puebla built exports up to some 17,500 Beetles for Germany each year plus 2,500 Safaris (the 181) for Germany and Latin America as well as Indonesia in CKD kit form, a project which came to an end late in the summer of 1979. As a German Beetle driver put it, 'I don't really care in the slightest where it's built, just so long as it is a Beetle'.

★   ★   ★

A good many Americans would feel the same, nostalgic way but limits there on noise and exhaust emissions combined to keep Escarabajo south of the border. When the country which had propped up VW better than any other finally got its own, oft-mooted Volkswagen construction plant, it would build Rabbits rather than Beetles. Before that, of course, the US had enjoyed an ample supply of the VW wonder, following a slow start.

Phase one of Volkswagen's American effort was a free-wheeling approach marked by little close planning and growing out of an almost imperceptible start. Dutchman Pon tried first, early in 1949, followed by Nordhoff himself later the same year. But neither found US car dealers even mildly interested. Max Hoffman, who handled just about every European car at some point, sold 330 Beetles in 1950 largely by making dealers, who wanted something else from his list, take VWs too.

The usually prescient Hoffman could not see much future for the VW which was still verging on the fly-by-night as late as 1953 and certainly not up to VW standards in any way. A year later half the cars were sold on the US west coast, key weather-vane market for American motoring matters, and by the middle-50s a fast-moving man named van de Kamp was overwhelming all opposition, operating as a visionary, out of his hotel suite. The first proper US VW company was formed in June 1955, the same year Volkswagen bought an ex-Studebaker plant in New Jersey. This early idea of American production was dropped within six months, however.

The company under one man's hat finally became more organised in 1958 when Nordhoff sent in Carl Hahn, a man with the boss's total confidence. Hahn began to apply marketing science and even launched the first of those famous self-kidding VW ads. As for service, they took a leaf from Ford's Model T book and sent out travelling representatives.

With the Beetle finally selling as VW believed it must, a whole range of company and independent magazines devoted to the marque sprang up, reporting every door-handle change and promising later, more exotic air-cooled cars some day. Those were for true fans. Most of America thought 'VW' and 'Beetle' were interchangeable. If they could not get enough of them, they might even build them out of the spare parts bin. This game occurred several times. As late as 1961 it took teams from New York area dealers six months and 400 spare-time man hours to put together such a genuine, American-built beetle, for instance.

A year later Volkswagen of America moved into its new, $2.5 million New Jersey headquarters. From there they could keep strict watch on nearly 700 dealers whose sales had grown from a scant thousand cars in 1953 to 200 times that figure ten years later. One of their first headaches was a vast grey market which sprang up in the Type 3, the 'real Nordhoff VW'. Soon Los Angeles alone was buying 1,000 'used' ones every month and expecting VW service. This hastened official import. US buyers listed economy, reliability and resale as their main reasons for buying a VW while five per cent admitted the Beetle was a status symbol and another two per cent bought one because the car was 'cute'. When VW sought the oldest in the land it turned out to be a December 1945 model.

In the mid-60s Hahn returned to Wolfsburg as head of world-wide sales and Nordhoff heir-apparent until marketing at home ran into its late-60s problems. He was succeeded at VW of America by Stuart Perkins who arrived from Canada, which had been an entirely separate VW operation up to that time. Under Perkins VW decided Volkswagen cars sold in the United States because they were 'honest' cars, so they aimed their advertising at this one factor. Before long even Wolfsburg was using the same ad campaign. And American sales boomed even further, causing a real order backlog until sagging German demand at the end of the 60s allowed Americans to reduce their waiting list with sales well above the half-million mark per year.

Not even a three-month US dock strike in 1969, just when VW of America was planning a special sales push, could dampen their once-endless upward spiral. America had long since bought its three-millionth VW but the Japanese were now crowding them in California, traditionally the first area to accept a new car. The official reason for a delay in releasing 1970 models was 'no shipping space', with excess stocks only mentioned off the record. The days when VW was automatic number one, selling ten times as many cars as the second-best imported make, were suddenly behind them.

This US market had become so important to Wolfsburg they would tailor models to suit—a Type 2 engine in the Beetle, for instance, to retain some power while meeting emission standards. They even wrung a promise out of Washington not to use the Beetle as its target vehicle in crash tests designed to show full-size American saloons were safer.

VW of America blunted a strongly chauvinistic American mood in the early 70s by trumpeting its US purchases, including up to 6,000 tons of steel monthly. However 1971 price cutting found the smallest new American cars selling for less than a Super Beetle which suffered from a dollar lag. It foreshadowed the day when VW must seek 'special car' buyers rather than the economy minded. They even sold a few thousand 411s to the true enthusiasts before facing yet another price increase for 1972, due in part to import levies stiff enough to bring threats of German retaliation against American goods. In the midst of this struggle, Nader's anti-VW rhetoric, however poorly founded, took its toll as well. Wolfsburg countered with a Washington contract for a safety car study. For the regular models, power, torque and sales were all down and VW of America would be posting real losses by 1974, just as Wolfsburg went into a loss year as well.

Since all American car builders now had spare plant capacity too, Volkswagen sent scouts to look over possible US factories. This production transfer would be vital by 1976 when sales sank to half the 1970 level. Leiding was pushed out for trying to set up US operations but his successor finally put the long-time idea across.

All this woe paralleled the end of the Beetle in America. Seven of 19-plus million Beetles had been sold there but the yearly figure had dropped to 27,000 by 1976, hardly 5 per cent of what it had been less than a decade before, so they turned full attention to the Rabbit for US production.

The chronology of this single most important overseas venture by VW goes back to the autumn of 1973 when a 'US Team' studied the idea even before their Golf (Rabbit) was introduced to Germany. Deciding the time for production was not yet ripe VW introduced the Rabbit to America as an imported product in February 1975. By May of that same year Toni Schmücker was meeting with US financial and industrial leaders. A month later he had assembled a new project team in Wolfsburg. His board voted unanimously for ultimate US production in April 1976, with union and government members agreeing at last. They were finally convinced it would not take any cars away from German production since those were virtually priced out of the American market anyway.

By June a survey of every state except Hawaii and Alaska had narrowed to two Ohio sites and New Stanton Pennsylvania, a town of 3,500, 30 minutes outside Pittsburg. Chrysler had started a plant there in 1968 and left its shell standing. By July 1976 VW was losing up to $100 on every car sent to America while their market share had eroded to 2.5 per cent. When Pennsylvania made attractive financial offers, including new road and rail links plus credits, VW took a 30-year lease with an option to buy and received the key in October. Now the real rush began on what VW likes to call the first car plant ever built in the US as a subsidiary of a foreign firm—ignoring Rolls-Royce.

VW Manufacturing of America at the same time acquired a stamping plant in South Charleston, West Virginia, from American Motors, using it to produce Rabbit panels as well as those contracted to the previous owner. They planned from the first to buy as much as possible from the US and Canada so management offices were located in Warren Michigan, the heart of America's supplier industry. Senior managers were hired from America's big-three car firms as well. Plant manager at Westmoreland, as the Pennsylvania operation came to be known, was a ten-year Chrysler man while both Vice President Richard Dauch and their key catch, James McLernon as President, came from

Below right *A model designed as well as built for America, the long-chassis Rabbit (Golf) Pick-up, announced at the end of 1979, to put the Pennsylvania operation up with the few like Brazil which was allowed to have its very own car.*

General Motors where McLernon had worked for 27 years, the last of those as manager of manufacturing for Chevrolet.

The clear goal was to regain 5 per cent of the American market, doubling their 1978 standing when the first Rabbit shell for regular production started down the new assembly line. This had been preceded by 1,000 MKD (medium knocked down) cars sent from West Germany as trainer units, along with some 65 key German overseers, later cut to a handful as the operation became wholly native.

Westmoreland has a potential of some 200,000 cars per year, built by 4,500 workers on two daily shifts. The original intention was to have 75 per cent local content by 1980 and while that proved hard to achieve, they could easily foresee a time when only gearboxes would come from abroad. As Schmücker put it, a trace smugly perhaps, in his plant-opening speech to notables including the Governor of the state and Treasury Secretary of the United States, 'This may be one small step for America, but it is one giant step for Volkswagen'. They were very aware that they must live down three decades of promoting 'made in Germany' as the best reason to buy a VW. Half the buyers polled that first year wanted a German Rabbit instead, yet that same survey found US-built cars then had fewer problems than German models.

Ever since the first Beetle, Volkswagen's major marketing problem had been to compete with its own legend. Westmoreland Rabbits even carried a VW emblem on the steering wheel, not a wolf and castle, although that home symbol is allowed on Mexican Beetles, for instance. Nonetheless, VW found 1979 sales reaching for 300,000 ten per cent better than forecasts. Americans willing to pay sky-high premiums for the imported Rabbit Diesel after the second oil crisis, also prompted VW to get a US-built version into production as soon as possible. There would even be a diesel engine for the Rabbit Pick-up, announced from Westmoreland at the end of the 70s.

This put them on a par with Sao Paulo as a builder of uniquely-native products on a VW base. Using a lengthened wheelbase and choice of petrol or diesel engine the only front-drive small truck available in America was called 'the first' VW to be designed in America, not the sole one. While its front end and two seats were Rabbit the truck bed and beam rear axle were pure American, as was the options list and range of colour combinations. Rabbits from the new factory, built on Mexican floorpans with West Virginian body panels, were 'Americanised' too: brighter plastics, colour-keyed interiors and non-reclining seat backs. Rectangular headlamps and a cleaner grille identified the US model while VW offered a five-speed manual gearbox there before it was available in Germany.

By 1980 the Westmoreland operation was a working arm of VW, producing 1,050 cars a day and so settled in that visiting Germans would insist even the rolling Pennsylvania landscape 'looked much like parts of Germany'. The work force was a little different, however. VW put this plant in Westmoreland originally because there was a pool of unemployed labour—ten applicants for every job—meaning somewhat lower wages than Detroit car workers could demand. Once the relatively young work force was hired (average age 27) it struck for Detroit-level money. Then came a dispute over an extra coffee break. Such US labour methods were more than curious to Wolfsburg people.

VW of America soon became the 12th member of the US Motor Vehicle Manufacturer's Association, however, the fifth of that group building passenger cars and one of the US team in effect. Very soon their capacity ranked them fourth, ahead of American Motors. Enjoying the most modern assembly plant in America VW could expect to show its first profit as early as 1981. Worldwide they were now 18th among all firms, largest non-US car builder, just ahead of Toyota and Renault. All this neatly defined their need for American production, a fact underlined in 1980 when VW had already outgrown its Westmoreland capacity and opened a second plant, even closer to Detroit, the traditional US car-building centre.

Volkswagen was so successful by 1979 that they became the focus of tales that Wolfsburg was about to buy up Chrysler, an idea both sides were quick to ridicule. They were seeking a third US factory in the land where VW sales had jumped 41 per cent since they became a producer there, compared to 13 per cent for the world. Soon engines would be built in America too, including those for Chrysler which wanted more than the 300,000

The US-built Golf is a Rabbit with rectangular headlights and 'Americanized' (meaning brighter plastics) interior.

VW could spare, but VW had little desire to swallow America's tenth-largest undertaking. The intriguing factor was simply that both press and stock market men could even speculate that they could or might.

★   ★   ★

If America was the most visible non-German market for VW, and later the most-discussed new producer abroad, the least-noticed would be that country which was first in length of VW service as well as nearness to home base: Belgium. The fine old coachbuilding firm of d'Iterean was putting Beetles together there as far back as the early 50s and had turned out some 1.7 million Volkswagens by the start of the 80s, belonging directly to VW for the last five years of that period. This quiet partner moved from Beetles to both saloon and estate versions of the Passat, delivering first to the Benelux area although they were always available to furnish cars to the home market as needed. At various times VW Bruxelles also sent automobiles to 30 different countries.

Yugoslavia is another country which had given VW assembly potential outside its direct sales area. In this case it was a toe-hold in the communist car world and a means of producing cars for that lower-priced market at a competitive price. The Yugoslavs began with Beetles of course, turning out 60 cars a day at Sarajevo in 1972, with expansion to as many as 60,000 per year. By the end of the 70s this car-conscious land had already moved on to assemble the Golf with total output by then topping 650,000 units.

As the Yugoslavs got into high gear Volkswagen was closing an attempt to assemble cars in Jakarta, Indonesia, a market once supplied from Australia. This island had begun in 1972 as well and put together Golfs, Transporters and Mexican-kit 181s before closing after a total production of only 16,000 cars.

Undaunted by this and earlier shut-downs of VW assembly efforts, Volkswagen was always ready to discuss tentative or promised openings and feelers when it came to new markets, giving them a multi-national range equal to any car company in the world and superior to most. Their Beetle was still a natural for any car-emerging country as late as the 80s. El Salvador, for instance, had given permission for a VW plant as early as 1964. They spoke of 5,000 cars per year but these never happened. VW also held a quarter of a light truck plant in Spain during the late 60s, inherited from DKW and used to service the Iberian market. Then there were feelers about a Greek assembly plant in the early 70s. VW was always an obvious partner.

From their own viewpoint, one key goal was a wedge into the east-block market area but, apart from independent Yugoslavia, none of these assembly or licence negotiations had borne fruit by the 80s, despite a total of roughly 65,000 VWs, largely Beetles, operating in various iron curtain countries.

Heinz Nordhoff was a passionate hunter who often shot in Hungary and always tried to sell his Beetles there, but could not manage it. In 1973, however, a contract was signed to send 10,000 of the VW 1300 to Hungary where electrics, lights and some plastic parts would be added before the cars in choice of red, white or pale blue were sold for about twice the western price. The Hungarian party paper quoted a 90-day delivery and there were ample buyers but the project ended with only 6,700 delivered. VW dropped the idea in 1974 when Hungary was unable to deliver the exchange goods specified.

A similar arrangement for 10,000 cars was signed with East Germany in 1978 when its leaders needed luxury goods to sop up some 80 million east marks from its hard-working subject's saving accounts. Since cars generally had a six to eight year waiting list in the DDR then, the other Germany was eager to offer precision tooling and even diesel injection pumps for those 10,000 Golfs. At first they were priced at a level which would buy a Porsche in the west—but still below the baby Volvo for instance.

This Golf price tag was later reduced in the face of buyer outrage, although not by much, and the entire order delivered. A West German joke insisted the total was actually 10,001 since their synonym for high society is the 'upper ten thousand' and that would never do for a workers' car. In any case, these gave Wolfsburg a small claim in the east, ahead of the Japanese, which was the point of the exercise. They later had discussions with both the Czechs, who sought 1.5 litre Golf engines for their Skoda line, and the Russians, who coveted a licence to build the Passat. In fact, Wolfsburg had been talking with the east for decades, ever since Nordhoff's era. But it never seemed to get much past the after-dinner toasts, about where similar discussions with South Korea ended.

The story was similar in South America where the one highly-successful operation in Brazil led all other lands to want the same. They spoke with Chrysler about taking over its Argentine operation and reached the signing stage in Ecuador over a DM 200 million assembly plant for the Golf with a 1982 projection of 30,000 cars per year for that land as well as nearby Bolivia, Columbia, Peru and Venezuela.

Cairo also agreed to a Suez Canal plant at the end of the 70s—to build up to 10,000 cars each year from CKD kits out of Brazil. The model would be a Beetle at first but the Golf was 'not impossible' at a later date.

Finally there was a foreign project which borders on all these although it would not have been a VW at all; but rather a (modern) Porsche-designed popular car for Austria where all the best Volkswagen engineers traditionally were born. That land's chancellor decided that if Poland or Spain could have thriving car industries, his country with its rich car traditions must again too. Kreisky saw all this in terms of Porsche engineering and Austrian labour as well as financial backing, but his dreams foundered on the idea of calling such a car the Austro-Porsche. The engineering firm naturally had nothing against such a design contract but baulked at fitting its sporty name to a project so far from its direct control. Any such non-German project by Volkswagen, for VW, or even touching upon VW myths, was always certain of ample public attention, in the 80s as it had been in the 30s.

Chapter 13

Volkswagen returns to the top

Toni Schmücker shared two conditions with Rudolf Leiding, whom he succeeded: all the raw materials for his eventual triumphs were inherited with the managing director's chair, but so were the basics for most of his subsequent headaches. Neither started with an easy road ahead.

Volkswagen's boom in the second half of the 70s was based solidly on a brilliant range of new cars which Leiding—and Kraus—had carefully prepared. It was even Leiding who sent up the first trial balloons for the American plant which would be so vital if VW was to remain in a key market. On the other hand, it was Schmücker's style which cajoled the German government and unions into approving the inevitable when he brought it up again. He took over the office on the 13th floor with the firm backing of a unanimous vote by all 21 members of the Supervisory Board, but realised full well that the press was right when it headlined; 'Toni Schmücker accepts the Wolfsburg ejection seat'.

Fortunately this was a man who had climbed the Matterhorn. Twice. He thrived on challenges. If he had remained at Ford in Cologne, Schmücker would very probably have been the first man there to rise from apprentice to board chairman. His father had worked at Ford and Toni put in two years there, as a sales trainee, before volunteering for the army which sent him to Murmansk in 1942. He returned to be a post-war buyer for Ford, the 'half-American' one who managed to get at least one English word into every sentence.

Schmücker joined the Ford board at 39, clearly in line for the top position. Then he left that car maker on the Rhine rather than move to England in 1968, in one of the typical Ford rotations of management. His next task was Rhinestahl, a very sick steel maker, where he could be the full boss although he was also taking on what observers then called 'the toughest job in German industry'. Schmücker later said it had cost him ten years of his life; that from a man whose sports are rock climbing and tennis which he plays aggressively. He soon straightened out the faltering steel operation, firing one director overnight for mistakes in his figures, and cutting away all Rhinestahl branches except its original steel-producing base—which he then sold to rival Thyssen, saving all the jobs and leaving himself out as sole boss but into a solid, high-level slot with Thyssen. When Volkswagen called he left to take up a new challenge, one which made the Rhinestahl task look like a mere dress rehearsal. It was just what the 53 year old Schmücker sought.

VW had lost a reported DM 600 million in 1974, and 1975 promised to be worse. Its plants were working at 60 per cent of capacity, US sales were down by 30 per cent—although the Rabbit would overtake the Beetle there in popularity by February 1975—and yet this slump was not his biggest worry. Chief spectre was the imminent total shutdown of their Neckarsulm plant. It seemed to be a choice of dropping up to a third of his work force at each of several plants or closing one entirely. The minister of Baden

Württemberg then was naturally fighting to save 'his' plant but doing it through wild public charges designed to inflame the public against parent VW.

The bare truth was that when Schmücker divided plant turnover by number of workers, each man in Neckarsulm only brought them DM 92,000 a year, the worst figure in German industry, whereas Audi, for instance had the second-best figure nation-wide, at DM 113,000 per worker. Thanks to many social benefits on the side VW workers then averaged DM 11.20 per hour against 9.90 for the German car industry in general. Even with sales looking up there had to be more austerity. Eventually Schmücker kept Neckarsulm open preferring that to a proposal from the Bavarian and Baden Württemberg governments, both conservative; they would solve his cash flow dilemma by buying 51 per cent of Audi-NSU at four times the nominal share price. In exchange for DM 450 million in ready money VW must drop the Passat in favour of Audi or NSU models. Not to mention later conditions.

The board now split; 14 for closing the plant, 7 against (7 board members were union men still) and that gave Schmücker the manoeuvring space he wanted. He received backing for the release of as many as 25,000 workers overall by the end of 1976, potentially the largest lay off in post-war Germany. The first 4,500 went in April 1975, a time when few really believed even cutting a fifth of the work force would prove sufficient surgery. Plans called for cuts at each plant, including nearly 6,000 from Wolfsburg proper, to blunt the charge that this was all a north German plot at the expense of their southern operations. In the end they only closed certain subsidiary plants inherited with NSU but that factory and Brussels both went on single shifts and Salzgitter assembly was moved to Wolfsburg, dropping the K70. Thus it became the shortest-lived model VW ever built. VW also retired from the Comotor project with Citroën.

They had slipped from first to seventh overall among German industrial giants when a Bonn leak revealed the 1974 losses had been DM 800 million, not 600. VW had to retrench or go under entirely and Toni Schmücker had just 100 days to sort it all out. Fortunately, he had always been known as a manager who considered the least of his workers first, a man thoroughly steeped in co-operation with the unions so he won his way when it was critical by explaining the situation fairly. His workers went along despite the lay offs, and most gingerly since they too realised that a strike, even a foot dragged slightly, could end it all. With some reason, Schmücker's first comment as director had been, 'the golden age of the automobile is behind us', although hindsight suggests this was among the least accurate of his predictions.

In an early interview the new director stated flatly there would never be another car like the Beetle, built in numbers up to 7,000 per day. At best they might aspire to build that many of the Audi 50/Polo/Golf combined, his most hopeful guess. He personally found the Polo too basic and decided to separate the VW and Audi images somewhat more by leaving functional cars to VW, the extra class to Audi.

Schmücker was fully aware that Volkswagen had produced half a dozen models almost simultaneously—having no choice at the time—and must be sure all of them did not pass into old age at once too. It turned out he was even willing to reconsider project 425, perhaps building as many as 80 sports cars a day jointly with Porsche, before finally deciding this was not really VW territory. Instead they sold the design back to Porsche which had created it in mid-1975 and contracted to build what became the Porsche 924 in Neckarsulm, using ex-Audi engines.

At his most optimistic, early in 1975, Schmücker would not predict profits again before 1977. At that time he personally kept a home in Essen on the Rhine and lived in the VW Guest House when in Wolfsburg. The new accent for VW would fall on sales rather than mindless production records, with a middle-road labour policy for the future.

If times turned good VW would live with waiting lists for their cars rather than hiring extra labour immediately, only to face seasonal lay offs later. They would also try harder on the European market, to reduce dependance on the US, but also shift production to America to take advantage of the low wages. One of Toni Schmücker's best moves had been the winning of German labour backing for Westmoreland Rabbits, cars they never would have sold from German stock anyway.

Furthermore, he moved to revitalise the VW Management Academy in Rhode which Leiding had been about to axe. He clearly sought a more homogenous director team which might prove more stable in any future crisis. They had found that young Wolfsburg men did not automatically aim at a career at any personal price, that perhaps half of them were already satisfied with whatever level they had reached when polled. Schmücker would tell each Rhode group to give its superiors constructive boosts. Twenty young managers would have the chance to speak freely with at least one board member at each one-week session. Many would later return to lecture at Rhode as well although only one of nine direct board members at the end of the 70s, the young head of production, had come up through VW ranks. At this same time VW was also spending DM 55 million to expand its already exemplary training scheme for all workers.

Meanwhile VW also had to deal with a persistent 1975 rumour that Ernst Fiala was contemplating a move to Mercedes which seemed more stable to outside observers then. The safety professor who had recently received a high award for Economy and Art from his native Austria elected to stay and help turn VW around.

It was a mixed year, when a Citroën would finish ahead of the Golf and Audi 50 in a leading car of the year poll because the two German products came so close together they effectively split the vote. Fiala promptly remarked, they did not mind at all. VW might have fewer votes but they would sell more cars. The mood was definitely up-beat. Symbolising that, they took part in a design symposium for a 'youth car' of the future. While Audi men chose solid values (a Polo with sail cloth interior and pop paint) Fiala's team proved the wildest of any German firm. They featured an inline, three-cylinder engine ('three is best for transverse mounting in a small car') fitted to a short wheelbase which would still carry four. Volkswagen did not mind dropping a few hints.

Schmücker had always believed in a long-range future for VW, no matter how involved the short-term prospects, but the actual turn around proved even more sensational than he had suspected. There was already a profit in August 1975 and they were back at number one for Germany in 1976, led by the Golf and Passat which were the two top-selling cars most months.

In figures, VW built 2.1 million cars in 1976 for a DM 1 billion profit—compared to the DM 800 million loss on 2 million cars in 1974. The nickname 'Toni the trickster' began to make Wolfsburg rounds. In his first five years, culminating in the 1980 models, Toni Schmücker of the silver hair and ever-present pipe could look back on the fully-updated new Transporter, on three new-generation models of cars well established when he arrived, and on two new models which appeared under his direct control.

★   ★   ★

The third-generation Type 2 was covered in Chapter 5. As for the cars Schmücker found on first reaching Wolfsburg, we now find VW operating very like any other car firm of the 70s, novel in itself. Engines were altered slightly to keep pace, several body shells were given small face-lifts, and special economy or boy-racer models added as appropriate. Trim could be altered any time sales might suggest it. There were even new badges on occasion.

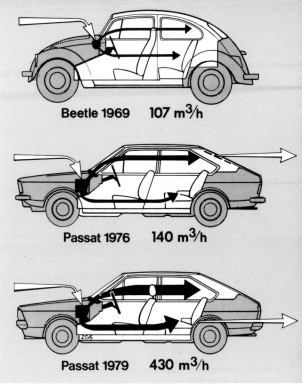

Beetle 1969   107 m³/h

Passat 1976   140 m³/h

Passat 1979   430 m³/h

Above left *Toni Schmücker.* **Above right** *Air through-flow over the past decade, showing VW concern with ventilation from the best Beetle to the original and latest Passats as aerodynamic work rushed ahead* (Autopress).

VW was far more concerned in this period with holding some sort of a lid on home-market prices than they were with new experiments. When buyers had to contemplate the second increase of the year before summer, or discovered they could re-import a Golf from France for DM 1,000 less than the new-car price at home, Wolfsburg concentrated on making the line shine more brightly. That meant a noise supression package for the Golf in the autumn of 1977, isolating suspension struts and steering from the body. Their aerodynamicists had changed nose radii some 1 or 2 mm, redefined the corners and front skirt, and gained 0.05 on their drag coefficient, a significant amount which maintained their position as 'slipperiest' in the field.

Along this same line, where a 1969 Beetle could only push some 107 m³/3,775 ft³ of air through the car each hour, a 1976 Golf or Passat with axial fan and new vents passed 140 m³/4,940 ft³ at a standstill and up to 430/15,000 underway, with the fan working fully. A major engine change was a return to 1.5 litres with a short-stroke powerplant which vibrated less. They achieved this by combining the 1.6 litre block with 1.3 litre crankshaft. Decibels fell by 2, horsepower by 5.

Even the most basic Golf was better trimmed as all models first received improved seat, gear change and pedal layouts. The first million Golfs were built within less than three years of the debut, a German record which may explain some of the early quality control troubles. Only a third of the first 100,000 had been entirely trouble-free, another third were truly problematic.

All that was behind them by 1977 when Golf accounted for 45 per cent of German VW registrations despite a price level about 20 per cent above that when it was first introduced. In 1977 the universal car came with choice of 1.1 or 1.5 litre engines, plus the 1.6 GTI and the diesel. Below that there was the Polo which had been upgraded in trim as well and would even receive a 1.3 litre engine option in 1978, one right out of their parallel Derby model which came in under Schmücker.

The Scirocco coupé was selling so briskly they confined updates to plastic-covered bumpers and larger front blinkers. A quarter million of this élite VW were sold in the first four years, moving it well out in front of all 2 + 2 rivals within six months of the launch, to the pleased surprise of its own builders. This Scirocco changed to the short-stroke engine when the Golf did.

The Passat, first of their new generation, had been a steady success ever since 1973 so the concept was left largely alone until 1978 when a new grille improved aerodynamics by 12 per cent, blinkers and tail-lights were altered and a small spoiler fitted below the plastic-sheathed bumper. Giugiaro performed this touch-up to his original idea which came out 10 cm/4 in longer. Interior noise dropped and the ride was softened at slight expense in handling, which seemed to deter no buyers.

As proof that VW had moved far from its 'one model' days, the Wolfsburg and Ingolstadt cars together now came in 72 varieties, 64 of them using water-cooled engines. Two further engine options were added for the 1978 Passat, one a diesel like the Golf which was mounted lengthwise here, the other their 110 hp four which gave the Passat GLI a top speed of 185 kph/115 mph. Ride was firmed up, but not to the extent of a GTI Golf. At the other end of the scale, a long-stroke 1300 was phased out, to be replaced by the new 1.3 with oversquare dimensions and the same 55 hp.

In 1977 the first new car under Schmücker appeared, dubbed Derby to continue their sporting line. It was actually a Polo, with a proper boot instead of the flat tail and opening hatch, but the three-box design gave it a much larger look which appealed to economy-minded but proud buyers who found the Polo looked too much like a city car. This Derby was 37 cm/14.6 in longer with twice the boot capacity of a Polo and 1.5 cm/0.6 in more rear headroom as well so two adults would just fit. Slightly firmer suspension allowed for greater load potential and their new 1.3 litre engine was reserved for the Derby at first.

Initially the car threatened to push its Polo brother right off the lists but sales later settled down to somewhat less than the hatchback model. A poll indicated just under a third of all Germans considered prestige vital in any car purchase. For a little more than a Polo cost those people could have a car which looked at least as—if not more—impressive than the Golf.

Volkswagen had got the proportions just right, the boot looked anything but tacked on. Also the rear window needed no wiper. After nearly a decade of telling customers what they really wanted—either bubble or two-box—VW actually offered a styling option on

Left *This small drawing-down of the bonnet line on the 1977-8 Passat, 'optimizing' as VW calls it, was worth a major gain in fuel consumption. This was justification for the finest wind tunnel on the continent.*

Above right *VW Derby, the boot on a baby Polo. This came before the Jetta and looks a larger car than it is, but they discovered it was not changed enough from the Polo and sold less than expected after an initial boom.*

one chassis/engine base. When the Derby first seemed likely to sweep the Polo away, Volkswagen began to give serious thought to a like alternative on the Golf chassis. During the gestation of that model, however, they realised the Derby had not been quite different enough. Their next effort would not only have a boot but altered nose and interior as well.

With the decision taken to bring out a three-box car based on the Golf chassis, VW needed only a name. The choice was Jetta, supposed to sound right in all tongues and evoke images of the jet stream, to maintain their wind connections. A whiff of jet set would not disturb Wolfsburg either. Monsoon had seemed too negative a wind and Wolf too stern while Regatta, the other prime contender, seemed likely to appear on a rival car. Tonny—to mean fancy—was suggested too, doubtless by a marketing man who felt the boss would be flattered. But the choice was Jetta.

Initially this model, like the Derby, did not offer the least engine known for its class, but appeared with either a 1.3 litre, the ubiquitous 1.5 or 110 hp to make a GLI. A diesel version came later. The key dimension was 630 1/22 ft^3 of boot space versus 370/13 for the Golf and only 502/17.6 for the Passat.

Their new 'sporting compact' theme for the 80s showed in such options as choice of five-speed manual gearboxes; either an economy version with long-legged top gear, or close-ratio model for maximum acceleration. In a wider sense it also meant Wolfsburg no longer would leave notch-back 'prestige' saloons to Audi but cover the spectrum with VW badges and leave Audi to find its slot through trim, wheelbase or panache. This was generally perceived as a victory for Wolfsburg in the long-running image battle with its own branch in Ingolstadt.

Technically Jetta was the first VW to use a new 'fist saddle' type of disc brake caliper developed by VW. By eliminating the frame of a floating saddle caliper they saved space within the limited wheel yet offered better self-adjustment than fixed-saddle calipers could provide. Above all they wanted to avoid the idea that this Jetta was just another Golf, a lesson learned from the Derby. It was the model which took their corporate interest to open the 80s, from the stage of the 1979 Frankfurt motor show where economy was an industry-wide watchword.

In Volkswagen terms this meant a thermo-choke which combined a cheaper manual choke with a bi-metal override spring which would finally turn the choke off when the engine was warm if a driver completely ignored it. It suggested their view of the 80s VW buyer, perhaps a less car-aware person than those old Beetle fans. If this new driver forgot to check the water temperature after so many decades of air cooling, VW would help: with two lights in place of the dial, showing yellow for too cold, red for overheated. The Scirocco also introduced electronic ignition to their 80s line-up, with other models to follow.

Jetta in cutaway.

At the end of the 70s Volkswagen was riding high again, even in comparison to a generally good German car picture. They held well over 30 per cent of inland sales for VW alone while the Audi division was fourth in Germany, the two combined built close to one million cars at home for the year. The work force was again close to 200,000 and a handsome dividend was paid to share holders while investment cash outstripped projects as Schmücker spoke of 'controlled expansion' which looked very like a boom to outsiders. Among other moves VW bought 55 per cent of the Triumph office machinery and computer company from the US to diversify. This also brought them the Triumph and Adler car names of the 30s.

The firm built 11,000 automobiles per day around the world and expected to increase that figure by ten per cent for 1981. At their first General Meeting in Berlin since the war Schmuecker announced the largest expansion programme in VW history, one designed to meet 'massive' price increases expected for all cars everywhere. Confident that oil crises could only help the builders of sensible size cars on the one hand, VW also planned expansion on the truck side in both Brazil and with MAN in Germany. In fact they now seemed so settled and all-knowing that the political jibes began to appear again. A conservative politician in Bonn who was also a union official—a common enough mix in Germany—grabbed headlines by asking when Volkswagen would finally build that proper economy car for the 'Volk' one he interpreted as doing nicely on just 4 litres per 100 km/70 mpg.

This rather smug question was loosely based on an automobile VW had already built for US government consideration, an extension of their most visible engineering break-through of the late 70s. This combined a small passenger car diesel engine, something they had brought closer to everyday viability than any other firm, with turbocharging and other consumption-optimising means.

With technology like this IRVW on hand, Volkswagen could contemplate its US market prospects with comfort, even pride. Their everyday Rabbit and Dasher diesels were leading all cars in government-measured consumption figures and enjoying a long waiting list. Compression ignition to new levels of refinement had opened a new world of credibility for Wolfsburg as the builder of peoples' cars.

Chapter 14

The viable diesel and thereafter

Diesel-powered automobiles appeared relatively late in Volkswagen's short history, but they quickly proved worthy of that firm's tendency to do it differently. This was the first marque to manage the technical breakthrough of a small passenger car diesel powerplant for the general market, one based entirely on a petrol engine and yet equal or superior to purpose-built diesels without their weight. That accomplishment ensured a VW place in the compression ignition world.

If diesel saloons should indeed prove the saviour of motoring, thanks to their low consumption and acceptable emissions, then this line of Wolfsburg engines could provide the most critical technical trophy Volkswagen has captured since it introduced the flat four.

Virtually every automobile engineer of the last half-century has dreamed at some time of turning his everyday Otto (spark ignition) engine into an equally light, compact and handy diesel with a minimum of special design or tooling. Several, including Porsche himself for the original Beetle engine, tried the task but few came anywhere near success and the diesel automobile remained an outsider. In 1973, however, Volkswagen engineers decided they badly needed a future diesel line-up to parallel and protect their now-successful petrol powerplants. While they were at the job, they aimed for the position of number one in passenger car diesel production as well. This ambitious operation was based on three pre-conditions: their engine must be light as a unit while overall vehicle weight as such must be kept low as well, and they would need a wider than usual revolution range by diesel standards. None of these factors was precisely common among small diesels at the time.

However, finite element experiments indicated that the VW 1.5 litre engine, based on Kraus' Type 827 as first seen publicly in the Audi 80, would do just fine. Next step was a test series with a Peugeot 204 diesel, then the smallest automobile diesel sold in Europe. They lifted that to 70 hp with turbocharging, clearly indicating that VW intended to supercharge its own diesels from the first.

Leiding liked this Peugeot well enough to give his team a mandate to do better. In only three more months they had their own engine on the test bed, one producing the target 50 hp immediately so they could move right to optimisation, with the aid of Bosch who provided the vital injection system.

By mid-1974 VW was running durability tests and pushing its first cars around the Ehra test ground. This phase was especially intensive, despite a relatively short list of problems, because they were using petrol engine parts and had to be doubly sure these would stand up. Such maximum use of common parts was part of their concept from the first—to keep costs down. Tight manufacturing tolerances would even allow them to build both engines on one line.

Furthermore, VW found they could use a Golf drive line without change. One test

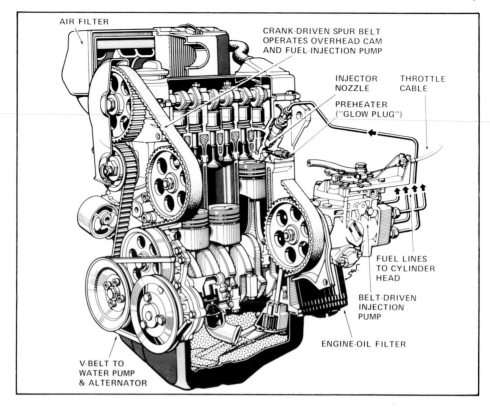

AIR FILTER

CRANK-DRIVEN SPUR BELT
OPERATES OVERHEAD CAM
AND FUEL-INJECTION PUMP

INJECTOR   THROTTLE
NOZZLE   CABLE

PREHEATER
("GLOW PLUG")

FUEL LINES
TO CYLINDER
HEAD

BELT-DRIVEN
INJECTION
PUMP

ENGINE-OIL FILTER

V-BELT TO
WATER PUMP
& ALTERNATOR

engine passed the 100,000 km/62,000 mile mark by the autumn of 1974 without causing any notable problems to chassis or body. Wolfsburg had actually been so confident of this outcome they had started production planning the previous August, with all goals met.

They needed high volumetric efficiency at high (for a diesel) engine speeds, high compression temperatures at cranking speed for easy start and idle, and a silenced induction system. This led to a swirl chamber design for low consumption with decent performance. The aim was a 5,000 rpm peak and specific output of 25 kW/litre. Peak pressures were held close to final compression pressure to minimise stress, but also to contain noise. Their tall, stiff aluminium head proved easy to adapt since it was almost diesel-type anyway. Valves were all on one side so their swirl chamber could go on the other, with injector nozzles fitted where the spark plug holes had been. Ribs cast into this head served to direct coolant flow as well.

Any diesel needs a compression ratio of at least 20:1 for acceptable cold start and idle, while 16 or 18:1 gives lower consumption. VW settled on 23:1, just on the high side of average.

In production they actually used three different head gasket thicknesses to maintain ideal piston:valve clearances and thus have a compression range of 22.5 to 23.7:1. Tight fit between combustion chamber, pistons and valves set a limit on valve lift so the intake camshaft was timed to close early and open late, for proper filling.

Early cold-start problems were overcome by containing heat loss, allowing them to claim that any production engine will still fire at -20 degrees C/-4 degrees F. A cold-start knob, used much like a petrol engine choke, advanced ignition timing then disengaged at

Left *The first viable small diesel engine for passenger cars, from VW and based on a petrol engine, which was once thought impossible.*

Right *Turbocharged diesel engine by VW.*

2,000 rpm. This reduced the characteristic blue cloud, improved throttle response and speeded warm-up.

The radiator from their 'tropic' kit handled extra cooling needs while exhaust ports were water jacketed. New, resistor glow plugs provided high initial current flow, then tapered off. Autothermic pistons with special rings set very tight limits on blow-by so oil changes could be stretched to 7,500 km/4,650 mile intervals. The belt driving their overhead camshaft was completely enclosed for the diesel, with a new tooth pattern as well.

Bosch injection works at 130 bar/1,870 psi, with dynamic injection-ram effect. Engine operation is controlled by altering the amount injected while air flow remains constant, a small but key factor in diesel driving for the everyday user. Should he run the tank dry, once a diesel car trauma, it would not be necessary to bleed the pump before restarting.

None of these technical features covered totally new ground but VW achieved an excellent mix and did it with a petrol engine base. Their engine surprised even its own designers (slightly) by the time it went into production at their Salzgitter plant, just 24 months after plans were first laid. Then the launch was set back somewhat at the last minute to solve a problem with broken exhaust pipes and to have ample cars for every dealer on day one. The limiting factor then, and ever since, proved to be enough injection pumps.

By debut day Volkswagen had mass-tested 300 cars, including some engines in the larger Passat, between Christmas 1975 and September 1976. Of those, 50 were sent to America for everyday use.

Once an engine completed its 100,000 km/62,000 miles, it was torn down and checked minutely. VW confidently predicted twice the engine life span of their petrol Golf and pressed forward with work on a hardly-secret turbocharged version.

Their unsupercharged 1.5 litre diesel was already changing many minds about this type of engine. It was sufficiently lively, revved more freely than its peers from the competition, and produced performance to equal their 1.1 litre petrol Golf, with the bonus of a very flat torque curve offering 75 Nm/55.2 lb-ft all the way from 2,000 rpm to 4,400. This engine came out only 5 kg/11 lb heavier than its petrol progenitor, although the complete car runs out at some 25 kg/55 lb more, due to additional sound dampening: an expansion chamber upstream of the exhaust pipe, induction dampening, silencing substance on the cowl, and an extra sheet of sound proofing material under the bonnet.

This added up to a new era, a diesel you could not hear at cruising speeds although it retained the typical rattling tone when idling. Even non-diesel drivers could not only live with but like it. All of this soon suggested a very pleasant future for the engine's spiritual father, a cocky young Austro-Czech named Peter Hofbauer.

This young wonder-worker in Fiala's team was born in 1941 at Znaim, Czechoslovakia, and schooled in Vienna which would seem the only possible path for an engineer with VW ambitions. Hofbauer took his master's degree at the technical college in Austria's capital, then joined Volkswagen in 1967 to work initially on all powerplants, including a rotary which was not the Wankel design. Within a year he had been promoted, to head 'special projects', and he would soon manage the VW engineering group responsible for unconventional propulsion systems. But it was the outstanding success of this diesel engine in the early 70s which ensured his promotion to head of all engine development at Wolfsburg in 1978. Four years earlier he had also been named to professorial rank at Berlin Technical University.

Today the slightly stocky Hofbauer, a man addicted to dark blue suits and black ankle boots with noticeable heels, can survey a range of four-, five- and six-cylinder diesel engines second to none. They have made him much in demand for such things as reading technical papers before the American Society of Automobile Engineers and given VW a fresh road to follow.

The first car to appear with this four-cylinder diesel was the Golf, of course, and it soon boasted a waiting list of over a year, despite production which quickly escalated from 100 to 800 per day, with an early goal of 1,500 daily. VW even worked at bringing English injection pumps to their teutonic standards in the hopes of easing the Bosch bottleneck, and explored the idea of East German pumps as well.

This automobile appeared at precisely the right time for drivers faced by sudden fuel price jumps—Golf D consumption came out to a mere 5.4 litres per 100 km/52 mpg at a steady 90 kph/56 mph. Yet one would still reach 100 kph/62 mph from 0 in 18 seconds and top 140 kph/84 mph, enough to outpace any other conventional saloon diesel of whatever size. At a stroke, VW had snatched small-car diesel leadership from the French. Of course a Golf D cost roughly ten per cent more than the same machine with a petrol engine so that true monetary savings were only possible with high yearly mileages. Early cost estimates showed that a Golf D would cost about two-thirds as much to run per mile as a Beetle or petrol Golf.

Volkswagen never meant the Golf D as a universal answer, although it soon accounted for a tenth of their sales, even in otherwise poor export areas, and became a small-taxi favourite in many countries. Like any diesel, the Golf does best in stop-start use and has less of an advantage for high-speed motoring. This same Golf D proved a key car in VW efforts to penetrate the Japanese market where half their sales had compression-ignition engines, including several purchased 'for study' by a major builder there.

Golf Diesels for Europe used the 1100 Golf gearbox and 4.57 final drive while US and

Australian cars carried the gearbox from their 1.5 machine and a 3.9 final drive. By 1980 US models also had a five-speed gearbox to further stretch the fuel. Only the big Oldsmobile V8 or turbocharged Mercedes 300 D of twice the capacity could beat a little Golf D and then it was a close-run thing. Soon US buyers were paying as much as a third above list price for a low-mileage, used Golf D, or following VW delivery trucks bearing diesels to a dealership. VW had to limit deliveries to each dealer for what soon became a cult—this Golf D was dubbed the only possible replacement car for the man who had already had 25 years of service from his split-window 1953 Beetle.

With a five-speed Rabbit D leading all cars in the official American EPA consumption standings for 1980, followed closely by the four-speed Rabbit D and Dasher (Passat) D, and the next-best diesel only 20th overall, sales of 60,000 for the last year of the 70s were no surprise and VW of America could hardly wait to get diesel production going in Pennsylvania. The car was an import from Germany at first.

Despite this acute engine shortage, VW soon chose to fit some into the Passat D as well, giving a more opulent trim level as well as a proper estate option. With marginally better streamlining this Passat D was 2 kph or barely over 1 mph faster than the Golf D but slightly slower in acceleration. Most impressive, it had a sound reading of only 72 dB at 96 kph/60 mph.

VW faced considerably more diesel competition in the Passat class, with Italian models coming along to match the French, but knew too that the only car to challenge a Passat D in performance was their own, smaller Golf D. In only two years they had become the largest diesel builder in the world. For America the Passat D even had a five-speed gearbox option by 1980, to the intense annoyance of German buyers.

In pure VW terms the next step up would be a six-cylinder diesel, drawing on the same parts bin, but before that they took a sideways pace as well, when their Audi branch came out with a five-cylinder diesel version of its Audi 100, one based on the Ingolstadt petrol powerplant but produced by Hofbauer's team in Wolfsburg.

Piëch believes engineers have a duty to conserve finite fuel supplies and that must mean a diesel for the corporation's largest model. They did not offer this option in the Audi 80 at first since the Passat could cover that segment. However, a turbo-diesel five would come soon after the turbocharged petrol five in their 1980 Audi 200.

The first Audi diesel, at the end of 1978, was best described as brother to the VW diesel six, first cousin to the fours. While Piëch did not do it directly, he had previously influenced the Mercedes five-cylinder diesel and always been intrigued by the inline five as a concept. In the Audi 100 5D case, bore was reduced to decrease capacity from 2.2 to 2.0 litres since they wanted coolant flow completely around the bores as well as a better gasket face. Audi's engine received stronger rod bearings and wider camshaft drive belt, again fully enclosed. Grouped accessory drive met the latest Audi theories.

This car embodied the first direct challenge to Mercedes diesels on home turf but Audi produced it one price class lower on the scale and originally fitted only a manual four-speed gearbox, although US cars soon had five forward speeds as standard—really a saloon-diesel must. Original projections were for some 15 per cent of all Audi 100s in diesel form but demand was twice that, at home as well as abroad.

The new size in VW-Audi diesels felt like a bigger Golf on the road—moving off briskly and showing no taint of the ponderous. Piëch's answer to 'why now' was simply that they felt they had tamed the diesel, 'now'. Of course a performance loss from 115 or even 135 hp to only 85 in the bigger saloon proved more of a handicap in the up-market class.

Next step in their building-block approach was the inline diesel six which Volkswagen designed but used only in its LT range of medium vans originally, although a joint venture with Volvo gave the Swedish firm access to a diesel six for its heavier saloon.

A five-cylinder version of the VW diesel for the Audi 100 line-up. Piëch was always a fan of fives.

They had paid a part of the research and development costs and had some voice in development.

The LT came with either an Audi 5D of 2.0 litres or VW 6D of 2.4, depending on which model you preferred. As a van engine the six produced 75 hp while Volvo enjoyed 82. Salzgitter was soon building a fifth of its engines in diesel form to keep up with all these varying demands, even though VW was becoming sceptical of errant US rules by 1980 so that they declined at first to even certify their diesels for California that year.

Like their five, the six has stronger journals, bearings and wrist pins, the same kind of alloy head with belt-driven single overhead camshaft and vertical valves, as well as water passages between all bores. Five and six share their stroke, and swirl chambers are larger than those in the four. Cold-start aid is automatic on the larger diesel engines, eliminating the Golf D knob. The five weighs only 172 kg/380 lb, the six a svelte 198 kg/435 lb. This achievement is a key factor in VW's diesel breakthrough.

Whereas the six is mated to a five-speed gearbox, geared to climb walls in low and give perhaps 90 kph/55 mph in top when used in their LT trucks, Volvo calls it a 'comfort diesel' using their familiar four-speed manual plus electric overdrive. The Swedish car will touch 150 kph/95 mph in top yet returns 10.7 litres per 100 km/26.4 mpg in spite of the car's weight.

Both VW and Volvo stress the point that their six benefited from a late entry into the diesel field. As a van engine the 2.4 litre produces more power than an earlier, 2.7 litre, English diesel VW also used, yet the Wolfsburg product is quieter in operation.

Before making any of these diesel moves VW did a vast amount of theoretical research which could then be spread into 'future' projects, once the basic saloons were well launched. Most visible of such efforts was a car they called IRVW for Integrated Research VolksWagen. It was built to show the US Department of Transportation that neither safety nor low emissions necessarily required vast bulk nor astronomical outlays. Under Fiala VW had moved in remarkably short time from a firm which ignored the initials R&D, to a leader in that expensive discipline, one other car makers scouted when recruiting special engineering talent.

Hofbauer explained in an SAE paper, to quote one instance, that they had studied a

The electric van fleet from VW is now undergoing road tests. The feature is the battery pack fed in one side while discharged batteries go out the other.

diesel range of 50 to 100 hp for the one Washington contract, including both turbocharged sixes and normally-aspirated V8s well outside their road car programme.

This was the point where VW-Audi decided to prefer a normally-aspirated diesel five over a turbocharged four despite its roughly 10 per cent penalty in consumption. The blown engine might well require Exhaust Gas Recirculation and would certainly cost more.

Nonetheless, VW was pleased to build their IRVW for American authorities to provide a fully driveable synthesis of late-70s engine and safety-cell technology within the reasonable dimensions of a Golf. VW felt then that diesels would be vital for any firm

Beyond today, the VW IRVW with turbo-diesel engine in a safety shell, developed for the US government, yet entirely possible for production within a couple of years.

long before the end of the 80s, although Hofbauer always stressed that he did not expect them to replace petrol engines in this century.

Whereas their everyday Golf D has the performance of a 1.1 litre petrol Golf, the IRVW which the author drove upon its return from the US performed just like a brisk 1.5 litre petrol Golf, used far less fuel, made a good deal less noise—and was safer. One feature was the AiResearch turbocharger mounted right at the exhaust manifold for optimum heat/pulse operation. It pumps only air, to reduce lag. A short intake manifold with aluminium elbow to the blower fits against the right wing with direct ducting to the compressor's inlet side. Compression was reduced by half a number and boost, which comes in softly as low as 1,500 rpm, has reached its peak by 2,500.

This IRVW also featured a special, five-speed manual gearbox essential to its overall economy—both fourth and fifth were 'overdrive' ratios. The car would pull easily in fourth from 30 kph/18 mph on its 75 hp/4,500 rpm, would touch 160 kph/100 mph and do 0-100 kph/62 mph in 13.5 s, yet average consumption was only 3.95 l/100 km or 71.4 mpg. Emissions easily exceeded mid-80s' US standards. Of course a production version would easily cost anywhere from a quarter to a third more than a normal diesel Golf so that even after investing DM 2 million in the project, VW would only say it was 'close' to production status. As for safety, IRVW was based closely on ESVW II, their second-generation safety cell with hydraulic bumper rams, frame built to withstand 65 kph/40 mph frontal crashes, knee bolster and rear shoulder bolsters as well as load-sensor belts, side-intrusion bars and integral roll-over cage. Yet all this weighed a mere 75 kg/165 lb more than your usual Golf D.

The next stage for VW was to encapsulate the engine, making it actually inaudible. This unit, displayed at the 1979 International Vehicle Fair in Hamburg, dropped the noise level by a full 6 dB with the bonus of a 10 per cent consumption improvement for city driving, thanks to more rapid warm-up.

Both Wolfsburg and Ingolstadt were working simultaneously on turbocharged petrol engines too, of course, with the first shown by Audi in the form of its 200 for 1980. This allowed a figure of 1.5 kg/3.3 lb/kW. VW even admitted to engines weighing a good third less for every kW they produced—but that would double the price. Much of this turbo work was done under another US contract, using AiResearch blowers with separate waste gates, preheated air and two-barrel carburettors initially, then fuel injection, EGR and lambda-sond electronic feedback control.

Late in the 70s Audi also developed its 'hedgehog' which inserts a bunch of fingers into the exhaust manifold to use that heat for quick warm-up, since 80 per cent of US emissions compliance comes in the first three minutes after a cold start. It underlined the fact that 35 major rules, plus subheads, had to be considered for a US Rabbit alone.

Ironically enough, much of Volkswagen's problem for the 80s stemmed from the fact that their latest engines had already been designed for low consumption, leaving much less 'fat' to pare away. They explored stratified charge and pre-chamber ignition for the air-cooled boxer (keeping the Transporter contemporary) as well as later water-cooled models. This brought petrol engine efficiency close to end-70s diesel levels.

Fiala and Hofbauer could naturally discuss far-future projects more openly than their next customer model, in part because these are done under government contract in many cases and hard to keep secret anyway. They are the jobs achieved by pure engineering with only a passing nod to eventual production costing. They foresaw two probable engine paths. One would be a smaller, even three-cylinder, diesel of about 975 cc and 30 hp which would be the VW economy powerplant. It might need a mechanical supercharger activated by an electro-mechanical clutch when 42 hp are needed briefly. Hofbauer also favoured direct injection such as trucks use, to eliminate glow plugs and idle pinging, providing they can eliminate high noise at peak power as well.

For their petrol engine, the comfort powerplant, some 75 hp seemed necessary but capacity must also be reduced, to the 0.9 to 1.3 litre realm, so a supercharger of some sort would again be required. Their goal was 180 kph/110 mph with consumption of 7.5 litres per 100 km (nearly 40 mpg). Micro-computer engine control and overrun cut-off to reduce city consumption by 20 per cent would be necessary features. It will be difficult to remove much weight from the cars which carry such powerplants without applying exotic (expensive) materials but such power figures would only be viable if a machine with Golf wheelbase and track, yet as much or more interior and boot space, could be brought down to 650 kg/1,435 lb as a diesel three or 700 kg/1,545 lb with a petrol engine.

At the same time they were working hard on the GT 70, a twin-shaft gas turbine with regenerator and integral gearing to suit its action to car conditions. This turbine was designed to fit most VW models and mated to their standard automatic gearbox. It would run on petrol, diesel, kerosene or even methanol, producing 75 hp.

The first methanol (alcohol) propelled VW was a Passat in South Africa but their Brazilian branch ultimately led the search into biomass fuels since they had the land areas to produce sugar cane, beets or manioc. As VW pointed out, a European land like Germany would have to plant almost its entire area to beets to produce sufficient fuel for the cars which would have no place left to run. Further problems came from tank

Above left *IRVW hardly looks different yet it meets all 1985 consumption and emission standards, with the performance of a current petrol Golf.*

Right *The encapsulated engine, in a car where it has its separate lid under the bonnet, on display at the international traffic show, 1979, is the next VW direction. Noise emissions are met without further worry, the radiator must be enlarged, but emissions in city (cold-start) cycle are actually better through faster warm-up.*

capacity, the hydroscopic properties of alcohol fuels and cold-start problems in colder climes, due to lean-burn engines. Methanol shows best when compared to pre-1967 engines. Even so, VW was running a fleet of 45 methanol-powered vehicles by 1979, largely in their own north German area to ease refuelling. Their aim was to gather 30,000 km/18,000 miles per year on each vehicle, in all environments and usage conditions, an interesting comparison with their heritage of W30 tests in 1937.

Since aerodynamics are as valuable in saving fuel as weight reduction, VW gloried in the finest wind tunnel of any European car builder and built up a large staff of air flow specialists. When they cut 10 per cent from the coefficient of drag it meant a 4.5 per cent reduction in diesel car consumption or 3.5 per cent saved by a petrol model. In fact, VW aimed at as much as a 30 per cent drop in the C_d, worth up to 15 per cent improvement in fuel consumption figures. That was to come from a Golf whose C_d of 0.41 was already more than a tenth below the European norm for its class. By the early 80s they would have this down to 0.35, with the Passat even more favourable.

Styling had indeed come a long way from those 36 random prototypes Nordhoff saved up to show when critics claimed he was far too Beetle-besotted. By the late 70s the Volkswagen preoccupation was 'optimising,' which came down to changing radii by as little as a millimetre (0.04 in) to make significant air flow gains. VW now maintained a proper inhouse styling department but also gave contracts to firms like Ital Design. Their wildest effort came from a contract for Luigi Colani, who claimed he could fit the interior space of a Passat into the exterior dimensions of a Polo. When Schmücker and Fiala were annoyed by his further attacks on their current line it seems inevitable that Colani's effort would disappear into the VW basement with the firm saying only that they had learned from the car. It was at least clear proof of more pragmatic Wolfsburg thinking.

When it came to drive train research, VW admitted first to a hybrid system for its Type 2 bus. A petrol engine either charged the batteries—a parallel to Porsche thinking six decades earlier—or ran the car when it was not feasible to use its battery drive. This van would start electrically but its engine would take over gradually as speed increased, with its surplus energy diverted to charge the batteries again. Their obvious problems were space, weight and cost, particularly with both petrol engine and electric motor involved. A next step might be stored kinetic energy with a flywheel reservoir 'fed' under braking. This project, with the Aachen technical institute, was supposed to effect a 20 per cent energy saving.

Wolfsburg soon found such futuristic plans were moving beyond the capabilities of normal test methods. They dictated increasingly sophisticated devices to sample such hopes. An electronically guided, hydraulically-activated, radio-controlled and pre-programmed driving machine with outrigger wheels was one answer. This quarter-million DM toy could repeat any manoeuvre with great accuracy and go to the dynamic limits without endangering a driver.

A further advance over the 60s, when the head of their safety team rode out crashes in person, came with a driving simulator on gimbals so it could move in all planes and feed audible, visual and mechanical inputs to the test driver with perfect reproduceability, regardless of wind or weather. Steering, acceleration or deceleration forces could be programmed at any desired force level.

All this came in a single decade from the time when ESVW I was built with the exterior of a European luxury saloon but interior freedom of a Beetle. By 1980 they employed some 500 men in six groups on such safety work alone. The first group produced visible safety car studies along with traffic system projections and projects for greater pedestrian safety. The second explored engines and drive trains. A third was devoted to fluid mechanics, gas turbines and their wind tunnel. A fourth group worked on systems simulation and electronics, largely in the analytical realm. That left groups five and six to concentrate on measurement techniques and process controls. They backed up the other four, in effect.

Their various studies might range as far afield as a project to determine the sound-dampening effects of different numbers of passengers—a Golf is up to 2 decibels quieter with three aboard than with two, when accelerating hard in third gear between 4,200 and 5,200 rpm, as one instance. Looking further down such roads, Peter Hofbauer sees Volkswagen building a mix of petrol, diesel and turbocharged cars.

Over the first decade after they chose a new path, their Golf became a car which was shorter, lighter and 'slipperier' than the Beetle, yet one offering 11 per cent more interior space, 36 per cent more boot room and 100 per cent more power. Their next stage would offer equal road performance from a quarter less raw engine output, be a fifth less

Above left *VW is fully involved in the methanol fuel programme of West Germany, using the Golf as prime vehicle but running a fleet including the Audi 80 and Type 2 as well.*

Right *A driving simulator from VW for quantifying driver modes in the future and trying to eliminate the human factor for a given road situation. The subject in the simulator sees a normal road picture with programmed hazards.*

Despite the use of driving simulators VW still have an interest in crash testing where the subject is a human, not a dummy, to gain a better base line. Rauno Aaltonen the rally driver took the ride here.

thirsty—but admittedly cost much more, if only because of the rare materials required.

Electronics, 10 per cent of a VW's cost by 1979 to quote one instance, would be up to 15 per cent of the total price by 1988. By 1995 their throttle would be a command control, not a direct link between foot and engine. With all this said, the keen new engineering breed at VW was sure this pedal-replacement would still dictate to a machine which would be fun to drive.

When Toni Schmücker arrived at Wolfsburg, his job was to fit together hard, high-pressure work already done and to present a smooth whole to the public. By 1980 he could view their future with 'self confidence and realistic optimism', despite ever-stiffer market competition. He could do this precisely because VW had moved into a leading technological position as an innovator with the pragmatic approach.

This firm had long-since grown from the factory which made only 'Volkswagens', to the producer of Golfs, Passats, Rabbits and all the rest. In the course of finding true survival VW had also become a past master at wiping past abberations from the corporate mind. Mention a 412 or K70 in 1980 and it drew a blank stare. These had become 'non-cars'.

As the end of their first half-century came within view the only direction which mattered in once-conservative Wolfsburg was forward. It was not the concept of a high-quality machine for the 'volk' which had changed at Wolfsburg. Rather, it was a realisation of the boundless sophistication which was necessary to achieve something like that for the 80s.

Volkswagen—the concept even more than the car—began as one man's vision and another's passion, survived both an immoderate boom and a period of stagnation, only to enter the 80s as the joint project of not one but several individualists willing to work within a multi-national framework. The key to their even reaching the 50th anniversary, never mind contemplating their next half-century with real anticipation, was far more the individualists and what they pushed forward than the framework around them. Volkswagen began as something different and survived each of its crises by remembering that trait, often only just in time.

Nobody ever promised that building a peoples' car was going to be easy.

Appendices

1 VW (Porsche) type numbers—Selected List

Porsche Design Offices 1936-1945

60		Porsche Design Office, Beetle or KdF
V3		Hand-built prototypes
W30		DB-built series for endurance testing
VW38		Reutter-built, pre-production prototypes
	K1	Saloon body, 985 cc engine (also K3-6-7)
	K8	Saloon, folding roof
	K9	Four-seater convertible
	K10	Berlin-Rome streamliner body
	K11	Plastic saloon body study
	K12	Cross-country body, saloon chassis
61		Down-sizing Beetle study
62		Cross-country prototype
66		RHD Beetle
67		Beetle for handicapped drivers
68		Panel van, PO
82		Kuebel, 985/later 1,131 cc engines
	E	Kuebel chassis, KdF body (later type 51)
	820	Four-seater Kuebel
	821	Three-seater Kuebel
	822 823	Two-seater Kuebels
	825	Two-seater pick-up (also 92 chassis)
	826	Tropical van
	828	Three-seat wooden body
83		Automatic gearbox (same number used later on closed van body)
86		Original four-wheel drive design
87		Four-wheel drive Kuebel
	877	Kommandeur (287 chassis)
88		Panel van, 2nd version
92		Two-wheel drive Kuebel chassis, KdF body (later 51)
	SS	Two-wheel drive Kommandeur
98		KdF study, convertible with four-wheel drive
107		Exhaust turbocharger
110		Volks-tractor, 1st version
111		with 2-cylinder engine

111 H	Wood gas generator
115	Supercharged 1.1 litre engine, study
120	Stationary engine
126	All-synchronised gearbox, study
127	Sleeve-valve engine
128	Amphibian on KdF wheelbase, based on type 87
138	Amphibian, backbone frame
155	Snow tracks for type 82
160	Beetle with unitary body/chassis
164	Six-wheel drive cross-country prototype
166	Amphibian, short wheelbase, as produced
174	Assault boat, KdF engine
177, 178	Five-speed, cross-country gearbox
182	Two-wheel drive cross-country, unitary body/chassis
187	Four-wheel drive for type 182
230	KdF, wood gas generator
235	KdF, electric drive, study
237, 238	Stationary engines
239	Kuebel, wood gas generator
247	Aviation engine variation, prototype
287	Kommandeur chassis, type 87 with 877 body
309	Diesel engine variation

Volkswagen Works (GB) 1945-1948

13	Beetle, folding roof
15	Two-seater cabriolet
21	Kuebel (previously type 82)
25	As fire tender
27	As open van
28	As closed van
51	Beetle, type 82 chassis (previously type 82E)
53	with sliding roof
55	Cabriolet, type 82 chassis
81	Pick-up, Beetle chassis
83	Panel van, Beetle chassis
91	Open two-wheeler trailer
93	Closed two-wheeler trailer
100	Road tractor (short-wheelbase Beetle)

Air-cooled VW 1949-present

1	(11)	Standard Beetle saloon
	13	Export saloon
	133	1302, new front suspension
	138	Remote-control test version
	14	Karmann Ghia coupé
	14A	Hebmüller 2-seater cabriolet (originally type 14)
	143	KG cabriolet
	147	Westphalia PO van
	15	Karmann 4-seater cabriolet
	17	Miesen ambulance
	179	Injected two-stroke engine, crankcase charging

	18A	Hebmüller police car, 4 canvas doors
181		The Thing
2		Transporter
	28	LT transporter (water-cooled)
3		VW 1500/1600
	31	Notchback and fastback body styles
	33	RHD
	34	KG 1500 coupé
	36	Variant (estate)
4		411/412
	41	Two-door saloon
	43	Four-door saloon
	46	Variant (estate)

Water-cooled VW 1973-present

16		Jetta (although last car released in series)
17		Golf
	171	Two-door saloon
	173	Four-door saloon
53		Scirocco
86		Polo and Derby
	861	Polo
	865	Derby
32		Passat
	321	Two-door saloon
	323	Four-door saloon
	33	Variant (estate)

2 VW/Audi production figures

Year	VW	Audi/NSU	Year	VW	Audi/NSU
1945	1,785	—	1963	1,209,591	—
1946	10,020	—	1964	1,410,715	—
1947	8,987	—	1965	1,542,654	52,207
1948	19,244	—	1966	1,583,239	67,248
1949	46,154	—	1967	1,300,761	39,062
1950	90,038	—	1968	1,707,402	69,918
1951	105,712	—	1969	1,830,018	264,420
1952	136,013	—	1970	1,989,422	316,515
1953	179,740	—	1971	2,071,533	282,296
1954	242,373	—	1972	1,895,192	297,332
1955	329,893	—	1973	1,927,809	407,360
1956	395,690	—	1974	1,778,738	289,242
1957	472,554	—	1975	1,649,895	299,044
1958	557,088	—	1976	1,862,711	302,916
1959	705,243	—	1977	1,806,750	412,130
1960	890,673	—	1978	1,439,000	295,000
1961	1,007,113	—	1979	1,397,000	323,000
1962	1,184,675	—			

Note The 35 millionth VW vehicle, a Golf, was produced in Wolfsburg during June 1979. One third of these were sold in Germany, the remaining 23.6 million to more than 150 countries abroad. Of the 35,000,000, 56 per cent or 19,657,000 were Beetles. Nearly one quarter of the 35 million, approximately 8.3 million vehicles, were assembled or produced by non-German plants: Brazil 4,783,000, Brussels 1,636,000, Mexico 868,000, South Africa 572,000, Australia 337,000. 18 production and assembly plants were building approximately 9,600 VW/Audi vehicles per day in 1979.

3 Technical milestones

Beetle/KdF Established classic 240 cm/94.6 in wheelbase and air-cooled boxer engine; 24 hp/985 cc.
Kuebel Continued wheelbase and engine dimensions in shorter, military tub shape.
Amphibian Prototype carried 25 hp/1,131 cc engine in standard wheelbase, production model wheelbase 200 cm/78.8 in.
Type 1 Post-war Beetle, 25 hp/1,131 cc and 240 cm/98.4 in wheelbase. Engine raised to 30 hp in 1954, then 34 hp/1,192 cc in 1961.
VW 1300 Engine of 40 hp/1,285 cc.
1302 44 hp/1,285 cc in 242 cm/95.4 in wheelbase.
VW 1500 44 hp/1,493 cc.
1302 S 50 hp/1,585 cc engine in 1302 wheelbase with MacPherson strut front suspension.
Type 3/1500 Flat fan engine, 45 hp/1,493 cc, 240 cm/94.6 in wheelbase.
1500 S Dual carburettors, 54 hp/1,493 cc.
VW 1600 Engine enlarged to 1,584 cc, same 54 hp.
Type 4/411 68 hp/1,679 cc four in 250 cm/98.5 in wheelbase.
411 E Fuel injection and 80 hp/1,679 cc.
412 72 hp/1,795 cc engine.
VW K 70 FWD, water-cooling, ex-NSU of 90 hp/1,607 cc. VW introduced with 75 and 90 hp, 269 cm/106.0 in wheelbase.
K 70 LS 100 hp/1,807 cc.
NSU Ro80 115 hp, dual-rotor Wankel engine, nominal 2 × 498 cc in 286 cm/112.7 in wheelbase.
VW Passat (Paralleling Audi 80) 247 cm/97.3 in wheelbase, engines of 55/60 hp (1,272 cc), 75 hp (1,588 cc) and 85 hp (1,588 cc), later 110 hp/1.6 litre and 50 hp/1,471 cc diesel.
Scirocco Golf 240 cm/94.6 in wheelbase, same 50/70/85/110 hp engine range.
Golf 240 cm/94.6 in wheelbase. Engine range; 50 hp/1,093 cc, 70 hp/1,457 cc, 75 hp/ 1,588 cc and later 1,457 cc, 110 hp/1,588 cc, 50 hp/1,471 cc diesel.
Polo 233 cm/91.8 in wheelbase. Engine range; 40 hp/0.9 litre, 50 hp/1,093 cc and 60 hp/ 1,272 cc. (Audi 50 paralleled).
Derby Wheelbase and engine options of Polo, added overall length due to boot.
Jetta Wheelbase and engines of Golf, added overall length due to boot.
Audi 100 Wheelbase 267.6 cm/105.4 in. Engine range; 85 hp/1,588 cc four, 115 and 136 hp/2,144 cc fives, 70 hp/1,986 cc five-cylinder diesel.
Audi 200 Wheelbase 267.6 cm/105.4 in. 136 hp/2,144 cc five or 170 hp with turbocharging.

Type 2/Transporter Beetle wheelbase and engines of 25/30/34/42/44 hp up to 1967, then 47/50/66 hp. Currently 50 and 70 hp from two litres. Last German-built, air-cooled, flat-fours.

LT/Transporter Larger transporters with 75 hp petrol or 65 hp Perkins diesel engines of four cylinders, later 75 hp VW diesel six.

4   Production runs/Key models

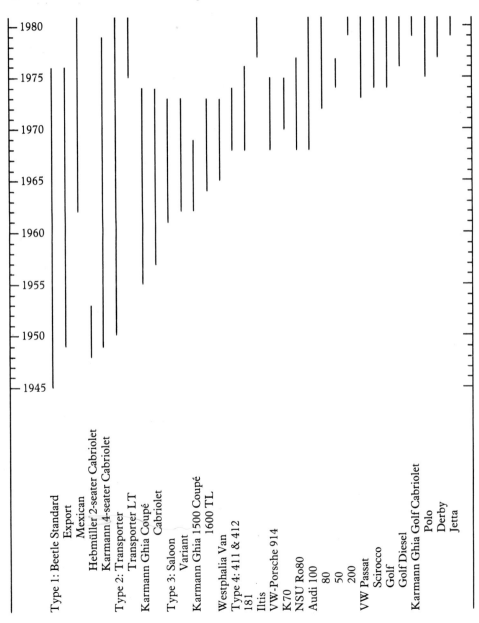

Index

The car which bids fair to replace the Beetle after all, the VW Golf (Rabbit in America) in its original form.